TEACHING SCIENCE

IN THE PRIMARY CLASSROOM

SAGE was founded in 1965 by Sara Miller McCune to support the dissemination of usable knowledge by publishing innovative and high-quality research and teaching content. Today, we publish over 900 journals, including those of more than 400 learned societies, more than 800 new books per year, and a growing range of library products including archives, data, case studies, reports, and video. SAGE remains majority-owned by our founder, and after Sara's lifetime will become owned by a charitable trust that secures our continued independence.

Los Angeles | London | New Delhi | Singapore | Washington DC | Melbourne

TEACHING SCIENCE

IN THE PRIMARY CLASSROOM

3RD EDITION

EDITED BY
HELLEN WARD & JUDITH RODEN

Los Angeles | London | New Delhi
Singapore | Washington DC | Melbourne

Los Angeles | London | New Delhi
Singapore | Washington DC | Melbourne

SAGE Publications Ltd
1 Oliver's Yard
55 City Road
London EC1Y 1SP

SAGE Publications Inc.
2455 Teller Road
Thousand Oaks, California 91320

SAGE Publications India Pvt Ltd
B 1/I 1 Mohan Cooperative Industrial Area
Mathura Road
New Delhi 110 044

SAGE Publications Asia-Pacific Pte Ltd
3 Church Street
#10-04 Samsung Hub
Singapore 049483

Editor: Jude Bowen
Assistant editor: George Knowles
Production editor: Tom Bedford
Copyeditor: Andy Baxter
Proofreader: Elaine Leek
Indexer: Charmian Parkin
Marketing manager: Dilhara Attygalle
Cover design: Wendy Scott
Typeset by: C&M Digitals (P) Ltd, Chennai, India
Printed and bound by CPI Group (UK) Ltd,
Croydon, CR0 4YY

Editorial Arrangement © Hellen Ward and Judith
    Roden, 2016
Chapter 1 © Hellen Ward, 2016
Chapter 2 © Hellen Ward, 2016
Chapter 3 © Judith Roden, 2016
Chapter 4 © Judith Roden, 2016
Chapter 5 © Hellen Ward, 2016
Chapter 6 © Hellen Ward and Keith Remnant, 2016
Chapter 7 © Claire Hewlett, 2016
Chapter 8 © Maria Elsam and Julie Foreman, 2016
Chapter 9 © Hellen Ward, 2016
Chapter 10 © Manette Carroll and Hellen Ward, 2016
Chapter 11 © Andrew Berry, 2016

First Edition published 2005 (reprinted 2005 and 2006)
Second Edition published 2008 (reprinted 2010, 2011
    and 2012)

Library of Congress Control Number: 2015949458

British Library Cataloguing in Publication data

A catalogue record for this book is available from
the British Library

MIX
Paper from
responsible sources
FSC
www.fsc.org   FSC® C013604

ISBN 978-1-4739-1204-5
ISBN 978-1-4739-1205-2 (pbk)

CONTENTS

ABOUT THE EDITORS

Hellen Ward is actively involved in science education, working as a Principal Lecturer at Canterbury Christ Church University and with teachers in a number of local authorities. Hellen has written several books and a number of other publications, and has developed teaching resources and teaching materials to support the teaching and learning of science. She has also contributed to science television programmes, websites and teaching resources for the BBC. Hellen is Faculty Director for Science, Technology, Engineering and Mathematics at Christ Church and is also an independent education consultant. Hellen is an active member of the Association for Science Education, and a regular contributor to both national and regional conferences. She is also a member of the Association for Achievement and Improvement through Assessment and has published materials on assessment. Hellen is a hub leader for the Primary Science Quality Mark working with teachers across the Kent and Medway region.

Judith Roden is an experienced teacher of science in all phases of education. Currently she is a Principal Lecturer working in the Faculty of Education, Canterbury Christ Church University, where she has held a number of roles including the role of crossphase science team leader, managing a large team of science tutors. She has written a number of science books, including the *Reflective Reader in Primary Science Education*, co-wrote *Extending Knowledge in Practice*, as well as writing a number of journal articles, and chapters in respected science books. Judith now works part time for Canterbury Christ Church University on the Teach First programme in the South East Region. In 2014 she was awarded a Teaching Fellowship Award for her contribution to Teacher Education over many years.

ABOUT THE CONTRIBUTORS

Andrew Berry has worked in primary education for 20 years. After teaching in primary schools in Kent for 10 years, Andrew worked for Kent County Council as their Primary Science Adviser. During this time he worked in over 200 schools, modelling teaching, and supporting and training science leaders and their colleagues. Andrew continues to provide support for primary schools all across the south east of England as part of his present position as the manager of Horton Kirby Environmental Education Centre. This current role also entails a lot of teaching in the outdoors and in many different schools. Andrew wrote the 2009 and 2014 versions of the Kent Scheme of Work for Primary Science.

Manette Carroll came into teaching as a mature student having had a varied career before going into teaching. Initially she trained to teach science to 7–14-year-old children in a middle school setting. Having taught for a number of years in the UK she moved to Germany to teach for Service Children's Education. She currently teaches from Foundation Stage 2 to Year 6 having undertaken recent training in Early Years as well as science subject leadership. Manette has been a science co-ordinator for at least seven years and has the unusual role of only teaching science and forest schools across the whole school; her classroom is set up as a science lab for primary school children.

Maria Elsam is a Senior Lecturer in Education within the Department of Primary Education at Canterbury Christ Church University. She is the Programme Director for the BA 7–11 Part-time Primary Education Programme. She teaches on numerous undergraduate and postgraduate science programmes, and is module lead for Full-time Year 2 BA Primary Education Science. She has a background in working as a research scientist in both the pharmaceuticals and interior/exterior surface coatings industries. She completed her PGCE Post-Compulsory training whilst teaching on a science degree programme at Canterbury Christ Church University. Maria is a member of the Association of Science Educators and is registered as a Chartered Science Teacher; she is also a Science, Technology, Engineering and Mathematics Ambassador.

Julie Foreman has retired from Initial Teacher Education and now enjoys photography and spending time with her grandchildren.

Claire Hewlett has many years' experience teaching in primary schools in East Kent. She spent five years as a science co-ordinator prior to becoming a head-teacher. Claire is a Senior Lecturer in the Primary Education Department at Canterbury Christ Church University and has worked on projects in Malaysia and India.

Keith Remnant is an independent education adviser who works with schools as a School Improvement Partner. Keith is an active member of the Association for Science Education. He has been the President of the Association for Achievement and Improvement through Assessment and currently organises their conferences. Keith has published materials on assessment in his role as Assessment Adviser for two local authorities. He was involved with the first national science tasks in Key Stage 1 and has worked as an Ofsted inspector. Keith is also a Science, Technology, Engineering and Mathematics Ambassador.

ACKNOWLEDGEMENTS

We would like to thank the many people who have contributed to this book, both directly and indirectly, including colleagues, both past and present, who have helped to shape the science courses upon which this book is based.

Thanks are due to the many ex-students and teachers, in the institutions in which we have worked, who have provided the inspiration and opportunities for us to develop our ideas about teaching science over the years.

In particular we would like to thank the head-teachers, teachers and children of the following schools:

All Souls Church of England Primary School, Dover, Kent

Bielefeld Primary School, Bielefeld, Germany

Bobbing Village School, Sittingbourne, Kent

Herne Bay Infant School, Herne Bay, Kent

Iwade Primary School, Iwade, Kent

Joy Lane Primary School, Whitstable, Kent

Sandwich Junior School, Sandwich, Kent

Senacre Wood Primary School, Maidstone, Kent

St James Church of England Primary School, Enfield, London

St Mary's Church of England Primary School, Ashford, Kent

St Mary's Church of England Primary School, Dover, Kent

Whitfield Aspen School, Dover, Kent

William Wordsworth First School, Sennelager, Germany

We would also like to thank Justine Swindells, Ellen Duggan-Strand, Amanda Sims, Katrine Shears, Becky Vincer, Charlotte Ward and James Bennett.

More specifically, we owe many thanks to Alf Lambert and are indebted to him for his work in producing many of the photographs included in the book.

1

WHAT IS SCIENCE?

Hellen Ward

In this chapter a pragmatic approach is taken to address the question, 'What is science?' There is evidence that learners do not enjoy science (Royal Society, 2010) and yet it is a subject with many opportunities for practical and enquiry learning approaches and has elements that promote awe and wonder. In addition, some people claim the subject has suffered for reasons specifically relating to teaching; for instance, teachers feeling they lack sufficient knowledge of the subject that results in poor interest, or the emphasis in the recent past upon teaching to the test, because Year 6 outcomes were nationally reported (Beggs and Murphy, 2005). In this chapter it will be suggested that there could be another reason, and therefore the issues are explored from a different perspective, proposing that perhaps the current view of science is outdated and therefore unrealistic in the 21st century. Learners' perceptions of science show they understand it to be a diverse and fascinating subject and therefore, by taking an 'ideas and evidence' approach to science, perhaps both teachers and learners would be able to leave the stereotypical approach to science in the past where it belongs.

WHAT IS SCIENCE?

Science is both a way of working and a body of knowledge. Science generates knowledge in the form of ideas, data, diagrams, theories and concepts (Ziman, 2000). Some of this knowledge is generally accepted (for example, that the sun is the centre of the solar system) while other aspects, such as the Higgs Boson, are questioned even by those who can access data from the CERN project. One view of science sees it as an accumulation of knowledge over time; this is the 'tablets of stone' approach (Solomon, 2013: 18). In this approach scientific literacy is laid down in books and is carefully built upon, and approved; the knowledge structures are certified and thus agreed to be truthful. The other view is one where knowledge is created and there is no ultimate truth. There is a reaction against science although Rorty suggests 'there is nothing wrong with science, there is only something wrong with trying to divinise it' (Rorty, 1991: 34). Ogborn (1985) identifies that science provides the answer to five distinct demands: 'What do we know?', 'How do we know?', 'Why do things happen?', 'What can we do with this knowledge?', 'How can we tell people what is known?' Science is a complex area of study but provides invaluable opportunities for learning.

Science is a relatively new subject, unlike the study of the classics or mathematics, and the name 'scientist' was first used as recently as 1834; although many men of science did not like this new term. While western science can be linked back to the Greeks it was then very different from what is currently thought of as science. Greek philosophy was a process of thinking, informed by observations. The Greeks thought that the world was composed of Earth, Fire, Water and Air. Aristotle, however, added Aether, because he did not believe that the things in the heavens could be constructed from the same sources as those on the earth. Aether was the fifth component (*Quinta* in Latin, leading to the word quintessential) and this filled the space between the earth and the rest of the known universe. Aether was a term, still in use in the 17th century, to explain how light travelled, as well as ideas in alchemy. So this Greek classification system lasted until the Renaissance although it seems rather rudimentary and not all philosophers held identical views. Democritus, another Greek philosopher, wondered in 460 BC what would happen if you continued to cut things into pieces until one piece could be cut no smaller. He decided this smallest thing, which could be cut no further, should be called an atom. This process involves the key features of science: wondering, questioning and then imagining an answer to explain what was happening. However, there was another feature of science happening: Aristotle did not believe the world was composed of atoms and because he was so influential neither did anyone else. Therefore, the idea of an atom was shelved until the 'Enlightenment' when the idea was resurrected. Science, like all knowledge, is a human process and is influenced by the humans who practise it. This is no different today as powerful people still influence what gets believed, or produced and published.

WAYS OF WORKING: THE IMAGE OF SCIENCE

An image that persists for many in the population is that of the lone scientist grappling with the mysteries of the world. This scientist is often pictured as being untouched by material ambition, or desire for personal prestige or glory, and one who will reject any subjective bias. Science is said to be objective; Osborne (1996) stated that science is able to make claim X about the world because:

X is a true statement about the world.

Scientists believe X.

Scientists have evidence of X.

Rorty (1991) argues that this objectivity is really a desire to win an argument against others who hold a different view. Science has a rational approach and seeks objective truth, although the ideas of 'truth', 'rationality', 'objectivity' and 'science' are often thought of as being the same thing. However, without a recognised and agreed system of 'finding out' there is little likelihood of getting any agreement and this results in a position called relativism. Science, however, is not about an uninterrupted series of instances of miraculous inspiration. The history of science is often neglected in science education and what is taught bears little relationship to the history of science as told by historians (Russell, 1981). There are many new ideas to explain the world but the acceptance of each new idea depends upon the network of support provided for the new idea. Latour (1989) suggested that the ideas were not as important as the people who supported them, and it was more how far the power and influence of this support stretched which affected what people believed. He studied scientists working in a Nobel prize winning laboratory in France and in his book, *Science in Action*, published in 1979 with Woolgar, suggested that what happens in a laboratory is inconsistent with the public perception of science as involving a search for truth and accuracy. Instead, he comments upon an approach that ignores any 'dodgy' or anomalous data that is not in line with the expected. Latour also describes science as culturally framed rather than as a set of fixed processes and procedures. Osborne (1996 rejects this view of science and explains that the reasons why there appeared to be inconsistencies in the research Latour observed were that it was ground breaking and involved complex approaches. Osborne went on to suggest that what happens in one place and at one time should not be considered as indicative of what happens everywhere at all times. 'Scientists work in communities of practice with established norms' (Osborne, 1996: 58). This notion of working together and relying on persuasion rather than force, and respecting curiosity and an eagerness for new data and ideas leads to the development of 'unforced agreement', which is the true value of science (Rorty, 1991: 39). Scientists, however, are human beings, with a range of human emotions, for example, Newton, working with Halley (the person after whom the comet is named) collaborated to publish the work of Flamsteed (the first Astronomer Royal), against his expressed wishes and despite the fact that his observations were incomplete. Newton wanted the data and regardless of Flamsteed's wishes used his immense network and power to get the work published and hence gain access to the data.

It can also be a trait of human nature to continue to believe something even when the evidence to support it does not exist. An example of this can be observed in relation to Joseph Priestley, the English scientist, who supported the idea of phlogiston. Priestley had many more supporters than the French chemist Lavoisier, who did not believe in phlogiston. The existence of phlogiston was the dominant theory of the time, and the theory stated that material that burnt contained a substance called phlogiston ('to burn' in Greek) which was released during burning. Although phlogiston was introduced by Swedish scientists in the 1700s, Priestley like most men of science at the time believed in its existence. They thought that when a candle was burned the phlogiston came from the candle into the air around it, then, when the air was saturated by this phlogiston (i.e. there was no more space), the candle would be extinguished. Phlogiston was colourless, had no smell and had no mass! It was also thought that when breathing, phlogiston was removed from a person's body and as a way of testing, to prove the existence of phlogiston, a mouse was placed in a sealed container. The notion was that when the air became full of phlogiston the mouse would die. However, there were many experimental issues relating to this theory, which meant Priestley often had to make small adjustments and changes over time to ensure his measurements remained constant. Therefore, although the results did not match the theory, the scientific community stuck with the phlogiston idea long after it was found to be false. Lavoisier, who went on, with others, to develop the way chemicals are named today, was executed during the French revolution, but not before he burnt all the books he could find that mentioned phlogiston. Priestley died never accepting that phlogiston did not exist.

There are many examples of theories, such as phlogiston, that have to be thrown out because of changing ideas, or instances where the science was found to lack believable evidence. Sometimes, the way scientific discoveries are reported and recorded is also unbelievable. Galileo, for example, is said to have been in a church and it was while watching a pendulum swing that he noted its laws; and yet many thousands of people, over time, would have seen the same thing (Matthews, 1994). The textbook story tells of his genius, sitting there making observations, but in reality it was not only 'the genius' who was observing. Like Newton, who was probably not hit on the head by an apple, Galileo had the ability to imagine a different idea from other observers and thereby create a new and different explanation that was exceptional. In each of these situations the two men arrived at their conclusions not by observation alone, as it was not possible for others to repeat these events and gain the same readings, but by the use of mathematics.

By 'jobbing backwards' it is easy to misrepresent the history of science as a tale of unqualified success, in which one enlightened genius after another was driven by the logic of the situation to take the inevitable step forward – 'such optimal paths are historical fictions, arrived at by belief ignoring a vast body of knowledge that was no less scientific in its time' (Ziman, 1976: 130).

This view of science as a changing story of endeavour, challenge and creativity is more appealing than the image of genius and an approach with only one 'method' that is termed 'the legend of science' (Kitcher, 1993). Whilst most people are aware that knowledge has developed and moved forward, as evidenced by the fact that few today believe that illness is caused by 'humours' or that 'all life on earth was created at one time', the view of how this science knowledge has been produced has remained constant. 'The legend of science' is a stereotypical view of the subject, an idealised viewpoint with only one method of guaranteed, unassailable competence (Campbell, 1974; Kitcher, 1993); and this ideal is what is taught in school

Yet science has much more to offer and perhaps it would have a greater appeal to learners if the approach to teaching the subject did not hide behind an elitist view that often results in many considering the subject as uninteresting and irrelevant. This is important because contrary to the numbers of interested learners in schools and colleges, television programmes and museums focusing on science are popular. There were 3.1 million general visitors in 2012/13 visiting the Science Museum in London. One value of science is that it produces knowledge that can be utilised to solve real problems; for example, advances in biochemistry can be utilised to create drugs and vaccinations that reduce childhood mortality, or advances in genetics which may, even within the next generation, produce 'three-parent' children who will have no genetic disorders. These are some of the ways in which science is contributing to improving human life. Yet science that is taught without the history of changing methodology and challenge fails to tell a story of science which can foster involvement. Science is not static, it is forever developing and that development began in earnest with scientists like Mendeleyev and Galileo.

One of these developments was the inclusion of mathematics, meaning that the qualitative medieval science began its transformation to that of the modern era. Science was providing technological advancement. Francis Bacon argued that the true value of science was its increasing ability to predict and control nature. He contended that the old way of debating things was not scientific and that in order to find truth, evidence was needed from nature. Galileo apparently observed the swinging of the lights in a cathedral, and from these observations he devised and developed his work on pendulums that resulted in a critical discovery which allowed the study of momentum, the measurement of time, and the development of the gravitational constant – ideas and inventions that are still used today. Although evidence in terms of observations and measurements was reported, the mathematics Galileo used was based on how the world should behave but not how it actually does! He identified that his 'world on paper' was not the same as the world of his observations. A number of scientists have tried to recreate his findings, some of which were found at the time to be 'falsifiable'. Naylor (1974) tried out a number of Galileo's famous experiments and concluded they would not provide the evidence for the theories proposed. Galileo however had powerful sponsors, and although he did not use a recognisable scientific method, because of this power his ideas were accepted. However, hindsight has shown his ideas had merit and without this step forward other discoveries might not have happened. It is unfortunate that these challenges and examples, where the discoveries do not hold to the idealistic view of science, are hidden from primary school children (and their teachers) by textbooks and stories which adhere to 'the legend'.

INDUCTION AND DEVELOPING THEORIES

This example of evidence not fitting the theory is not a feature within primary science because learners are only told 'the facts' that are in line with an idealised view of science. In learning to learn, it is advised that the journey might be hard and that some of the best learning comes from initial failure and mistakes; yet in science the perceived thoughts are those of correctness and accuracy. History demonstrates that there is not always one idea, or that initial ideas are subsequently further developed and new 'truths' emerge. Yet when, on occasions, the results of practical work do not give the 'expected' answer this is not anticipated because learners are taught that science is something that naturally follows from observation to the answer. In reality, the unexplained outcome can be used to truly review and evaluate what is happening, thus enriching the learning. Duschl (1990) suggested that science education needs to address not just what is known but how that knowledge has come to be accepted. There are many types of science and ways of gaining knowledge about science, and only one of these is from direct observation. Inductive reasoning is where observations are made and then theories are developed from these observations. The fundamental idea behind this is that knowledge is gained from direct sensory experiences. There are many stories in science where this process is said to have operated. Charles Darwin was supposed to have observed birds on the Galapagos islands and from noticing their differing shapes developed the idea of evolution.

> Darwin's conversion to the theory of evolution – once thought to have been a typical 'eureka' experience stemming from his famous voyage to the Galapagos Archipelago – is now generally seen as a slow and largely post-voyage development in his scientific thinking. (Sulloway, 1985: 122)

Observation and measurement play a vital part in science but, as Medawar (1969) argued, instead of just observations science also needed a theory, or an incentive to engage a scientist into making the observations in the first place. His comments were linked to his analogy that, otherwise scientists would 'browse a field like cows, looking for something to catch their eye'.

CASE STUDY

Shells in the fields

Whilst walking on a costal path in Cornwall I came across some sea shells in a field. They were at some distance from the sea, and as I collected them for a science teaching activity later that week, I speculated on how they had arrived there. Were they dropped by children who had collected them and, running back to their holiday cottage, had a few spilt out of their buckets? Could it be that they had been thrown up the cliffs and deposited in the field on a very windy or stormy day? Or, could there be another explanation, such as do shells grow in fields in Cornwall? The next day, in another field, again about 200 metres from the sea, while on a cliff walk, I found more shells, some of these had damage and so another thought occurred: could they have

(Continued)

been dropped by gulls? So was I, to use Medawar's view, 'browsing the field like a cow?' Or, when I observed something, did I begin to raise questions and make stories about how the shells might have arrived in the location? This in turn raises the question of, 'Is there only one method of science?'

Primary science in England has until recently only valued the fair test method of investigation and identified this as the only way to do science. In the current National Curriculum (DfE, 2013b) the inclusion of different methods of enquiry is encouraged, and this may help to break down the 'legend of science' approach. When developing learners to 'work scientifically', it is important not to just start with observations and follow an inductive approach, as induction does not operate well in a world without regularity or where objects cannot be seen at all. Many suggest that induction is not a valid scientific process and ask, 'Why would scientists make observations in the first place unless they had already spotted a problem or query?' In the shell example, was it by chance that the first shell was spotted? Whilst in some areas of science the question of why an observation would be made without a theory is a valid query, in other fields of science, such as observing the behaviour of people and other animals (surveying and pattern seeking), observing plants growing and seeing seasonal change (change over time), the very act of observation can and should be used to stimulate thoughts. The initial observations prompt questions and this can result in a hypothesis or idea (or story) being developed, and then decisions can be made on which further observations or measurements are needed to test this theory; this is a hypothetico-deductive process. It is possible I might have been looking at birds, chatting to my companion or thinking about dinner and would never have seen the shells at all!

Popper (1965) argued that induction does not exist; he said the starting point for all science is speculation and from this speculation observations are then made. Gibson (1977) identified that observer and the object are part of an energy flux which is perceived by the observer as something general before cognitive processes take place. Rorty (1991) suggested objects are printed as replicas on the retina and then this information is used in conjunction with information and previous experience to link to what is already known and thus to prompt a response, for example that 'shells do not grow in a field'. So was the image of the shell imprinted on the retina without intention and once there was the image linked to ideas already held and did a resulting speculation create further ideas and stories? Whilst Fleming was the first person to identify penicillin, it is thought that other plates in other labs at other times had shown the same results. Others therefore had seen the same things but not thought the same thoughts and the petri dishes were thrown away because they were thought to be contaminated. However, to be scientific there has to be a respect for curiosity, and an eagerness for new data. This is true in all aspects of science, so that further observations and measurements would be needed to even begin to decide on which theory might explain the spoilt petri dishes, or shells found in the field. In science others have to have access to the data to inspect the approaches and data and then approve the findings without being forced or bribed.

The shells in the field is an example of one way in which science works, it also demonstrates that a hypothetico-deductive method is more common than an inductive one. From the first observation a range of ideas emerged, but to be scientific a preferred theory would need to be selected and then checked against further evidence, rather than just collecting evidence without having a reason why it was being collected. It is now recognised that science is a hypothetico-deductive activity where theories are created, and falsified. It is a principle that is based upon a theory being in the mind of the scientist before observations were taken; and while this has become a more accepted approach, Lawson (2004) suggests that teachers and children still hold to inductivist approaches. Perhaps this is because science in school is more to do with following instructions and finding evidence to support 'the one idea' to which the answer is known. Ziman (1978: 23) goes one step further to explain why the hypothetico-deductive approach is the way scientists work, and suggests that this explains why some theories and models look like other things. Using the Rutherford–Bohr picture of the atom, as an example, in which the atoms are viewed as a planetary system of electrons in orbit around a nucleus. Ziman suggests that perhaps its basis was not just the principles of classic physics but also that it was familiar to scientists because they were used to such systems in astronomy. In the classroom some things can be explored just by using observation but for investigative work it is important that learners' own ideas and questions are used along with a range of approaches to finding answers.

KNOWLEDGE OF SCIENCE

The question of whether science tells the truth about the world and whether it explains nature is hotly debated outside primary science. Here, the issue of truth and reality will not be discussed; partly because it could form a book in its own right but also because in a practical guide to teaching science in primary school a focus on approaches that support teachers is more valuable. One starting point in finding a practical answer is to suggest a classification system to support the understanding of the different types of phenomena in science. Harré (1986) classified things into three Realms; the first Realm included all things that that are tangible and can be seen by the eye; examples of Realm 1 objects include an apple, the moon and springs. Realm 2 objects such as bacteria, viruses and atoms cannot be seen with the eye, only by using instruments and thus, in describing them, metaphors or analogies to things that can be seen are used. Whilst most of the scientific theories discussed in secondary schools involve Realm 2 objects there are some that are used in primary schools, such as forces at distance. Realm 3 objects are theoretical objects for which there is no direct evidence of their existence. In primary schools the majority of what is taught concerns items in the Realm 1 category, and it is vitally important that a basic understanding of these Realm 1 entities is developed at this phase of education because future scientific learning will be built upon this knowledge. However, some teachers will question the reality of science and its changing models and ideas, so in addition to understanding different types of phenomena it is useful to use a map analogy.

The building of science knowledge and its link to nature was first likened to a map by Korzybski (1931). When someone wants to get from A to B, a street map is useful but what is portrayed on the map is not the same as what is seen when one is in the street, although it is a helpful way of representing this reality. This metaphor of a map is a popular way to explain science (Korzybski, 1931; Toulmin, 1953; Ziman, 1978), because it can be used to clarify how ideas and concepts link together; for example, as more roads and motorways are built a map becomes more complex and it illustrates how even more places are linked; so too, as more in science is discovered there is an increase in complexity. Maps of one region can be linked to other areas and in the same way links can be made to other scientific theories which in turn make the scientific map more detailed, reliable and ultimately more worthwhile. This metaphor of a scientific map can also be used to discuss how science can be perceived at various levels of difficulty.

But in order to use a map, simple conventions first have to be taught; to begin, a learner must understand that a map is a 'bird's eye view' that is not necessarily to scale – that a map is a simplification and if you hold it in the wrong way then all sorts of trouble can ensue. In science, understanding the Realm 1 objects can start the process of understanding the directly observable. The abstract ideas should come later, in the same way that learning about maps would not provide concrete or first-hand experience because the symbols, conventions and signs on a map epitomise reality at an abstract level.

A perennial problem for learners is that at each new stage in science they are often told 'to forget what they were told previously'. Some materials, such as solids, are replaced by atoms, each of which has three elementary particles, which in turn are replaced by the ideas of quarks, and then the mind-blowing idea that a single atom contains more than 90 'things', and so it goes on. If the map analogy is used, then just in the way that maps can be produced with various scales and detail, so too with science; as concepts increase the 'science map' can be used to illustrate the increasing complexity. Thus at Key Stage 1 there might be a map of the whole of the world, but not in terms of detailed information. This large-scale map for young children is analogous to the idea that there are things called materials and they have simple properties, just like a map of broad generality. The map will contain Realm 1 objects. If more detail is needed, for instance, at the level of particles, then a higher resolution is needed to discuss and understand Realm 2 objects, but the basic skill of holding the map the right way up, knowing the language, and having engaged with the process can make learning more meaningful.

This grounding will eventually lead to an understanding of more complexity and abstraction. The analogy of science as a map also helps with the idea of reality, as no one imagines a map to be exactly the same as standing in a street. This can be shown simply by switching from a 'Google map' to a 'satellite view'. A map is an abstract representation. Just as with maps and places, as learners become more proficient through experience and practice, an unfamiliar place becomes familiar and the map is no longer needed to get from A to B. It is the same in science, as scientific theory becomes accepted so it becomes part of the known.

Science is an intellectual construct and the laws of nature are prescribed as a result of this human activity, and this is why sometimes scientific knowledge changes – in the same way as the maps of old, including those that contained 'here be dragons', altered because more first-hand information was available. Voyages of discovery meant that more was known and as a result more detail could be added to the map; even if sometimes the details were not completely accurate. However, as more specialised equipment became available then accuracy and detail improved. Despite this greater detail and precision, however, a map is still a map, a representation, and no matter how many maps are produced, reality can never be truly replicated.

THE NATURE OF SCIENTIFIC IDEAS

Enabling learners to make the link between their ideas and the evidence for them can be encouraged through simple activities. A good activity to make explicit the need to look objectively and to respect evidence to support conclusions follows, starting with Figure 1.1.

FIGURE 1.1
What ideas
are generated
by this
picture?

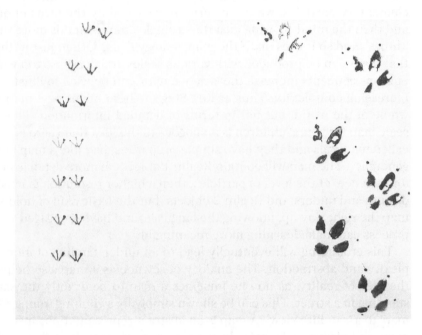

Many ancient sets of footprints have been found and these have fascinated scientists for centuries. Learners can be asked to reveal the ideas they hold as a result of looking at Figure 1.1. When shown this drawing recently, some learners stated that they thought the drawings were of footprints. When asked why they thought this, it was clear that they had brought evidence from everyday life to their interpretation of the drawing, for example having seen birds' footprints in the snow. They also stated that one animal was bigger than the other, as evidenced by the size of the footprint, and that the animal with larger prints had claws. While the smaller animal moved with both feet together, the larger footprints were made one at a time. An adult learner suggested that the small footprints were made by an animal with a small brain who had not evolved a brain big enough to have co-ordinated movement.

When more evidence (Figure 1.2) was presented, the learners put forward ideas of a meeting between the two animals, resulting in the smaller animal flying away, having a piggyback or coming to a 'sticky end'. The evidence that supported these ideas was elicited and questions were asked which focused the learners on what evidence explicitly supported their ideas and whether all the ideas could be correct.

FIGURE 1.2
More evidence
is provided;
have the ideas
changed?

In this case all the ideas had merit, although learners developed their favourite story, but it was not possible to discount the other views. In fact, there was no evidence to suggest that both footprints were made at the same time! Once the learners realised that in this type of science lesson the expectation was for them to promote ideas, to discuss evidence, and that their responses could be modified as more evidence came to light, they were ready and willing to use their enthusiasm and creativity in other activities. Challenging learners to use their ideas and collect evidence can occur in most activities, and as it starts to form their ideas, is more in line with Popper's view of science.

Tracks in everyday modern life provide as many challenges as using examples from pre-history. The tracks in Figure 1.3 were made on a beach in the USA in 2004. Looking at the different tracks should provide some evidence as to the 'animals' that made them. Enabling learners to be creative just requires less teacher direction and an understanding that science can be meaningful. Making tracks at school to solve problems is discussed in Chapter 5.

FIGURE 1.3
What made
these tracks?

On another occasion, everyday materials were used to link science to real life. Learners were asked to apply this approach to an everyday setting. A range of cans of proprietary soft drinks, i.e. a 'Coke', a 'Diet Coke' and a '7 Up', and a tank of water were used to challenge learners to provide ideas of what would happen when the cans were placed in water. Learners used previous knowledge of floating and sinking to arrive at suggestions. These included 'Diet Coke will float as it is lighter' and 'They will all sink because they are heavy'. The cans were placed into the water one by one, with an opportunity for the learners to observe what happened to each can, and learners were asked if they would like to alter their ideas based on the new evidence. In the event, the '7 Up' sank, the 'Coke' floated just off the bottom and the 'Diet Coke' floated just below the surface, which resulted in amazement and quick suggestions as to why this might be. The learners then had to think of ways to test out their ideas.

Suggested tests included weighing the cans, measuring the liquid, counting the number of bubbles in set amounts of each liquid and the use of secondary sources to research the composition of each liquid (for example, amount of sugar). One child suggested that if the cans had been placed in the tank in a different order a different result would have occurred. Identifying learners who require support or challenge is an additional advantage of working in this way. Although no writing was involved in the original part of the session, this did not make this activity less valuable. When the learners tried out their tests they recorded their results and communicated their findings in poster form later in the week.

PUPILS' PERCEPTIONS OF SCIENCE

Many people know that scientific ideas have changed; for example, that the world was thought to be flat, that coelacanths were thought to be extinct or that gold cannot be made from lead. The world has changed significantly from that of 100 years ago and so somehow thinking that a learner will be confused if a more up-to-date idea of science is provided seems inadequate. There is a link between the economic development of a country and its citizens' attitudes to science. The ROSE (Relevance of Science Education) project showed that in developing countries there is a strong positive correlation, whilst in developed countries the trend is a negative one (www.uv.uio.no/ils/english/research/projects/rose/index. html [accessed 29 May 2015]).

This report also identified that there was little evidence that the public at large were disinterested in science or that their interest in science was waning. In fact the interest in science as judged by the number of science books purchased, the viewing of science media and visits to science museums and fairs, suggests that there was little evidence to support a drop in the public interest in science. The researchers therefore concluded that this is a school phenomenon (Sjøberg, and Schreiner, 2005: 11). The latest PISA report suggests this has not changed (OECD, 2012).

Chambers (1983) was the first researcher to ask learners to draw a picture of a scientist and to investigate the age at which stereotypes of science emerged. This has been linked with the pupils' poor image of science and often issues of gender. The drawings by the learners are very entertaining, and as a result this research tool has continued to be used widely. There is a downside to this approach: if asking for a stereotype then it is rather less than surprising that this is what is provided. Instead of only asking learners to draw a scientist, these learners were also asked to use collage materials, to provide their perception of science. Whilst collage has been used since early times in China and has been used to assess individual subjective perception and subsequent behaviour (Stabler, 1988) it is still an unusual choice for scientific research. The benefit of using the collage is that it does not require written communication skills and can 'Express the views, opinion and projections of the participants in nonverbal form (the old adage that a picture is worth a 1,000 words)' (Stephen, 2009: 23). Learners who had previously been asked to draw a scientist (Figure 1.4) were then asked as part of their homework to create a collage of science without searching for 'science' on the internet.

FIGURE 1.4
Draw a
scientist

TEACHING SCIENCE IN THE PRIMARY CLASSROOM

The outcomes were thought-provoking, but it was what these learners said about science and their understanding of the word as they discussed their collages that was more fascinating.

It appears that the learners are far more aware of the world they live in than the drawing a picture of a scientist activity might suggest. They know about positive and negative aspects of science, they show interest in some aspects, like exploring the universe and how science helps with health and wellbeing. Some were able to identify the 'bad bits' of science, like making bombs and war. The collages helped the learners to express their knowledge and understanding in a far more sophisticated way than might have been expected.

FIGURE 1.5
Collage 'What is science?'

CASE STUDY

Katie's conversations with her learners

Sam (not his real name) was asked about his drawing of a scientist (Figure 1.4) and whether this was what he really thought scientists looked like. He said, 'If you had asked me to draw a dog I would have drawn you one type, but I know there are many types and most of them would not look like this!'

The learners had very positive things to say about science both out of school and in school, particularly the practical aspects; they disliked writing about something that is found in other research (Beggs and Murphy, 2005). Part of their conversation is produced below.

Girl 2: It's very simple at school most of the time. Some days can be good. It's easy though.

Teacher: Do you feel challenged with your science lessons in school?

Girl 1: Not always no.

Boy 1: Well put it this way … once we had to write about a digestive biscuit, to describe it. We had to just look at it and then write it down. I even had to write the word digestive. Fantastic!

Boy 2: It should be more real. They should teach us about the stuff we need to know about the different jobs.

Boy 1: I want to build a rocket in the classroom and see what happens.

Boy 3: But then not write about it. It's annoying having to keep doing it again. If I had to write about a football game every time and I love playing football I would hate football.

These learners' drawings of scientists showed the expected view of science, but their collages suggested that they were aware of new ways of thinking in line with technological advances. In discussions about school science it is proposed that learners could welcome more challenge, be involved in more real-life opportunities and have a chance to develop a different 'map' of science. Working scientifically provides this opportunity.

Recently this activity has been included in the first science sessions for the Initial Teacher Education postgraduate course at Christ Church University. Ellen's collage (Figure 1.5) is included along with her understanding of what science meant to her. Her understanding and interests are wide ranging.

ELLEN'S COLLAGE

The immediate ideas that sprang to mind were test tubes, circuits and scientists, including Newton and Einstein. I then thought about how science connects to all life on Earth. I thought about field trips and experiments including collecting and studying bugs, then thought about habitats of different animals (represented by the Nemo poster, where each fish is shown at their correct depth in the sea). I enjoyed studying genetics and the human body when I was at school, and the brain interested me. I then wanted to represent how science covers everything from the atom, to the universe.

Some will continue to point to teachers and a perceived lack of knowledge and confidence, and yet teachers, as evidenced by the Ellen's statement of what science means to her, now have more science knowledge than when the National Curriculum began. Possibly it is time to focus on a different notion of primary science teachers rather than a deficit model.

SUMMARY

The rest of this book provides practical examples of science in the classroom. The learners who took part in these activities are from schools across a large geographical area. Many of their teachers will say when asked that they lack confidence and so instead the approach is to focus on linking science across the curriculum, suggesting a range of learning and teaching approaches in order to try and rewrite the story of primary science teaching from one of incompetence (Osborne and Simon, 1996) and a lack of confidence (Royal Society, 2010), to a more realistic picture where teachers and children are discovering and drawing their own 'maps' of science. Before proceeding to the practical aspects of the book this chapter will end with an analogy used by Einstein, who many would identify as one of the most successful scientists, but who identified clearly there are many things that are unknown.

Einstein used the analogy of a watch when attempting to explain the universe, suggesting it was like trying to explain the operation of a watch without ever being able to open it. You can hear it ticking and see the movements of the hands, but you are unable to image the mechanism that produces these effects. This he said, 'was the limitation of human understanding'.

(Continued)

(Continued)

FURTHER READING

Mansfield, C.F. and Woods-McConney, A. (2012) '"I didn't always perceive myself as a 'science person'": Examining efficacy for primary science teaching', *Australian Journal of Teacher Education*, 37(10): 37–52.

Özel, M. (2012) 'Children's images of scientists: Does grade level make a difference?', *Educational Sciences: Theory & Practice* – Special Issue, Autumn, Educational Consultancy and Research Centre.

Yilmaz, C. and Eylem, B. (2012) 'Developing children's views of the nature of science through role play', *International Journal of Science Education*, 34(7): 1075–91.

2

THE SKILLS LEARNERS NEED TO LEARN SCIENCE: PROCESS SKILLS

Hellen Ward

This chapter will explore the process skills and their role in developing learners' knowledge and understanding of science. It will identify and consider the importance of developing these skills. Although termed the process skills – the skills needed to learn science, in everyday teaching and learning in schools – they are the basic skills. These basic skills, while sometimes implicit rather than explicit, are embedded into working scientifically: the backbone of the National Curriculum. The main aim of this chapter is to look at ways in which teachers can structure the experiences they provide to learners to develop these skills within the science topic or unit of work.

DEVELOPING LEARNERS' PROCESS SKILLS

Initially, learners' process skills are limited and unsystematic and are characterised by trial and error exploration. It is part of the teacher's role to help to develop learners' acquisition and competence in using these skills so that, as they make progress in learning science, they can approach the exploration of the world in a more systematic, organised and meaningful way. Instinctively, young learners make use of simple individual process skills all the time during their exploration of the world but, as they get older, individual skills become more important in formal education. The simpler skills involve observing, identifying, classifying, questioning and performing simple tests, but are fundamental to the development of more advanced skills such as planning, predicting and data interpretation.

FIGURE 2.1
Process
skills

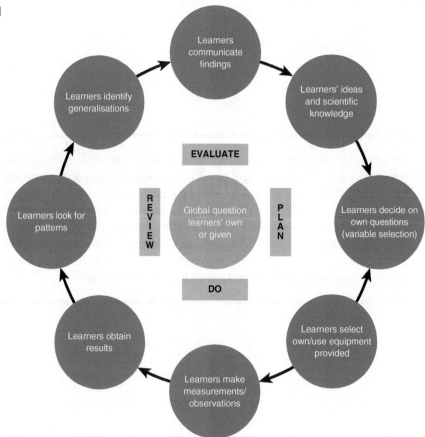

As learners move through school, teachers need to identify the individual process skills that together make up procedural understanding. Gott and Duggan characterise procedural understanding as 'the thinking behind the doing' (1995: 26), and argue that this thinking is the building block for understanding the notion of evidence. Science is built on the idea of cause and effect; something happens and there is a reason for it. If an evidence-based approach is taken, science learners will 'engage with and challenge the science that impacts on their lives' (Roberts et al., 2010). This process begins in the Early Years with a focus on how things are either the same or different as a result of carrying out simple tests; for example, blowing bubbles using different size blowers and observing if there is any difference in the size of the bubbles, or making suggestions and then testing the ideas to see the outcomes. The process skills are needed to develop procedural understanding and it is vital to provide opportunities for learners to practise these individually within activities where the learning intention is related explicitly to the chosen process skill. This will allow improved application of individual skills and over time, more sophisticated use of the whole process. There is research evidence that the process skills develop hierarchically (Russell, 1988). This suggests that teachers need to identify individual process skills at the planning stage and to focus learning intentions specifically on them. Millar and Driver (1987) maintain that the process approach should be seen as the means by which science concepts are learned, and not that they are a by-product of learning science; and Klahr and Simon (1999) encouraged the specific teaching of process skills to primary-aged learners.

Within a scientific activity learners may use a number of process skills separately or together depending on the context presented to them. Observation is a basic skill that links many of the other identified processes, often leading into and enhancing the quality of other process skills. Questions identified either by the teacher or learners as a result of observation can be used as a starting point for investigations of all kinds. Process skills are important, but their use depends on the learners' previous experience and on their previous knowledge and understanding of the topic under study.

HMI (2013) reported that science achievement was highest when pupils were fully involved in planning, carrying out and evaluating investigations that they had, partially, proposed themselves. However, they also noted that in a quarter of schools there was not enough challenge for higher-ability pupils because teachers did not see the purpose of constructing activities that enabled learners to discover the scientific ideas for themselves. Yet the process skills are an ideal vehicle to enable such scientific discovery.

Performing simple tests enables learners to make measurements using both standard and non-standard units and to use equipment with varying degrees of precision. Once data is collected, learners need to look for patterns and trends in order to draw their own conclusions, and explaining what they have found out enables them to make sense of their findings and allows them to use their increasing scientific vocabulary to enhance overall learning.

QUESTIONING AND QUESTION-RAISING

It is widely accepted that learners bring previous knowledge to a new situation and this forms the basis upon which to extend their understanding (Driver et al., 1985). In order to extend their knowledge further, learners should be encouraged to ask questions about the world around them. Being asked to raise questions and to find their own answers enables them to relate new ideas to a previous experience and to draw upon their current knowledge and understanding. Although they find this challenging, learners will, and do with encouragement, raise their own appropriate questions that can be investigated. Questioning, alongside observation and simple testing, is a key aspect of developing learners' understanding of the world. They need to understand the difference between the questions they raise that can be investigated, those that will be answered using other approaches and those that do not have an answer. Clearly, therefore, it is important to encourage learners to question, and there are a variety of ways to do this.

The use of a 'question box' in the classroom helps involve learners in the learning process. They post their questions about the unit of work being studied and these questions are then selected by the teacher and become the focus for planning the learning on a weekly basis. This method helps show the learners that their questions are important and valued, and that they can be effectively linked into classroom work. It is also a good idea to have a 'problem corner' or a 'question of the week' as this allows learners to pursue questions in their free time. Displays can include enquiry questions, and including a 'question board' is another strategy that encourages the involvement of learners. Here the questions are shared in a visual way and learners can then find the answers and add these to the working wall display. The answers can come from work in lessons as well as self-study or homework activities.

The KWHL grid (K = What I **Know**? W = **What** I want to know? H = **How** I will find out? L = What I have **Learned**?), also facilitates learners' raising questions at the start of a unit of work. The items in the 'Know' column can be used as a focus on areas of misconception and the questions raised can encourage learners' interest in lessons. Although not all of the questions will be asked in a form that can be investigated practically, many can be used as a starting point for appropriate practical work and others will be answered by using research in secondary sources.

While pre-school children seem continually to ask questions, some older learners seem to have lost this ability. This might be because traditional teaching has not required them to ask questions or, more often, learners are not encouraged to ask questions because teachers have not had time within the curriculum to allow these. In recent years learners' questions have been seen as somewhat irrelevant, with the trend towards the widespread use of inflexible schemes of work that provide little opportunity for work to be tailored to meet the needs of individuals. The *Maintaining Curiosity* report indicates that curriculum approaches that focus on questions set up:

> a climate of enquiry at the start of topics by asking pupils what they want to find out. That approach is particularly effective for science, because it allows teachers to set up practical investigations to answer questions that pupils have raised, providing a motivating purpose and context for learning. (HMI, 2013: 44)

Enabling learners to define their own questions is an important feature of investigative work. This could take place initially in basic skills lessons, with learners being taught how to ask investigative questions. It would be ideal if learners could, following this starting point, go on to try out their ideas. However, time for science in the primary curriculum has become squeezed in recent years and *Tomorrow's World* (CBI, 2015) suggested that 'unless science is exciting, interesting and challenging in primary school, the pipeline will clog long before secondary level', and that 53% of the primary teachers they questioned thought that science was less of a priority in the primary school curriculum over the last 5 years (www.cbi. org.uk/tomorrows-world/primary_schools_are_critical_t.html [accessed 29 May 2015]).

GLOBAL QUESTIONS

Teachers can help to scaffold learning related to investigative work by providing a 'global question' as the starting point. This enables learners to begin to identify variables and offers a way whereby they can generate a range of appropriate questions within an investigative framework.

Using the global question 'How can we keep a drink hot for the longest time?' provides an opportunity to identify many variables. However, in a lesson where the focus is upon the skill of question-raising, it is important for the teacher to select the variables to be used; for example, selecting the factor to change (independent variable) as 'the type of liquid' and the factor to measure (the dependent variable) as 'temperature over time'. From this starting point learners can then identify specific questions and the process should be supported by modelling and shared writing. The questions that result could be 'What happens to the temperature of different liquids over time?' or 'What happens to the temperature of liquids over time?' or even 'Which liquid will cool the quickest?' Discussion, alteration and refinement of these questions can then occur, further developing the learners' skills in question-raising.

Modelling allows learners to develop their skills further than if they were unaided; however, the degree of support should be reduced over time. Learners should be provided with opportunities to practise their newly developed skills, i.e. given the opportunity to generate new questions using the same global question but with different variables. For example, if, instead of the type of liquid, the independent variable could be changed to 'the type of materials the cup is made from', different questions will be formulated, such as 'Which material will keep a drink hotter for longer?' or 'Which material is the most effective at keeping a drink hot?' or 'What happens to the temperature of the liquid in different types of cup?' Some learners' questions will be more refined than others and discussion of this should be a teaching point so that gradually each learner begins to identify better questions. Eventually learners will be able to pose better questions, and then they can go further and identify global questions of their own.

VARIABLE IDENTIFICATION AND SELECTION

Variables are also called 'factors'. Those that can be changed are termed the independent variables, while those that can be observed and/or measured are called the dependent variables.

At the beginning it is useful to ask learners to identify all the variables for an investigation. Using a global question is a good starting point. For example, if the global question 'How can we keep an ice balloon from melting?' is used, learners should be able to identify, with some prompting from the teacher, what could be changed in order to keep the ice balloon as a solid. (An ice balloon is a balloon filled with water and chilled for 48 hours until frozen solid.) In this example, the independent variables include: the type of material, the amount of material, the size of the ice balloon, the shape of the ice balloon and where the ice balloon is placed (e.g. on a windowsill, on a desk or outside). When given the opportunity, learners do not usually find identifying variables difficult; in fact, they often enjoy the challenge.

Identifying the dependent variables is more problematic. These will provide the outcomes of the test, the temperature drop of the liquid or the time taken for the ice balloon to melt. Some learners will identify with the term 'measurement' and will think of measuring the ice. However, the amount of ice is one of the variables that can be changed and just measuring the amount of ice will not lead to data that will answer the question. Highlighting the different variables for changing and measuring using different coloured 'Post-it' notes, one colour for the variables that can be changed and another colour for those that can be measured, helps the learners to identify and recognise these different features (Figure 2.2).

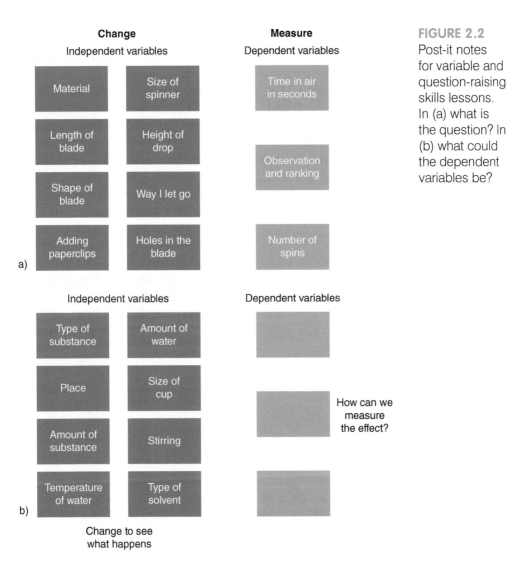

FIGURE 2.2
Post-it notes for variable and question-raising skills lessons. In (a) what is the question? In (b) what could the dependent variables be?

PREDICTING

Prediction is commonly practised in most primary classrooms. In fact, this could be seen as one of the key outcomes of the National Curriculum's impact on practice at Key Stages 1 and 2. Many lessons start with the question 'What do you think will happen?' before any equipment is used or any activity is undertaken. While prediction is an important skill, perhaps this emphasis or overemphasis should be evaluated.

With very young learners, asking for a prediction will often result in the response 'I don't know'. Using the ubiquitous 'cars down ramps' scenario, where learners are asked which car will travel the furthest, after being let go at the top of a ramp, often results in learners selecting a car of a particular colour because it is their favourite. When asked why, this in turn prompts a response such as: 'I like blue, because blue is the best'. Learners, at this stage, do not have a well-defined or developed understanding of why things happen and yet they are frequently asked to make a prediction. The result of this emphasis is twofold. First, learners are asked to make a prediction when their knowledge and understanding of the aspect are limited and, second, teachers pre-judge an outcome. When carrying out work with the cars, the learners either find that their ideas are wrong, so they 'cheat' to ensure their prediction 'becomes correct', or they change their prediction to match the findings, understanding only that they were wrong. In this scenario learners unconsciously receive the inappropriate message that making a prediction is an element of science that 'proves' that science has the right answer and that perhaps their role is to find it.

Teachers often also expect that the outcomes of activities will 'prove' a fact. It is really important that learners are allowed to carry out their own investigation, collect and interpret their own data and then consider what their data tells them, i.e. draw their own conclusions based on consideration of the collected evidence. It is tempting for teachers, anxious for their learners to get the 'right answer', to suggest that some data might be disregarded.

CASE STUDY

Mini-beasts

One group of Year 6 learners, working on a topic of mini-beasts, carried out a simple practical task to find out where woodlice like to live. The learners were asked to test different materials and to set up a survey. They were given a shoebox with a lid and a range of materials with which to line various sections of the box and in this way to find out if the woodlice had preferences. The learners carried out their observational activities and recorded the time the woodlice spent in the different places by time sampling and tallying the numbers of individuals in each location. The results of all the groups were fed back to the teacher at the end of 30 minutes.

The outcome was that all but one of the groups demonstrated that the woodlice preferred the damp area. However, one group found that their woodlice spent more time in the straw. Although their findings did not concur with other groups', their results were consistent with the data collected by their observations. These unexpected results neither tallied with their own prediction, nor with that of their class teacher. Unfortunately, the teacher stated that their results were wrong and that they should not write their findings as their conclusion. Ominously, they were required to write the conclusions obtained by the rest of the class.

This pre-judging an outcome is problematic because it promotes the idea that there is one answer and that the learners' role is to hunt it out! This is not helpful to the promotion of learning and does not reflect the way in which scientists work. Francesca Happé, one of the Acclaim scientists (www.nationalstemcentre.org.uk/elibrary/resource/6614/francesca-happ), when asked what she would do if her experiment did not work, stated

Think about why it didn't work, every finding tells you something if you can think about it laterally. It is important here to note that science develops through things that do not work as much as through those that do and that this is true also of how learners' understanding of science develops.

If young learners are continually asked to give a reason for why things might happen in advance of any exploration, they can image science as the hunt for what the teacher wants. Even adults if they have no previous experience or knowledge to use are actually put off when asked to give a prediction. Therefore, rather than always starting by asking, 'What do you think will happen?' as a direct question, teachers could instead allow the learners to talk about what they will do to answer a question. This view does not, however, preclude the teacher from taking notice, if learners spontaneously provide suggestions, about what they think might happen. This could be recorded in the learners' work and reflected upon with them, at a later time. In fact, this would indicate good practice, not least in terms of differentiation.

EQUIPMENT SELECTION AND USE

In the Early Years of primary education, learners are often expected to use equipment provided for them by their teacher and only later are they required to select their own. However, it is difficult for learners to choose appropriate instruments to use if they have had limited experience of using relevant resources. Therefore, learners need to be shown particular pieces of equipment and need to be taught explicitly how to use them. While it is common practice in mathematics for time to be spent on teaching learners how to use equipment by employing a range of approaches, in science, equipment is often introduced as part of an activity. It is better for scientific equipment to be introduced to the learners and that this should be the focus of the learning intention within an illustrative activity. This approach will not only lead to learners making informed choices about the equipment to use in an activity, but will enable them to use the equipment correctly and make more accurate measurements.

CASE STUDY

Using a Newton meter

Using a Newton meter is a prime example of a resource that is often not introduced before it is used. Initially, many learners are often not aware of forces in everyday life, let alone of how they may be measured. Before the Newton meter or spring balance is introduced to learners they need to have had opportunities to push objects with springs to see the effects this process has on the spring. Following this, they should go on to pull and contract springs as part of simple work on forces. (Springs are not expensive pieces of equipment and bags of 500 springs suitable for this purpose can be bought very cheaply.) Learners should then be introduced to a range of Newton meters and asked to find similarities and differences between them (10 N and 20 N, or 10 N and 5 N). The teachers should then model how a Newton meter is used before allowing the learners to explore using them. Using this approach results in less equipment being broken and learners who are more competent in the use of the equipment before any testing is undertaken. Learners need to be taught how to hold the meters correctly (to hold the Newton meter at the top with one hand and to place the little finger of the other hand in the hook at the bottom) then read the measurement accurately (pulling down on the hook gently, using only the little finger) reading from the scale. Next, the teacher should ask questions to focus the learners' attention, 'What happens to the spring when you pull down gently?', 'What happens to the spring when you stop pulling and allow the spring to return?' Changing over to different types of

Newton meters enables learners to obtain information in order to make generalisations. The bigger and thicker the spring, the harder it is to pull. Playing a guessing game in pairs helps learners to gain an understanding of this measurement of force. While one learner places their little finger on the hook of the Newton meter and closes their eyes, the other learner holds the top and asks the first learner to pull a force of a set number of Newtons, e.g. 4 N. When the learner who is pulling thinks he or she has pulled the requested amount of force, the pupil then opens their eyes and checks the scale. With learners changing over roles and using different force meters they not only become very accurate in estimation and scale reading, but also gain a clearer idea of what a Newton feels like.

It is crucial that, before learners are asked to make and record any measurements, they have been introduced to the relevant equipment in this way, otherwise their results will not be accurate, and therefore not reliable, and they will not be able to explain their findings.

COMPARATIVE AND FAIR TESTING

Working scientifically requires learners to use scientific methods, processes and skills (DfE, 2013b). For too long the methods in primary science have focused around the 'fair test'. Goldsworthy et al. noted that

the range of investigations used in fair testing is limited with dissolving in water being used as a context for fair testing by every child in the country an average of three times during key stage 2 and 3. (1998: 6)

There are many other methods of working scientifically, as discussed in Chapter 1, and the National Curriculum (DfE, 2013a) identifies that scientific enquiry should include: observing over time; pattern seeking; identifying, classifying and grouping; comparative and fair testing (controlled investigations); and researching using secondary sources. Learners need some guidance when they are identifying the independent and the dependent variables. Although often identified as one of the process skills, fair testing is actually a method of science. This method provides a platform to enable learners to carry out the work in one scientific way (the fair test). Although fair testing is only one aspect of working scientifically, it is the aspect focused upon extensively in the primary classroom. This has led to many learners and teachers seeing the 'fair test' as the only method of practical science and, often, most science activities are carried out using the fair-test model whether this is appropriate or not. The method is confusing for young learners because of the term 'fair', which to them means not to cheat or everyone 'having a turn'.

Scientifically, a fair test is one where only one variable is changed and all the rest remain constant. A comparative test is one where the learners compare the effect of two or more different factors and set up a number of tests at the same time. In a fair test it is the inability to keep all the factors constant that makes this method ineffective for some investigations. Plants, humans and other animals are living things with genetic differences. These differences can play havoc with the results unless large enough samples are used. There are other factors, the hidden ones that also affect results. A good example of a hidden factor can be demonstrated using the simple plants experiment.

CASE STUDY

Factors affecting plant growth

In a typical lesson on plants the factors that affect growth are selected. The teacher and learners talk about what to test, and decide upon changing/altering the amount of light, keeping the amount of water, soil, type of plant, etc., the same. The outcome is to be measured by comparing the height or colour of the leaves. One plant is placed on a windowsill, one in a cupboard and another under a table, and a 'fair test' is started. However, the plant on the windowsill does not grow as expected. This plant experiences the greatest range of temperatures, as it is in one of the hottest places during the day and the coldest place at night, sometimes it experiences a temperature change of as much as 20°C. This temperature change is a hidden factor which can cause the plant, and the teacher, stress. Another hidden factor is the genetic make-up of the plant. Both will impact upon the results and make it difficult to 'prove' the point being illustrated. A survey using more plants and obtaining a greater range of information would have been scientifically more accurate or 'fair'.

Extending the types of investigations that the learners are exposed to is essential. Going back to watching and recording change over time, surveying, problem-solving and making observations are vital. The class could plant a number of bean seeds in a plastic bag with some damp cotton wool at the bottom, at the rate of one a day for two weeks, and then monitor their growth. This will provide the opportunity for developing practical skills in a far better way than a situation where each learner in the class plants one seed at the same time. This is not an investigation but an observational task – a valid science activity – and will provide the learners with opportunities to learn about science and then use these skills to carry out their own investigations. This activity also allows for comparisons to be made between day 2 and day 10 for example. However, in order for this to take place, more value and status must be given to non-fair-test activities and a greater under-standing of methods of science is needed. In the 1800s, about 300 stones fell from the sky near a village in France called L'Aigle. Before the stones landed there were bright lights in the sky and the stones made craters in the ground. Using data collected from observations, scientists decided that the rocks had come from space. This deduction had no fair test element or planning attached to it; however, it was still effective science. The scientists obviously did not plan this event, but the method of gaining understanding about the world was still a valid one. Observations can be planned, and an immense amount of plan-ning and testing occurred prior to the invention of the first microscope. Allowing the learners to watch the growth and change of living things over time is a type of observation that can be planned and is an ele-ment of working scientifically that has much to recommend it. Darwin walked the same pathway in his garden every day and many of his ideas were developed as a result of the observations he made, these observa-tions also needed theories and speculation to be provided too. Perhaps a 'Darwin Walk' could be created in a school or local area, where the learners follow the same pathway throughout the year and observe and record how things change. Valuing other aspects of science, in addition to the fair test, is vital if progress is to be made in developing creative-thinking individuals for the future.

CHECKING OBSERVATION AND DATA

Once observations and measurements have been made it is important that learners review these. Taking more than one reading in a practi-cal investigation is expected from the end of Key Stage 1, although the expectation is that seven-year-olds will add the totals or take the mid-dle number. At this stage, looking at the readings and checking for odd results must be taught simply. Checking readings allows the reliability of the readings to be gauged. Learners can be taught to identify unusual results and, it is suggested, to repeat these. This skill should be taught in basic skills lessons and then should be practised during complete investigations.

USING A RANGE OF RECORDING STRATEGIES

There is a view that science is about doing and not communicating. Where communication happens it is sometimes focused around a writing frame or a photocopied worksheet. These forms of communication make it difficult to identify what learners know and can do. Creativity in science can be stifled by the use of a limited number of approaches and outdated recording strategies. Instead learners could be encouraged to record their findings in more imaginative ways; this will support both the less literate and more literate alike. Starting a topic with a mind map will provide evidence of prior learning. Using pictures to plan their simple tests can help children work in a systematic way and provide excellent evidence for assessment. Both of these activities also link with computer science: the sequence drawings are a type of algorithm and mind maps are useful to teach the skill of decomposition. Each child being given the opportunity to record in their own way encourages individualisation as well as indicating that there is not one particular way to record. Encouraging quick and simple recording throughout the lesson rather than having a lesson for practical work and a lesson for recording will make the recording more significant to the learners. Children's drawings provide a wealth of information about what they know. Using labelled diagrams, children can demonstrate their understanding of parts of the plant, recording the equipment they used in a comparative test or even showing what they think will happen. Writing in science can provide a context for development of English. Learners do need to have something to write about (Figure 2.3).

Learners may need to be introduced to different ways of recording in the same way as they need to be introduced to resources. Teachers could select a different method of recording to model each lesson. This then enables a range of recording opportunities to be provided throughout the year so that at a later stage, when learners are asked to choose their own, most appropriate, method, they will have a repertoire from which to select. Communicating their science understanding can also occur with newsletters and magazines. A great example of this is provided in Figure 2.4. The school sensibly covers the cost by charging a little for each copy.

The use of word banks and individual science dictionaries promotes learner independence. It is suggested that learners should be able to read and spell scientific vocabulary correctly and with confidence, using their growing word reading and spelling knowledge (DfE, 2013b). Recording in science also requires mathematical skills of drawing tables and graphs. Modelling and breaking these activities down into small steps helps learners to develop their recording skills.

FIGURE 2.3
Fleece

FIGURE 2.4
School
newsletter

THE SKILLS LEARNERS NEED TO LEARN SCIENCE

IDENTIFYING PATTERNS, TRENDS IN DATA AND DATA INTERPRETATION

Learners need to be taught how to present data: for example, drawing diagrams and graphs, as well as having the opportunity to interpret these. Interpreting data relies heavily on seeing patterns or relationships between things that can be observed. This skill is closely linked with the skill of evaluating. Specific lessons need to be planned across the Key Stage where time is devoted to this skill, enabling learners to find the patterns and draw inferences for themselves. An important part of pattern seeking is being able to describe what is seen. Learners therefore need the support of the teacher to develop the appropriate vocabulary and to know what to identify. Pattern seeking is about describing what is seen rather than explaining why it happens. Providing graphs and asking questions related to these enables learners to learn how to interpret the graphs. This is initially difficult for many learners as graphing skills usually focus upon the drawing of the minutiae rather than the broad patterns within.

Identifying the patterns and trends would rarely take up a complete science lesson, so after identifying the patterns and trends the learners can then try out one of the tasks. As learners often have difficulties in interpreting patterns and trends, starting a lesson in this way is helpful. Frequently, insufficient time is devoted to this aspect of learning in science as these tasks are often left to the end of an illustrative or investigative activity. Consequently, for many learners, their ability to identify patterns, to see trends in data and to interpret what their data tell them is often underdeveloped. They are not being provided with sufficient opportunity to develop the higher-order skills in science, because carrying out the activity and recording the result are viewed as more important.

DRAWING GRAPHS

Drawing graphs is hard, and teachers need to provide learners with support for graph-making. A good introduction is to start with examples of graphs that have a mistake in them, as asking learners to 'spot the deliberate mistakes' helps them to identify what features a graph should contain (see Figure 2.5). Teaching learners graph-drawing skills and allowing opportunities to practise these skills does work. Learners can become very good at drawing graphs, and this can be related directly to detailed teaching. When interpreting data is the learning intention, rather than the drawing of a graph itself, the time involved in drawing a graph can be minimised by use of a computer program. Graphs work is a central part of mathematics, and science provides a good context for graphs.

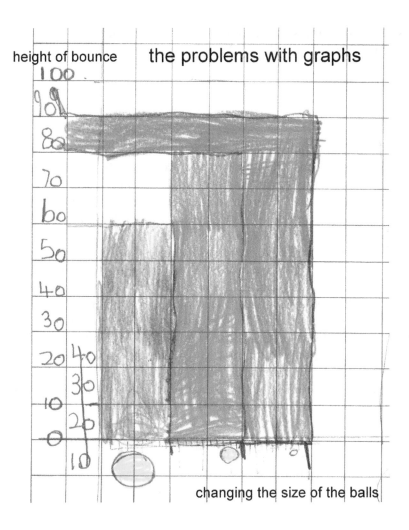

FIGURE 2.5
Is my graph
correct?

the problems with graphs

height of bounce

changing the size of the balls

CONCLUSIONS

Drawing conclusions makes learners aware of what they have discovered and why it is relevant, but few learners find this easy. Concluding is a crucial, basic skill that is made easier if learners have developed enough appropriate scientific vocabulary. Providing opportunities for learners to evaluate conclusions written by others, especially if this is undertaken as an aspect of peer assessment, supports this process and helps learners to identify what are the features of good explanations and how they differ from descriptions. Providing skills lessons that focus upon a set of prewritten conclusions with modelling and scaffolding by the teacher is vital. Learners should not write down the statements or conclusions that have been modelled for them, but should always try to improve or alter the ones that have been discussed. This process also supports scientific understanding and the content of the statements can be altered in order to target the skill of drawing appropriate conclusions based on evidence.

EVALUATION

Evaluation is an important process skill following an investigation. The evaluation of the way in which an activity proceeded is required, as is questioning the reliability of the data collected. Learners need to review, critically, the methods used in order to make suggestions for future work. They also need to discuss what they have done and why, and to think about how else they might have completed the task or recorded the information. This allows learners to actively evaluate their own and others' learning and by providing a structure for this to happen, such as a series of questions, scaffolds the process. Where learners are not supported in this process they often evaluate the work in a non-scientific way; for example, in one case a group of 10-year-olds were asked to evaluate the work: 'It would have been better if Kirsty had not been sick in the bucket' was the response. A group of infants, who were not used to investigating or evaluating their work, suggested 'It was fun, do not change it at all'! However, the question needs to be asked if learners are to become more skilled in their ability to evaluate. Evaluations have a strong link to the English curriculum and are an example of complex sentences where cause and effect are linked by the term 'because'. It is important that these opportunities are not missed. Science provides an opportunity for writing across the curriculum.

SUMMARY

The importance of the process skills that are needed in order to undertake scientific enquiry has been highlighted throughout this chapter. The chapter has shown the need to plan directly for the development of individual science process skills and to include activities in science that will enable learners to develop these progressively and systematically throughout their time in school. These approaches will develop learners' procedural understanding. The chapters that follow will consider these issues in more depth; for example, the next chapter will focus more specifically on the skill of observation. Chapter 5 will expand on these skills and show how they are linked in working scientifically.

FURTHER READING

Gillies, R.M., Nichols, K., Burgh, K. and Haynes, M. (2014) 'Primary students' scientific reasoning and discourse during cooperative inquiry-based science activities', *International Journal of Educational Research*, 63: 127–40.

Jirout, J. and Klahr, D. (2012) 'Children's scientific curiosity: In search of an operational definition of an elusive concept', *Developmental Review*, 32(2): 125–60.

Milne, I. (2007) 'Children's science', *Primary Science Review*, Issue 100: 33–4.

Osman, K. (2012) 'Primary science: Knowing about the world through science process skills', *Asian Social Science*, 8(16). DOI: 10.5539/ass.v8n16p1.

3

OBSERVATION, MEASUREMENT AND CLASSIFICATION

Judith Roden

This chapter will explore why it is important for learners to be regularly provided with activities to develop their observation, measurement and classification skills, and also provide suggestions for a range of activities that will help teachers to plan systematic and worthwhile activities to help pupils to progress in their science studies. Additionally, it will provide an explanation of how these can contribute to progression in the scientific learning associated with developing an understanding of the world and working scientifically.

DEVELOPING THE SKILLS OF OBSERVATION, MEASUREMENT AND CLASSIFICATION

Observation, measurement and classification are fundamental aspects of scientific enquiry at all key stages of the primary school. The most important of these is observation, which makes the others possible. In order to develop learners' knowledge and understanding of the world at the Foundation Stage, practitioners should give particular attention to activities based on first-hand exploration. Building on this experience, it is important that older learners collect evidence by making observations and measurements when trying to answer a question, and later that they test ideas, including those of their own, using evidence from observation and measurement.

Clearly, accuracy and attention to detail within the skill of observation is crucial both for precision in making measurements when collecting data and for comparing things with each other. Comparison leads to grouping of objects and things both living and non-living that are similar and those that are different. Although it may not be obvious, classification based on close observation and accurate measurements is very important in science, whether the things to be grouped are living or non-living, animals or plants, chemical or other materials, or, for example, whether things conduct electricity or are electrical insulators. Observation forms the basis for fundamental classification systems such as the taxonomy of plants or animals and the classification of the periodic table of the elements.

One point of note here is that the systematic development of the process skills of observation, measurement and classification, which together form a simple type of investigation, should not be taught separately as isolated tasks, but should be set in the context of other specific scientific topics within a scheme of work. This means that teachers should focus learning intentions specifically on observation, measurement and classification, and they should regularly provide specific tasks that require learners to make observations and measurements in relation to things in the living and non-living world, materials, their properties and usage and functions, and within the physical sciences, using these important process skills as a basis for classification.

It is crucial that learners are provided with opportunities to observe, measure and classify, noticing the finer detail of things, and that this should be included in schemes of work across the whole of the 3–11-year age range. This not only helps to interrelate scientific enquiry with the other aspects of science, but also should enable learners to build up an understanding of things systematically across the various aspects of science. For example, when looking at aspects of the living world, learners could observe things from the natural world, such as small creatures, leaves or flowers, etc. By doing so, learners will also develop their understanding of, for example, the diversity of living things, the parts of a flower or parts of a leaf. Observation and drawing of a number of different kinds of pine cones, or rocks, or shells, will reveal the differences there are between things which are similar. In the same way, in relation to materials and their properties, learners could look closely at a variety of fabrics, or paper, or wood, which could lead to simple investigations to find out, for example, which fabric absorbs the most water, or which is the best wrapping paper with which to wrap up Christmas parcels, or which is the best paper for writing on. When the focus of study is on physical processes, learners might be encouraged to note the finer parts of unconnected small light bulbs. Here, noting similarities and differences between bulbs of different voltages may well lead directly to questions about the size of filaments and simple investigations to find out what happens when the different bulbs are connected, one by one, into the same simple electrical circuits.

Observational drawings provide excellent opportunities for learners to record their observations and measurements. Here, teacher questions should focus on learners looking for detail and patterns, etc. Some might argue that observational drawing is more of an art than a science activity; however, in science it is different because the learning intentions are different. The learning intention in science is not about the quality of the drawing, although accuracy in drawing might be encouraged, but more about recording observed features, noticing detail and patterns, and identifying similarities and differences.

The use of frames or 'peepholes' can focus learners' observations on a small area to view specific details rather than on gross external features. Use of peepholes is less threatening than asking learners to draw a whole object, as only one small part has to be focused on. It is important to realise that it is legitimate, and important, to have process skills learning intentions in addition to those relating to knowledge and understanding, or sometimes exclusively. These should be indicated explicitly in long- , medium- and short-term plans as well as in lesson plans. It is important to remember that here the focus is on developing the process skills.

Progression in what is expected from learners is important in terms of observation, measurement and classification as they progress through the early and primary years. Consequently, while activities provided for learners may be similar in nature at the different levels, teachers need to place different expectations on different individuals and groups of learners to ensure challenge and linear progression in learning.

WHY LEARNERS SHOULD BE TAUGHT TO OBSERVE

Clearly, observation is important: it is a fundamental aspect of the learning process and, although the skill is taken much for granted in everyday life, it is crucial for making sense of the world from an early age. Without this first-hand experience, learners may not question what is observed in their world. Observation provides the opportunity for learners to explore the nature of objects and the relationship between objects. Observation and, more importantly as they get older, critical observation, promotes scientific thinking and contributes to learners' understanding of science. Explanations can easily follow from close observation. Furthermore, initial observations can lead to the formulation of questions, hypotheses, predictions and conclusions.

Observation is also one of the most important process skills for developing knowledge of the natural and physical world. Here, observation provides a good starting point for further exploration and investigation. It is widely accepted that learners and adults learn about the world by using all their senses – touch, sight, smell, taste and hearing – and so learners should regularly, when appropriate and with care, be asked to undertake activities specifically planned to develop the skill. Observation is therefore an important process skill, because it develops the ability to use all the senses appropriately and safely, which enables learners to find patterns and develops the ability to sort and classify.

The role of the teacher in helping learners to observe is crucial here, as what teachers ask learners to look for can have a significant effect on what is observed. Additionally, what learners see is influenced by what they already know, or think they know. Therefore, focused observation not only helps learners to identify differences and similarities between objects or situations, but also helps them to see previously unnoticed patterns and to provide questions to be investigated further.

It is generally recognised that learners find it more difficult to notice similarities because differences are often more obvious. Learners also need to be encouraged to look for patterns and sequences in a series of observations, especially in illustrative activities and investigations. Ultimately, systematic observation, particularly when collecting data (for example, when measuring the temperature of water as it cools), results in accurate observations.

Developing the skill of observation is important in helping to seek explanations for observed phenomena. Learners come to understand better by being asked to articulate their ideas. While this is true for the individual, this also follows for the wider development of scientific knowledge and understanding within the larger scientific community. In the past, great leaps in the development of scientific ideas have come about from an initial starting point where a small, possibly unusual, observation has led to a search for a new explanation for the observation or inconsistency. This helps to explain how revolutions in scientific thinking have come about: for example, Newton's observation of the apple falling from a tree, Archimedes' observations of water levels or Priestley's exploration of what happens when something burns.

WHAT SORT OF ACTIVITIES CAN HELP LEARNERS TO DEVELOP THEIR OBSERVATION SKILLS?

There are many basic observation activities that can be used across the age range. For example, at the earliest stages of education, observation enables learners to gain information about a wide variety of different everyday objects helping them to better understand the world around them. Learners should regularly be asked to describe, for instance, a leaf, an apple, a book or a table fork, thus enabling them to see similarities and differences between things that are very different. Building on this foundation, older learners can be asked to describe objects that are very similar, such as a number of different leaves, pine cones, seashells, rocks, etc. This leads to the recognition of characteristics by which scientists group things together. Older learners need to be challenged to observe finer detail. This can be made more challenging by asking more able and older learners for measurements to be included in the description.

A good activity for making learners look more closely at objects makes use of a digital camera or tablet device. Providing learners with close-up photographs of an object and then asking them to identify the object from the picture is a good way to encourage fine observation. If learners cannot identify the object immediately they can be challenged to 'go find the object'. This is a fun way to improve finer observational skills and learners enjoy the experience. Younger learners can be provided with photographs that may well seem obvious to older learners and adults, for example see Figure 3.1.

Learners can be given a range of close-up photographs and the real objects can be placed around the room. Learners are then challenged to match the photo with the real object and asked to identify the object. Older learners will enjoy identifying a more difficult close-up photograph, acting as detectives to find the answer. Observational activities provide plenty of scope for exploration and questioning. Learners enjoy a challenge and 'mystery parcels' offer the opportunity to develop observation

FIGURE 3.1
Close-up
photograph
of broccoli

using a variety of senses and the development of vocabulary. An object can be wrapped in newspaper – a little like the party game 'pass the parcel'. Once it is wrapped, learners can be asked to feel the parcel and to note any words used to describe it. After a short time they can be asked to try to identify the object from their observations, then to unwrap the object and note down further words to describe the object. Alternatively, an object could be placed in a shoebox, or smaller items, such as paperclips, a magnet or a piece of Plasticine, could be placed in a matchbox.

Observational skills can also be developed through the use of simple games. 'Feely bags' are popular in many classrooms. Variations on the theme of 'Kim's game' (discussed in Chapter 9) provide learners with the opportunity to look at a tray full of objects including a range of different items made of different materials (e.g. a balloon, a plastic spoon, fabric and a rubber ball – fewer for younger learners, more for older learners) for a few minutes, before having to recall what is on the tray. This game, as well as developing memory, can be extended to differentiate not only what the object is, but learners can also be asked to recall finer details; for example, what colour the object is, how many wheels it has, and finer details about a wheel, such as how many spokes it has. Learners can play the 'yes/no' game where one child secretly chooses one item from the tray and others ask questions to try to identify the object. This will require learners to think about the detail of an object and/or what it is made of. Some variations might include hard/soft, shiny/dull, natural/human-made. From a planning perspective, differentiation is 'built in' and is achieved by outcome.

SORTING AND CLASSIFYING

Being asked to sort and classify provided objects naturally leads to seeing similarities and differences between objects. Sorting and classifying is also fundamental to science. Learners need to be given many opportunities, starting from observation using all their senses, and from their earliest days in school, to develop systematically the skills of sorting and classifying. At the Foundation Stage and Key Stage 1, this mainly involves sorting based on gross features. Can learners sort into two groups, three groups or four groups? A variation on this theme could be that the teacher sorts a group of objects and challenges the learners to state which criterion has been used to classify them. A further development could be where the teacher provides objects sorted into two groups and provides other objects for learners to add to one of the groups. Learners then need to explain why the new object belongs in the chosen group.

Learners group from an early age, but are not able to give reasons for doing so. Learners say that things just 'go together' instead of saying they have the same characteristics. It is tempting to think that older learners need not practise these basic skills, but they too need opportunities to notice more detail and to look for more sophisticated patterns within and between objects. Therefore, older learners should be challenged to make finer observations of everyday and more unusual objects.

Basic sorting not only leads to classification but, in itself, helps to develop learners' observation skills by asking them to examine detail to find out which groups they belong to. Observation in this context leads learners to notice patterns; for example, that all seashells have similarities and are made of the same material, but that differences between shells are often substantial. Finer observation of detail may reveal differences between other things that are basically 'the same', such as rocks, or a natural seasonal change like the discoloration of leaves in the autumn.

LEARNERS' OBSERVATIONS

Experience suggests that observations are frequently influenced by past experiences and therefore learners' observations are often not what might be expected. Learners will often observe what they think they can see, but actually it is often what is stored in their memory. Such observations are frequently 'contaminated' by their previous experience. For some learners, observation is important because they may be being asked to look closely at some objects for the first time. Young learners can often surprise adults by what they notice and it is important that their observations are not dismissed as irrelevant. Young learners make sense of things based on previous experience and therefore it should not be surprising when they appear to make what adults might think are irrelevant observations. In some ways, young learners' observations can be very limited, while often being influenced by other things in their real world, such as storybooks and other aspects of popular culture like videos and cartoons.

Johnson (2014) researched early scientific observations in children under four years of age and came to the conclusion that many responses of young children are non-verbal (Johnson, 2014: 9–11). However, she has also held the view for many years (Johnson, 2005) that children's creative approach to observation needs to be encouraged and she says that children's drawings often show their 'observation skills and creativity' and that these 'creative additions' indicate wider powers of observation (2005: 35). Furthermore, the way in which this manifests itself in learners' drawings often differs according to gender. Girls tend to include more 'touchy feely' additions while boys generally will be more imaginative in their additions. However, there is an obvious tension here because on the one hand we want to encourage learners to be creative, but on the other we want them to make accurate observations of things in their environment.

WHAT DO LEARNERS NOTICE?

The three observational drawings of fish shown in Figure 3.2 are all drawings of the same trout drawn on the same day by seven-year-old learners. The fish was placed on a white tray in the middle of a large table and learners were placed around the table and asked to draw the fish. The quality of the drawings varies enormously; fish 1 shows much immaturity in both observational and drawing skills, but indicates features observed by the child and reproduced in the drawing. Fish 2 has a noticeable head feature that is more reminiscent of a turtle, rather than a fish. Many people assessing fish 3 choose this as the best drawing of a fish, which it is; however, the drawing is typical of one that draws more from memory of pictures of fish than from observation of the fish on the table. The role of the teacher here is very important, as learners need to be asked regularly what is being noticed to enable them to discriminate fine detail.

On the other hand, the drawings of various small creatures, drawn by very young learners, indicate that they have been influenced by remembered images of the creatures from books of fiction or other aspects of

FIGURE 3.2
Fish drawings

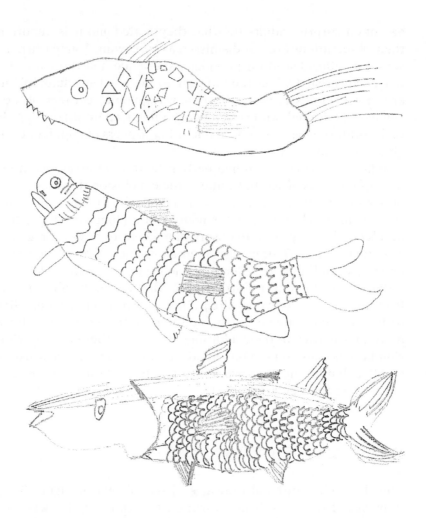

popular culture. Often, drawings of animals can have faces drawn on them. A drawing of a crane fly, while showing some very good observed features, provided a more creative impression rather than of the observed creature. One boy drew a crane fly that had almost fairy-like qualities and the lady-birds, drawn by girls, had been given human-like characteristics. These are typical of young learners' drawings of real things in their environment.

Children's observational skills can be enhanced by recording their observations using a range of media. Here, there is a need for practition-ers to emphasise that children should draw 'what they see' – in contrast to 'using their imagination' as children quite often are encouraged to do in other contexts. However, the need to embellish observational draw-ings seems to be deep-rooted. Using their imagination is often evident in learners' paintings and drawings of living things found in the environment. Even when prompted, children often draw faces on their drawings before realising that this was not what they were observing.

The above are fairly typical responses by younger children and demonstrate how children's ideas and perceptions of reality can be so easily influenced by the media and other aspects of their everyday lives. Children's views of the world are often very different from those of older children and adults.

Clearly, from a scientific point of view, while wanting to encourage creativity, it would be preferable that the drawings focused on observable features and did not include fanciful features perhaps influenced by learners' reading matter and other media. One further problem here is that teachers will regularly praise highly such drawings because of their artistic, creative content rather than their close observations. Thinking about progression in the skill of observation, it is likely, however, that older and more able children will make more realistic observational drawings than younger or less able children.

Other activities to promote the skill of observation

Other activities that do not require such intense teacher input, within the context of life processes and living things, could include learners sorting picture cards of plants or pictures or models of animals into groups based on observable features. This leads directly on to classification of living things. Younger learners will sort things familiar to themselves in various categories, for example whether they fly, walk or swim; alternatively they may group the 'scary' animals and the 'friendly' animals. Older learners should be more able to group animals into scientific groups and, if not, should be challenged to do so. An activity like this can assess the extent to which learners understand, for example, the vertebrate groups. Experience tells us that many adults as well as learners will group amphibians (frogs, toads, salamanders and newts) with reptiles (lizards, snakes, etc.). While both groups have some similar features, there are major differences which need to be identified. Talking to learners and beginning teachers in training it is clear that many become more, not less, confused about animal groups as they get older. This needs to be dealt with at a simple level at the primary stage.

There are a number of misconceptions relating to animal groups that are commonly held by learners and many adults. For example, young learners will often be confused because, although it can fly, a bat is a mammal not, as they might think, a bird. Similarly, a penguin can be confusing because, although it is a bird, it does not fly in the air. Dolphins are often considered to be fish rather than mammals, and the difference between reptiles and amphibians is not often clear. Amphibians have soft, damp bodies and start their lives in water, whereas reptiles tend to have scaly skins. Frogs, toads, newts and salamanders are amphibians; lizards, snakes, turtles, crocodiles and alligators are reptiles. The confusion arises because newts and sala-manders look like some lizards and many reptiles are amphibious, that is, they spend time in water and on land. Many adults are not clear about the difference between vertebrates, those animals with backbones, and invertebrates, those without backbones. In particular, worms, snakes and some lizards, such as slow-worms, are confused because at first glance they have similar features. Where invertebrates are concerned, many individu-als have problems in relation to 'insects' where in everyday usage this term often means all small creatures such as spiders, millipedes, etc., whereas the term 'insect', in science, relates specifically only to those creatures that have six legs, a thorax, a head and an abdomen.

Using models that are not made to scale, common in many Early Years classrooms, also might lead to misconceptions with younger learners. In addition, it needs to be borne in mind that sometimes even identifica-tion books can help to promote misconceptions. Teachers and parents need to be aware of the possibility that some identification books, even if entitled 'Insects', may well include animals of other subgroups, for example, spiders, molluscs and crustaceans.

MAKING AND USING KEYS

Basic sorting leads to classification. Learners of all ages need to be able to use classification keys: even Foundation Stage learners can be introduced to simple keys made up by their teacher or by older learn-ers especially for their younger peers. Using keys can help learners to become less confused about animal groups. This is one good reason for including them in teaching in the primary classroom. Use of keys should start off simply, based on a very few different objects with very different characteristics. Older learners need to be introduced progressively to more complex keys. The oldest and most able primary learners can be expected to be able to make keys. Once again, learners should be intro-duced to this by being given fewer and very different objects and then asked to draw up a list of characteristics for each object. They can then be asked to make up a simple branching key. Coins could provide a good starting point for this activity. Once made, learners could swap keys to see if they work.

OTHER ASPECTS OF OBSERVATION

It is important to remember that observation in science includes all the senses and therefore it is appropriate for learners to be asked to identify things using other senses than sight. Learners could undertake a 'senses survey' where they are asked to notice things deliberately placed in the room; for example, a fan blowing at foot level – did they notice? A smell in the room; for example, perfume or sliced onions revealed at a certain point in a session. There could be things to feel when blindfolded, such as a teddy bear or rough sandpaper, and things to listen to; for example, at what level of loudness can learners first identify a tune well known to them? Can they identify taped noises, of a tap running, a clock ticking, etc.?

Observation is very important when learners are carrying out practical work. Obviously it is important that data collected within an illustrative activity or an investigation is accurate and reliable. Learners need to be able to read scales on a thermometer or Newton meter with accuracy, as inaccuracy can lead to much wasted time. Accurate observations of change, over time, are also crucial to the outcome of an investigation and to what learners learn from the experience:

FIGURE 3.3
Salt dissolving in water over time

CASE STUDY

Separating mixtures

A class of Year 4 children (aged 8–9) were attempting to separate four mixtures. Included in the mixtures was one of gravel and salt. Having successfully separated the gravel from the salt using a sieve, one group added the remaining salt to water. In response to the adult helper's question, one child explained that they did this because the salt would dissolve in the water. The learner showed the resulting cloudy-looking liquid to the adult and said the salt had dissolved. The group then went straight to the next task without another thought about the salt water. However, their attention was re-focused on the salt–water mixture by the adult, who realised that something unexpected had been observed: the salt solution should be clear, not cloudy. This led to further exploration and close observation by the group. A teaspoon of salt was added to about 100 ml of water and stirred. The group watched what was happening in the beaker and noticed that at first the mixture looked cloudy and it was only after a number of seconds that the liquid became clear. At this point the adult introduced the word 'transparent' and emphasised the need for the liquid to be transparent to be able to say that the solute (in this instance the salt) had dissolved. Fascinated by the change over time, the learners went on to take photographs of the changes in the water as the salt dissolved (see Figure 3.2). Had the adult helper not taken action in this way, the children may well have continued to think that solutions look cloudy.

SUMMARY

Observing is the skill of absorbing all the information about the things around us. Learners need to be encouraged to notice fine detail and go beyond what they expect to see. Learners should develop the ability to distinguish what is relevant and what is not. They should be given the opportunity to record observations in a variety of ways, including talking, writing or through their drawings.

The teacher's role in developing observation skills is not to be the fount of all knowledge. Rather, the teacher should enable learners to see with 'new' eyes. The teacher can do this by carefully structuring opportunities for the development of observation skills. Plenty of resources need to be provided; materials need to be selected carefully. Learners need the opportunity to share their observations with others and need to be questioned about what they are noticing.

FURTHER READING

Harlen, W. and Symington, D. (1985) 'Helping children to observe', in Harlen, W. (ed.), *Primary Science: Taking the Plunge*. London: Heinemann.

Johnson, J. (2005) *Early Explorations in Science* (2nd edn). Maidenhead: Open University Press.

Johnson, J. (2014) Chapter 1 'The development of emergent skills', in *Emergent Science: Teaching Science from Birth to 8*. Abingdon: Routledge.

Roden, J. (1999) Chapter 9 'Young children are natural scientists', in David, T. (ed.), *Young Children Learning*. London: Sage.

Roden, J. (2015) Chapter 3 'An introduction to science', in Driscoll, P., Lanbirth, A. and Roden, J., *The Primary Curriculum: A Creative Approach* (2nd edn). London: Sage.

Roden, J. and Archer, J. (2014) Chapter 1 'Working scientifically', in *Primary Science for Trainee Teachers*. London: Learning Matters (Sage).

4

RAISING AND ANALYSING QUESTIONS AND USE OF SECONDARY SOURCES

Judith Roden

Chapter 3 explained how observation, as a fundamental skill, could lead learners naturally to seeing patterns and sorting into groups, leading to classification. Following on directly from Chapter 3, this chapter will focus more particularly on asking questions, which, along with measurement and classification, are often neglected aspects of scientific enquiry. The nature of learners' questions and how teachers can provide a role model will be explored. The chapter will also provide an analysis of teachers' and learners' questions that form the basis for productive learning at an appropriate level in the primary classroom, with examples of the questions that learners ask and how these can be responded to.

LEARNERS RAISING QUESTIONS WITHIN STATUTORY REQUIREMENTS

In the Early Years Foundation Stage, there is an increasing expectation, building on pre-school learning, that learners will ask questions. In England, The Early Years Foundation Stage (EYFS) (from birth to five years) science is part of Understanding the World. The EYFS Early Learning Goals, reflecting what is known about child development, expect that from birth learners will show interest in the world around them by observing and following objects that move and by interacting with things such as kicking a ball or shaking a rattle. Even at this very young stage in a learner's life, although the learner will not be able to articulate a question, questions can be identified from what learners are doing, for example 'What will happen if I kick the ball?' or 'What will happen if I shake the rattle?' Early Years practitioners are encouraged to look for instances when their learners make close observations such as what animals, people and vehicles do, or when they look for objects buried in the sand answering the unstated question 'What can I find hidden in the sand?' They also begin to explore scientific concepts such as sound and cause and effect when they explore what happens (e.g. when they bang two objects together or push a toy car along the ground).

The use of all the senses leads to questions about how different things taste and what happens if, for example, a finger is poked into play dough, or a button on a toy is pushed, or a toy duck in the bath is pushed under the water. They begin to recognise the similarities and differences between themselves and others by exploring unarticulated questions about how things are the same and how things are different (e.g. 'What is the difference between a lamb and its mother?' or 'What is the difference between a snail and a slug?'). Such explorations and raising of questions happen all the time and are frequently not recognised as indications of young learners beginning to 'work scientifically'.

In the Early Years there is a heavy emphasis on learners exploring the natural and man-made world so, for example, between one-and-a-half and two-and-a-quarter years learners are expected to make comments and ask questions about aspects of their familiar world such as the place where they live or the natural world. Whilst doing so they inevitably look closely at and identify similarities and differences, see patterns and notice change over time. These are all things that chime with the expectations of older learners in working scientifically and form a sound basis for more sophisticated responses in older learners.

The Early Years practitioner is crucial in providing a good role model when interacting with learners playing with and exploring materials.

This is particularly important when they are exploring materials at first hand in order to place them into simple groups as a precursor to classification.

During the primary years questioning forms part of working scientifically at both key stages. In England in Key Stage 1 (ages 5–7) learners need to be encouraged to ask simple questions and recognise that they can be answered in different ways. They should observe things closely, use simple equipment and use observations and ideas to suggest answers to questions. It is important that they collect and record data to help in answering their questions (DfE, 2013a).

At Key Stage 2 (ages 7–11), naturally, the requirement is more demanding. According to DfE (2013a), in working scientifically lower Key Stage 2 children should be taught to use practical scientific methods, processes and skills in asking relevant questions, using different types of scientific enquiries to answer them. In doing so they should set up simple practical enquiries, and comparative and fair tests. Learners at this stage should gather, record, classify and present data in a variety of ways to help in answering questions. Later on, in upper Key Stage 2, learners should plan different types of scientific enquiries to answer questions, including recognising and controlling variables.

While in the Early Years Foundation Stage learners will need help to find the answers to questions, by Key Stage 1 they should be encouraged to try to find their own answers, unaided, using a variety of books and internet sources, as well as being guided by the teacher to try to find answers to some questions by hands-on practical work. The role of the teacher here is to listen to learners' ideas and to modify and develop them into something that can be investigated. Building on this, Key Stage 2 learners should be able to access a wider range of sources to find answers to their 'Why?' and other questions, and should be regularly challenged to discuss whether or not their questions can be answered by practical investigation rather than merely the use of secondary sources.

Traditionally, some teachers have viewed learners' questions about science as a threat both to their authority and to their own knowledge and understanding, rather than as an aspect of learning to be encouraged. While there is more understanding now, it is still true that some teachers are afraid of their learners' questions on a subject they still feel less confident about. Frequently, this is due to teachers' perceptions that they should be able to answer all the questions asked of them, reflecting a now misguided view of the teacher as the 'fount of all knowledge'. This has led, perhaps unconsciously, to questioning being discouraged; although realistically, given the vastness of science, most teachers and even the most eminent of scientists cannot be expected to know the answers to all the questions learners might ask.

Although there is an expectation for teachers to focus on learners' questions and to help them to develop their ability to raise questions, in practice this rarely happens. Some argue that there is not enough time devoted to science for this to happen, but this is frequently just an excuse for avoiding this type of work. Teachers often argue that learners do not ask questions, and when those that do ask questions, teachers find difficulty in knowing how to deal with them. This is in part due to the unsophisticated way in which the questions are expressed and partly because many questions are difficult to answer directly. However, this is not a good enough reason to avoid questions because, when learners are given the opportunity to observe, explore and investigate for themselves, questions are often an important by-product.

Providing a good role model here is crucial. Learners of any age will not ask questions if they are not encouraged to look closely at things or to ask questions about them. Neither will they make progress in the types of questions to ask if the adults around them do not ask the kinds of questions that can lead to higher-order thinking skills. 'Wait time' in science teaching is still an area that could be developed further, with the time between asking the question and expecting an answer still pain-fully inadequate. When learners are given more time and the original question is not reworded or moved on to the next learner, they have to begin to think for themselves and often astound teachers with their understanding.

Extending the type and function of questions is also necessary. *Application questions*, i.e. those where the learners have to think about the knowledge in a new setting, help to promote and extend thinking far more than low-level knowledge questions in which the learners have a 50% chance of being right: for example, 'Is salt a solid or a liquid?' compared with, 'If aliens landed on earth and wanted to know what a solid was, how would you describe the properties of a solid so that they understood?'

Analytical questions require learners to discuss how things are the same and different or what are the major causes of an event. For example:

Q: 'Does sugar dissolve?' (Teacher)

A: 'No.' (Joseph, Year 6)

can be replaced with

Q: 'What are the differences between melting and dissolving?' (Teacher)

A: 'Melting is where the stuff changes shape, it goes runny and watery and a bit melty, but dissolving the stuff will go into the water so you cannot see it. Melting you can see but dissolving you cannot.' (Joseph, Year 6)

Synthesis questions start from the premise that learners can think for themselves, and link ideas together. For example, a group of Year 6 learners were looking at 'instant snow' which expands when water is added. They thought originally that the powder would dissolve, so were rather surprised by their observations. They thought that if you added more water it would dissolve and, so, a small amount of 'instant snow' powder was added to a large amount of water. It was still possible to see the granules.

Q: 'Based on your idea that when materials dissolve they are too small to see, can you explain if this is an example of dissolving?' (Teacher)

A: 'You can still see the small bits of the stuff; it is floating in the water. But if you add more water it will probably dissolve.' (Brett, Year 6)

Q: 'Do you agree with Brett?' (Teacher)

A: 'You can see the small bits but adding water will not make a difference - it would have done it by now if it was going to. I think you could put it on a radiator in the sun and get it back so it's like dissolving because it will evaporate.' (Joseph, Year 6)

Synthesis questions are ones that prompt learners to see links and enable the teacher to plan the next steps in their learning as a result of expressing their ideas verbally. Synthesis questions are very helpful and are typified as 'So, based on this fact, what would your conclusions be?' type questions.

It is also important to allow opportunities for learners to experience *evaluative questions*, which enable them to rank statements. For example, they can be asked to decide which definition they agree with the most, or make up one of their own.

It is also important to include some *interpretive questions*, which require an opinion from the learners, a useful strategy for responses that are scientifically inaccurate. So when one learner suggested 'Dissolving is when it disappears or disintegrates' (Libby, Year 6), this response was used as a question to the class, 'Why would you agree with this statement?', thus allowing thinking time and responses from the learners, with the teacher taking the role of moving learning forward rather than being controlling.

Whatever range of strategies are used there is safety in numbers for learners. Using talking pairs is helpful, but ensuring that the pairs are changed regularly is vital. Linking 'Talking pairs' into 'Thoughtful fours' (two pairs of learners asked to consider ideas in a thoughtful way) can ensure a range of ideas are raised. Although calling out and putting hands up occurs in some classrooms, this practice means that only a few learners have to 'do the work'. The hands-up strategy also leaves the problem of the learners who do not have to take part. Traditional questioning with hands up is found to be detrimental to the development of thinking and is a type of neural pruning. If the brain is not used effectively its ability to make links is reduced. But when 'wait time' is increased, response partners are used and the quality of questioning is improved, learners make thoughtful responses and become more involved in their learning. Neural branching is an outcome of effective questioning.

USING LEARNERS' QUESTIONS AS A STARTING POINT

Teachers should aim to use learners' questions as often as possible for a number of varied reasons. Questioning as a process skill is an important part of the scientific process. Learning to ask good questions is fundamental to 'working scientifically' and, in the long term, a scientifically literate person needs to be an effective questioner, someone who can use their knowledge and understanding alongside the ability and confidence to ask the right question at the right time. Primary-aged learners are living in an uncertain world where being able to question the world around them is increasingly important. Therefore, it is important to encourage learners' questions within formal education today.

LEARNERS' QUESTIONS

Pre-school children naturally raise many 'why' questions. This is typified in the book *Why* (Camp and Ross, 2008), a story of Lily and her father, who becomes increasingly exasperated trying to answer Lily's incessant 'why' questions. Experience suggests that 'why' questions are asked when children do not understand something, or when they need either to gain further information or to extend their knowledge of a familiar subject, or sometimes merely to gain attention from adults.

Although 'why' questions are important for developing learners' knowledge and understanding of science, they are not the most important for providing opportunities to develop science process skills. Starting from learners' own questions can provide some ownership of their own learning and, consequently, can be a terrific motivator.

It is crucial that they do not merely undertake practical activities to reinforce existing ideas or to illustrate a concept. While illustrative activities are important, it is also most important to provide opportunities for practical exploration and investigation of things with which they are not yet familiar. Merely asking questions that learners already know the answers to could lead to disaffection, characterised by unwelcome questions such as 'Why are we doing this?' However, if investigations are based on learners' own questions then the outcome will not be known before the exploration, research or investigation begins. Furthermore, learners' questions can also be a focus for formative assessment, not only to assess what they know or, more importantly, do not know, but also to provide an opportunity for teachers to assess the quality of their question-raising ability.

ANSWERING LEARNERS' QUESTIONS

Learners do need to ask questions to obtain information and to clarify unclear thinking. Many of the 'why' questions they ask can be easily answered by reference to textbooks set at the appropriate level. Children are fascinated by questions that ask, for example, about the tallest tree, the shortest man, etc. However, merely providing learners with the 'correct' answer will rarely provide the long-term solution. Clearly, though, it would not be realistic, or appropriate, to expect teachers never to answer their questions, and teachers need to use their professional judgement when learners ask questions. Before directly answering a question, teachers need to consider if doing so is in the best interest of the learner. Sometimes, as discussed above, it is appropriate to throw the question over to their peers, as other learners can often offer an answer that is set at the appropriate level using more learner-centred language, or that provides a new slant that will enable more discussion to occur.

Instead of always being provided with the answer, learners need to be taught to ask their own questions as a way of obtaining information and understanding in science. Learners also need to recognise that for some questions there is no known answer, and that there are various ways of finding out the answers to different kinds of questions. Older learners also need to learn how to make their initial questions into ones that can be investigated so they can find an answer by practical scientific enquiry. In order to gain this skill, learners need time and the opportunity, built into their learning time, to consider what sorts of questions are suitable for answering by practical enquiry. Some ideas for developing this further are provided in Chapter 5.

By helping children to clarify, qualify and refine the question, the teacher's role is actually enhanced. Throwing the problem back to the learners, asking 'What makes you ask that?' or 'What do you mean by that?', may well lead to more meaningful, longer-term learning than directly answering the question when the provided answer may or may not match the understanding of the learner. It is a common occurrence, even in adulthood, to be put off asking further questions because the answer to an initial question, even if accurate, was not understood. Answering learners' questions at the correct level, with differentiation, is a very difficult instructional skill and, more often than not, it is probably in the best interests of the learner if they are required to find out for themselves.

HELPING LEARNERS TO RAISE QUESTIONS

In order to help learners to develop their question-raising ability, teachers need to listen to their questions, analysing them to try to discover the reason for the question and whether or not they can be answered by practical enquiry. One of the most useful ways of promoting the questions that can lead to further practical enquiry is to provide learners with the opportunity to explore and observe some objects, using all the senses (where appropriate). Older learners can be given a simple resource and requested to ask questions about it. One Year 6 class provided with a potato as a stimulus raised 98 different questions. The teacher said that the questions ranged from 'Where did the original potato come from?' to 'How can we grow a potato?' So successful is this strategy that it is almost possible to base a whole term's cross-curricular work on the questions raised – very much in keeping with a view of the primary curriculum that emphasises topic work including more cross-curricular work! While the same range of questions may not be possible for all starting points, experience suggests that the latent potential of learners' raising their own questions may well be enormous. One strategy that helps learners to raise questions is the use of a question hand (Figure 4.1).

Learners were provided with some white powder (instant snow) in a transparent plastic cup and invited to think of questions they could ask about this and write them on their first hand. Then they were asked to add water to the powder and to observe what happened and to ask some more questions on their second hand. All learners asked 10 questions, many of which could have been answered using a practical activity. It was interesting that the quality of the questions improved greatly after the water was added.

FIGURE 4.1
The question
hand

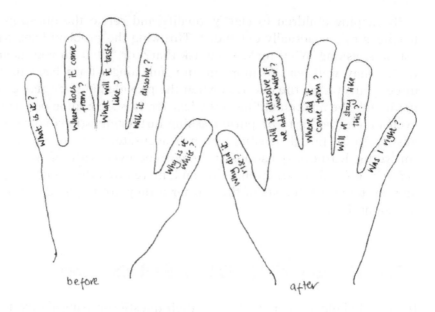

before

after

Learners looking at small animals

There is often a tendency for teachers to ask learners to research, prior to their exploration, the sorts of animals they may encounter in their local environment.

The argument used to justify this strategy is that learners will then be more informed about the animals they are likely to encounter before finding them. However, while important, knowing the names of animals is not the most important reason for observing them. Preparing learners in this way is tantamount to putting the cart before the horse in terms of learning because, inevitably, they are likely to notice those features that they have been prepared to notice, rather than observing features in an open-minded way (see Chapter 3). Learners' questioning ability and their knowledge and understanding of small animals can be extended if they are challenged to notice similarities and differences between animals while observing them, then they will not only begin to appreciate the wide diversity of living things, but will also develop the scientific skill of classification of invertebrates. This will be particularly so if they are encouraged to use classification keys to identify the animals they come across.

When learners are given the opportunity to observe a number of small animals it is almost impossible to stop them from asking questions about them. If they are asked to observe collected material for a few minutes, then to view the individuals, one at a time, in a viewer, they become fascinated. It is easy, for learners working in pairs, to record their questions, either in writing or electronically, and then to seek answers to their questions. This strategy is particularly motivating because learners themselves have ownership of the questions they ask and require little formal input from the teacher.

One reason why this activity can be such a good vehicle for raising questions is that learners will immediately compare the animal to themselves and, among the many 'why' questions, there will be more productive questions such as:

- What is it?
- What does it eat?
- How does it feed?
- How many legs has it got?
- What are the feelers for?
- Does it have eyes?
- Is it a boy or a girl?
- Is this a baby one of these?

Teachers can prompt learners, through questioning, into noticing missed features that are important to learning. Then learners can choose some of the questions that they would really like to be answered either through looking again more closely, using secondary sources or by setting up a practical situation to try to find the answer to the question. While consulting secondary sources when looking for the answers to specific questions, learners invariably not only find answers to questions that they had not even asked, but also begin to realise that some questions cannot easily be answered.

Of course, teachers need to provide a variety of resources and also to be aware themselves of which questions should be answered in a practical way, for example: 'What does the animal eat?', 'Under what conditions does it prefer to live?' or 'How far does the animal travel in five minutes?' etc. Teachers also need to know how this could be carried out practically; without giving too much information, they should scaffold learning so the learners can go about finding the answers to their questions. For a successful outcome, secondary resources set at an appropriate level need to be readily available. It is important here to be aware that some well-known and recently published materials may unintentionally transmit misconceptions. For example, one book of insects contains spiders and another aimed at the primary age range has a large heading of 'Insects' on the cover with a much smaller heading of 'and other small creatures that live in the soil', with large pictures of a variety of groups of small animals on both the back and front cover of the book.

One of the best things about approaching this topic in an open-ended 'learner-directed' way, starting with questions, is that it is highly likely that the questions asked by learners will follow curriculum guidance. Not only are learners introduced to the wide variety of living things by using such an approach, but also they are highly likely to explore the seven life processes of living things, namely, movement, reproduction, sensitivity, nutrition, respiration, growth and excretion – a topic very much of interest to children! In working in this way, learners are very motivated and this suggests that the teaching style adopted has an effect on learners' learning, which is not seen with a list drawn up by the teacher. This approach still requires intervention by the teacher, not to direct learning in a formal way, but to ask the questions that learners have not asked themselves.

BUBBLES

Playing with bubbles is a common play activity both inside the Early Years classroom and outside. Bubbles fascinate learners of all ages. They provide a wonderful starting point for simple investigations arising out of observation. The beauty of using bubbles as a starting point for simple observational activities is that a whole series of activities based on simple observation can be completed in a few minutes. When starting with all resources for exploration, it is important that teachers have explored the possibilities for themselves, before the activity is carried out with learners. It is also important to note that the learning outcomes here relate to process skills objectives and not, except incidentally, to those relating to knowledge and understanding.

Observing and raising questions about bubbles

Table 4.1 shows the types of questions that teachers can use not only to encourage further observation, but also to model the kinds of questions that can be investigated practically. Initially learners should be provided with a pot of bubble mixture and bubble wands of various shapes and sizes. Once they have begun to explore blowing bubbles, the possibilities for simple investigations arising out of frequently unstated questions are almost endless. The most important thing here is for the teacher not to ask questions too soon, or too quickly. Initially, it is better to watch what learners are doing and to listen to what they are saying and to take the questioning from them, rather than to have a predetermined list of questions that *have* to be delivered.

TABLE 4.1 Teacher questions to aid observation and promote simple investigations

Pupils' observations or statements	Teacher questions
What have you noticed about the bubble?	
The bubble is coloured	What colour is a bubble?
	How many colours can you see?
	What do the colours remind you of?
The bubble is round	Are all bubbles the same shape?
	What shape is a bubble?
	What shape is the bubble as you blow through the frame?
	Can you blow a square bubble?
The bubbles float	What happens if you use different size bubble frames?
	Can you make it touch the ceiling?
	Will it stay in the air forever?
	How long can you get it to stay off the ground?
	What do you think is inside the bubble?
	How is it different from the bubble mixture?
	Does it float up or down?
	Why do you think it moved that way?
	How did you make it move that way?
I can blow a big bubble	What happens to the size of the bubble when you blow slowly?
	What happens to the size of the bubble when you blow quickly?
	In which ways are big and small bubbles the same and in which ways are they different?
The bubble popped	What is the shape of the popped bubble?
	How long did the bubble last?
	Can you count how many seconds the bubble lasted before it popped?
	If the bubble was made out of a different material would it still pop?
Look, two bubbles bumped into each other	What happens to the shape of bubbles when two bubbles join together?
	How many bubbles can you make stick together?
	Magnets attract some metals. Do you think this is the same?
	What shape can you see inside the bubble?
I can see reflections	What can you see in the reflections?
	Are the reflections the right way up?
	Can your bubble make a shadow?
	How do a shadow and a reflection differ?
It is dripping	What words can you use to describe the bubble now?
	Could you get a dry bubble?

Observations and explorations need to be built upon, rather than superimposing a set diet of activity on the learners.

After just a few minutes learners can share their observations with the rest of the class. Some will have focused on some aspects and not noticed others. Sharing observations here allows a much wider range of observations and simple investigations to be undertaken in a relatively short time.

PROGRESSION IN LEARNERS RAISING QUESTIONS

CASE STUDY

Children's questions about bread

Bread is a very good starting point for scientific investigations and has the additional attraction of providing a multicultural dimension. What follows is a case study account of the response of four learners, two girls and two boys from each of Years R, 2, 4 and 6. All learners were provided with the same starting point, a variety of 'breads' from around the world to explore, to observe using all the senses and to raise questions about. The breads provided were:

- Baguette: typical French bread.
- Pitta bread: unleavened bread that can be split open to hold a filling.
- Chapatti: flat 'bread' with obvious herbs within it.
- Naan bread: leavened Indian bread in a flattened tear-drop shape.
- Mediterranean roll: a very colourful, rich bread with identifiable pieces of olive and tomato within it.
- Stay fresh white bread: 'long life'.
- Ciabatta: flattish Italian bread made with olive oil.
- Wholemeal brown bread: traditional sliced brown bread.

Initially all learners from each year group were asked what they noticed about the different breads at the exploration stage. If necessary they were then prompted with the following questions:

- What do you think it tastes like?
- What does it smell like?
- What does it look like?
- What might you eat it with?

- Where do you think it comes from?
- When would you eat it?
- Do you know what sort of bread it is?

Learners were asked to:

- Look at the bread.
- Think of any words to describe the bread.
- Choose one type of bread to draw.
- Ask any questions about the bread (the question hand was used again).

All learners were most interested in the Mediterranean bread (see Table 4.2), the chapatti and the naan bread. Of all the breads, the Mediterranean bread was the least familiar and white bread and wholemeal bread the most familiar.

TABLE 4.2   Pupils' observations of Mediterranean bread, and activities that could follow

Year group	Children's observations	Activities that could follow the observations
Foundation Stage	Tended not to comment about the bread, but their observational drawings suggested that they had noticed 'bits' of black pieces of olive and red pieces of tomato within the bread	The 'bits' could have been taken from the bread, put in piles and weights of each could be compared using simple scales, to find the proportion of each
Year 2	Looks like a currant bun with cracks on it. It looks like it has raisins in it. It tastes fruity – very yummy. Learners thought it came from a bakery in Dover	Comparison of the olives and tomatoes by sight, touch and taste to see if the learners' ideas were correct. Finding out what was in the bread by comparison of simple possible ingredients
Year 4	Jane noticed that the bread 'smells like garlic' and noticed herbs and 'fruit' in it. She thought that its texture was 'quite squidgey' and it tasted tomatoey like pasta sauce and came originally from Italy	It was interesting that Jane compared the taste of the bread to her experience of other food. She was trying to make sense of her observations. The smell of the bread could have been compared to a clove of garlic and a range of herbs used for baking

(Continued)

(Continued)

Year group	Children's observations	Activities that could follow the observations
Year 6	Mandy thought it had fruit inside and that the texture was hard, on the outside, but 'squidgey and lumpy on the inside'. She did not like the taste, describing it as disgusting because she detected the smell of garlic and herbs with the bread. Mandy commented on the smell	The Year 6 learners were much more sophisticated in their previous experience of foods and were able to correctly identify a number of tastes presented to them in the bread. They also had more understanding of the origin of various foodstuffs. However, they tended not to ask questions that could be investigated
	Egan thought the bread probably came from Italy. Sam thought it looked brown and bumpy and that it felt hard and lumpy. He thought it tasted like a pasta sauce and thought that the bread came from Italy because pasta comes from Italy. Tim thought the bread looked like a fruit cake, smelled like tomato purée, was hard and tasted a bit like pizza and came from Italy	Again though, these learners could have explored further the proportion of ingredients and compared tastes of herbs that might have been in the bread – acting like detectives, before looking on the bread packet

Inevitably, a number of questions were asked by learners of all years that were not particularly productive in terms of leading to further observation or investigation in science. Examples of these included 'Where did the bread come from?', 'What is the name of the bread?', 'Have you ever been to the country where this bread comes from?' However, other questions were potentially more useful (Table 4.3).

TABLE 4.3 Questions leading to further practical work

Year	Question	Questions that could lead to further practical work
Year R	Notices the 'bits' in the bread	How many different 'bits' are there in the bread? What are the 'bits' in the bread?
Year 2	How is the bread made?	Making bread using the ingredients listed on the packet

Year	Question	Questions that could lead to further practical work
Year 4	Why does the 'stay fresh' bread always stay fresh'?	How long does 'stay fresh' bread stay fresh?
		Looking on the packet for the 'use by' date
		Comparing bread packets to find out what ingredient helped to keep the bread fresher for longer
		Setting up a practical situation (taking care to do this safely) to find out which bread, e.g. 'stay fresh', ordinary white bread and wholemeal bread, stays freshest for longest
		Making bread using ingredients listed on packets (where possible)
		Omitting single ingredients systematically to find out what difference this makes to the bread
	Why did the Mediterranean bread taste like 'Domino's' pizza?	What ingredients give the bread its characteristic smell?
		Comparing herbs in pots to the smell of bread to try and determine the ingredients
	Why has the naan bread got 'bits' in it?	What would the naan bread taste like without the 'bits' in it?
		Find out what the 'bits' are
		Making naan bread without the 'bits'
	Why is the baguette my favourite?	Survey of children's preferences of the breads under study
Year 6	Why do you like it?	Survey of the reasons why learners like different breads
	Where does it come from?	Answers found by consulting secondary sources
	What is special about it?	Comparing breads by further observation and looking at lists of ingredients from packets or recipe books
	Why is it called chapatti?	Research of secondary sources
	What does it smell of?	Comparison of the smell of different breads
	What colour is it?	Describing the colour of different breads
	How would you describe it?	Asking learners to describe bread
	How do you think it was made?	Looking up recipes and trying to make the bread

(Continued)

(Continued)

While most of the learners involved in the case study knew what a question was, they were not very good at raising investigative questions. However, some questions could be derived from their spontaneous questions and some of these could lead to further observation or investigative work.

SUMMARY

Learners ask a wide variety of questions, but some of these are not as useful in promoting scientific enquiry as others. Observation works to encourage questioning because learners are starting with things they notice and in which they are interested. The teacher's role in this process is to encourage observation, to ask learners what they have noticed and to clarify questions.

Finally, it is important to know when and how to intervene when learners ask questions. It is pertinent to note at this point that in the Early Years teachers are warned that 'giving the game away' too early during an activity may limit the depth of learners' learning; telling learners before they have a chance to experience the 'eureka moment' provides information, but prevents the development of investigative skills. This message is true also of all teaching in science, and the implications of this may well be far-reaching for many teachers in the primary classroom.

FURTHER READING

Chin, C. and Brown, D. (2002) 'Student-generated questions: a meaningful aspect of learning in science', *International Journal of Science Education*, 24(5): 521–49.

Harlen, W. (2006) 'Teachers' and children's questioning', in Harlen, W. (ed.) *ASE Guide to Primary Science Education*. Hatfield: Association of Science Education.

Harlen, W., Macro, C., Reed, K. and Schilling, M. (2003) 'Teachers' questions and ways of responding to children's questions', in *Making Progress in Primary Science* (2nd edn). London: Routledge Falmer.

Lazonder, A.W. and Kamp, E. (2012) 'Bit by bit or all at once? Splitting up the inquiry task to promote children's scientific reasoning', *Learning and Instruction*, 22(6): 458–64.

Lord, R. (2011) 'Asking the right questions', *Primary Science*, Issue 117: 13–15.

Mills, C., Danovitch, J.H., Grant, M.G. and Elashi, F.B. (2012) 'Little pitchers use their big ears: Preschoolers solve problems by listening to others ask questions', *Child Development*, 83(2): 568–80.

University of Cambridge, Faculty of Education. 'Questioning Techniques in Primary Science'/Document. Available from: http://oer.educ.cam.ac.uk/wiki/Questioning_Techniques_in_Primary_Science/Document (accessed 18 August 2015).

5

SCIENTIFIC ENQUIRY AND WORKING SCIENTIFICALLY

Hellen Ward

In this chapter the importance of different types of investigative work is reviewed. The use of scaffolding is seen as a way to provide learners with opportunities to extend their skills and to provide teachers with expectations for each age group. Examples of different types of enquiry are provided with examples of outcomes from classrooms. Group size and expectations for ways of working are considered. Working scientifically provides the context for learners to practise their English and mathematics skills as well as learn more about their world.

Working scientifically is the latest term in primary science and comes from the Australian curriculum where it has been used for many years (Skamp, 2004). The change of name is not the only change,

> 'Working scientifically' specifies the understanding of the nature, processes and methods of science for each year group. It should not be taught as a separate strand (DfE, 2013b: 145).

SC1 was previously a separate strand and was double weighted for assessment purposes in Key Stage 1 (ages 5–7) (DfEE, 1999) and was worth 40% of the curriculum at Key Stage 2 (ages 7–11). Now it is the vehicle through which children learn biology, chemistry and physics. This focus is to ensure that learning takes place from practical work; this might seem an unusual statement but there is a debate about the role of practical work. Abrahams and Millar (2008) indicated that many teachers viewed practical work 'as central to the appeal and effectiveness of science education' (p. 1946). The Royal Society's third 'State of the Nation' report (2010: 70) states that pupils enjoy practical investigations and group work. However, others question what constitutes enquiry and whether it is an effective learning approach in science (Abrahams and Millar, 2008).

Scientific enquiry, working scientifically or the methods and processes of science emerged in the 1830s in Britain as a result of interest from the British Science Association, and the term scientist only came into existence in 1830s. Huxley suggested that science was 'nothing but trained and organized common sense, differing from the latter only as a veteran may differ from a raw recruit' (Huxley, 1905: 45). How different from today when the language is all about how elite and difficult science is and how many teachers cannot teach it (Beggs and Murphy, 2005; Royal Society, 2010). Perhaps lessons should be learned from Armstrong (1903), the father of science education, who suggested that science was a game with rules and the learners just had to know what the rules were. In early science education, there is much to recommend an approach that is more inclusive and aims to involve all learners and their teachers.

Another downside of regarding working scientifically as a game with rules is to suggest that scientific method is only one approach and it is undertaken in only one way. There are a number of approaches to working scientifically, and these include fair testing, comparative tests, pattern seeking or surveying, exploring, sorting and grouping and monitoring changes over time.

WORKING SCIENTIFICALLY

The ASE/King's College Science Investigations in Schools (AKSIS) project in 1998 found that fair testing was the predominant activity in primary science. The project report (Watson et al., 1999) recommended that different types of science should be encouraged. The National Curriculum (DfE, 2013b) suggests that learners should select the most appropriate ways to answer science questions using different types of scientific enquiry, including observing changes over different periods of time, noticing patterns, grouping and classifying things, carrying out comparative and fair tests and finding things out using a wide range of secondary sources of information. The type of investigation depends on the approach or context taken rather than the area of the curriculum, so it is possible to investigate the same artefact in different ways depending on what is to be achieved. Using a global question 'What is the best cup of tea?' as an example it would be possible to investigate using a fair test changing just one variable (for example the type of tea, temperature of water, amount of tea, type of container, etc.) and keeping the rest the same, or as a comparative test, where a number of variables might be changed, resulting in learners needing to monitor more cups. It could also be an activity over time where observations are made of how things have changed every minute, with each child having one cup and making observations and recording what is happening using scientific diagrams and measurements and then adding their results to the class results. They might survey 'What is the best cup of tea?', finding out what happens with different temperatures of water, sorting and grouping different tea bags according to the type of material or shape as a classification or grouping exercise, which might then raise questions that could be investigated further. It is also possible to explore what happens when tea bags from different shops are used, and to measure the colour of the tea (for example, by using a paint colour palette strip). One group of learners was astonished when they placed blackcurrant tea bags in sparkling water; this raised a great deal of debate about the processes at work. Whichever type of science enquiry is undertaken, Millar suggests it

 encourages students to be more independent and self-reliant. In this way it supports general educational goals such as the development of individuals' capacity for purposeful, autonomous action in the world. (2004: 3)

OVER TIME

Changes over time can be over different time spans (for example, how things change in an hour, or a day, a month, a year or longer [evolution]), but the key skills involved are making a series of observations or measurements and making comparisons The emphasis is on identifying how things are the same and how they have changed. There are many examples of changes over time; for example, plants changing over the seasons, looking at how plants and animals change through their life cycles – frog spawn and caterpillars are a classroom favourite but mealworms are a cheap and exciting alternative. Learning can be gained from looking at how things rust, burn or decay. The changing position of a shadow during the day, looking at the changing position of the sun in the sky across the seasons, or by making measurements of length of the day using secondary sources as well as direct observations are useful activities for studying the movement of the planet, as is keeping a moon diary over a month,

PROBLEM-SOLVING, MAKING THINGS OR DETECTING

Often a science and technological application is the starting point for this type of science. Making a simple vacuum cleaner out of a plastic water bottle, a paper bag and a simple circuit with a fan is a great example of problem-solving. This activity also helps learners understand what happens when the motor is reversed. Other electrical examples include making a lighthouse, a moving fairground ride, lights for dolls houses, or using electricity to illuminate a Christmas tree or provide a flashing nose for Rudolph. Other kinds of applications such as making bath bombs and making bubble bath all have a science and technology starting point and can be linked to other areas of the curriculum.

CLASSIFICATION, SORTING AND GROUPING

Sorting is placing things into groups, and discussing these groups; Venn diagrams or Carroll diagrams can be developed from this, and here the link to mathematics and logical thinking is vital. A suitable question is 'Are all coins magnetic?' This activity helps learners understand that not all metals are magnetic and develops their understanding of patterns as they search to find out which year coins changed their composition. Sorting rocks and soils provides opportunities to develop language, such as 'sedimentary' (layers and softer rocks) and 'igneous' (they will contain crystals). Sorting materials of all kinds according to their properties, such as rough, smooth, hard, soft, flexible, transparent, magnetic, etc., helps link scientific vocabulary and support learners in developing their ability to discriminate between different objects. Matching pictures of items and the shadows they make is a more unusual classification activity (Figure 5.1). A more complex sort might involve asking if a chef's fruits are the same as a scientist's fruits. So rhubarb might be a fruit according to a chef, but a stem not a fruit according to a scientist (Figure 5.2).

FIGURE 5.1
Matching
shadow (a)
and the object
that makes the
shadow (b)

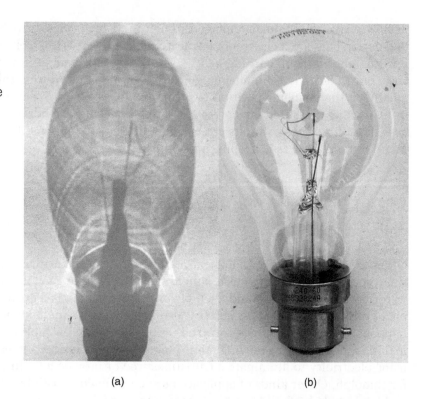

(a)   (b)

FIGURE 5.2
Carroll diagram
for types of
fruit. Where
should she
place the
mushroom?

PATTERNS, TRENDS AND SURVEYS

Pattern seeking involves observing natural phenomena and searching for patterns; the learners do not need to decide what to change as the survey question identifies the thing that is being changed, and the learning is centred upon measuring and/or observing to find out if there is a relationship. Example questions include 'What lives where?', 'Are all leaves on a plant the same size?', 'Do all trees have opposite leaves?', 'Do all infants have the same length of leg?', or other examples which focus on any observable features or measurable attributes – 'Can people with shorter legs jump as far as those with longer legs?', 'Does the heart beat per minute change with exercise', 'Do babies eat as much as adults?', 'How many different types of food are provided by school over one week?'; or comparing the size of feet and the length of the ulna, or counting the number of plants and animals in one habitat or the number of habitats that one animal is found in.

Other helpful questions are:

- Does the size of the spring affect the amount of force that can be suspended on it?
- Would the thickness of the elastic band influence the amount it can stretch?
- Will more seedlings be found further from the tree?
- Will the size of the puddle influence the time taken for water to evaporate?
- Is it only temperature that affects evaporation?
- Does the type of butter affect the temperature it melts at?
- Will the roughness of the surface affect the distance a sledge will move?

CASE STUDY

Dinosaur footprints

Making science part of cross-curricular work provides an opportunity to engage learners' interest and link to core skills. In schools where science is less valued, this type of work can be promoted as a mathematics and English activity. The lesson started with a footprint of a dinosaur on the floor of the classroom. The learners were asked to

(Continued)

(Continued)

discuss what they thought it was and anything else they knew. Without any prompting they were sure it was made by a large thing and decided it was an animal. So their prior experience from footprints in the snow and mud had enabled them to know that the size of the footprint in some way was related to the size of the animal. They were then introduced to large wooden footprints and tape measures and were told that a scientist a long time ago found fossil footprints and did not know how to work out how big was the thing that made them. They were asked if they could come up with a way of helping the scientist by using the size of their own footprints and measurements of their own heights. They were also told that the scientist first calculated the size of the foot and then the height to the animals' hip. It did not take long for them to come up with how many times they needed to multiply the size of their feet to get their height. As a class the data was collated and a scatter graph constructed. It is possible to draw around feet and then use these feet to measure distance as well as measuring in centimetres with older children

After the relationship of a footprint to the height of the animal was identified, the learners were introduced to the idea that the distance between footprints could provide information about how fast an animal was travelling. In the next lesson learners made wet footprints and measured the distance of their stride when walking, jogging and running. The distance each footprint was apart when divided by the leg length provided evidence of the speed at which an animal was moving. If the dinosaur footprints are placed on the grass this provides an excellent opportunity to remind the learners why the footprints have turned yellow and about the importance of light for plant growth.

FIGURE 5.3
Dinosaur footprints provide a pattern-seeking activity on the size of the dinosaur and how fast it was moving

An investigation is more than an activity that involves equipment and practical tasks. The following box denotes the stages. It can be seen that there are many steps, and when undertaking an investigation the learners will follow and be involved in all the steps. In illustrative work the teacher will plan steps 1–5. Basic skill lessons focus on only one step at a time, as discussed in detail in Chapter 2.

THE STAGES USED IN WORKING SCIENTIFICALLY

1   Selection of the global question*
2   Identification of the independent variables
3   Thinking of how to measure/observe the outcome (dependent variable)
4   Question generation
5   Selecting the equipment and deciding how to use it
6   Deciding what might happen (making a prediction) if needed*
7   Data collection methods – type and amount of data to be collected*
8   Making observations and measurements
9   Recording and evaluating the data (reliability)
10 Interpreting the data
11 Drawing conclusions
12 Evaluating the process*

*Using secondary sources of information can occur at a number of points. It will differ according to the investigation as well as age of learners, but is an important part of the process.

A global question starts the process, so it could be the question of how to make a spinner that takes the longest time to get to the ground. This question then can be answered in a number of ways and if it is a survey the global question will be refined by the teacher who also selects the independent variables. The term 'investigation' is used explicitly for activities which require learners to think and make choices about 'what to vary' and 'what to measure' (NCC, 1993). It is this choice that is important as it enables the learners to plan their own work. In investigative work learners plan by selecting the variable (factor) they will change and then deciding how to measure and record the effect of the changes. It is suited to simple tests, comparative and fair tests. It is also useful in investigations over time, although the learners might decide early on which plant or habitat they wish to monitor over time and the rest of their time will be spent looking at the changes. The over time activity might also be useful in watching changes, for example when sweets are added to water or beans growing in a measuring cylinder (Figure 5.4).

FIGURE 5.4
Bean growing
upside down in a
measuring cylinder

This also might be an exploration and provide a starting point, with the learners then carrying out the whole process of investigating their own idea, using basic skills they have acquired. This approach enables learners to make choices and is more effective than teacher-directed practical tasks. In *Maintaining Curiosity: A Survey into Science Education in Schools* (Ofsted, 2013) debate about the content of science and step-by-step instructions were identified as a weakness.

> Some of the teachers were keener to cover the content than to develop pupils as independent, inquisitive young scientists. It also explains why many lessons were controlled by the teacher, with detailed, step-by-step instructions (Ofsted, 2013: 13)

Whilst investigations are important, so too is illustrative work as it enables learners to learn about science in a practical way by focusing upon a limited number of skills at any one time. These activities enable learners to concentrate upon the outcomes, as the 'what to do' and the 'how to do it' are prearranged by the teacher. Due to the formal nature of the illustration it is easy to focus learners' attention directly upon what is required. The methods of communication and recording can also be prescribed in illustrative work, and the activities undertaken provide experiences upon which future learning can be based. Illustrative work provides opportunities for learners to experience many aspects of working scientifically.

It is a myth that learners will become investigative scientists by a process similar to osmosis, picking up skills, attitudes and concepts by 'being there'. Learners generate ideas and questions, but enabling them to answer these questions in a scientific way requires procedural understanding to be developed throughout primary education. The process should be started in the Early Years, and the degree of challenge and the complexity of tasks increased as they progress through the school. In order for the process to be successful there needs to be a common approach across the school, with all adults working in similar ways. This is known as continuity, and without a continuous approach it is unlikely that learners' learning will progress. In order to make this easier to manage there needs to be agreement about progression in procedural understanding, which will result in all teachers knowing what learners have already been taught and where they are expected to progress to next. This is easier to achieve if the expectation for ways of working in all aspects of science is clearly stated for each year group. From a simple starting point in the Early Years, learners will develop more independence. The expected outcomes for each key stage could make it clear where progress should be focused at each year. Using this information together with extensive opportunities to work with learners in whole-class investigative activities and in real settings allows a suggested framework for progression to be constructed. Tables 5.1 and 5.2 provide an opportunity for teachers to gain an understanding of where the age range they teach fits within the whole schema, and are a starting point for future discussion in schools.

The theory supporting this framework has as the central tenet that learners will make gains in understanding and skills, if development is in small steps and there is support from teachers and others. Vygotsky (1978) created the idea of the zone of proximal development. For learners to be successful, teachers have continually to aim to extend unaided achievement, by planning small steps and increasing the challenge. This is only effective when all teachers work to the same goals, and realistic but challenging expectations are set from the start. It also requires a belief in the importance of procedural understanding.

METHODS OF WORKING

Young learners have their own ideas and are keen to find out about the world. When learners start school the whole process of investigation should begin, with the teacher supporting the work at all stages. A suitable idea can be generated from work already occurring in the classroom.

Sometimes this can result from a suggestion made by a learner or it might be teacher-directed: the teacher then models the investigative approach with the same variable being investigated by all the learners. Learners in the Early Years will spend a lot of time exploring their world. By the age of seven, learners should have experience of a number of investigations. They should be used to working in groups and being supported by the teacher and their peers. They will be used to working with their teacher to identify variables from a global question and will be able to think of a question their group can answer. The learners will begin to take a more independent role and build upon the skills and experiences gained earlier in their education. The teachers/adults have an important role here in facilitating the work but not controlling it. By the time the learners are nine years old the process should be further developed, with teachers supporting not directing. It is found to be most effective if direct adult support is reduced over time, with the reduction corresponding to the development of the learners' skills and abilities. Thus the role of the teacher is to model and support the learning processes throughout.

TABLE 5.1   Progression of procedural understanding KS1 (ages 5–7)

Aspects	Reception	Year 1	Year 2
Methods of working	Adults scaffold the activities, individuals work alongside each other following explorative activity	Beginning to work in groups supported by adults carrying out simple tests, classifications, groupings and seeing how things change	Groups working on their own investigations supported by planning format and class teachers. Carrying out comparative tests, pattern seeking and changes over time
Question formation	Child generates an area of interest and adult helps to focus the question	Adult sets a question. Pupils begin to raise own questions	Questions and suggestions made by pupils and they respond to teacher questions
Prediction	Pupils formulate idea/guess in their head. Pupils are not asked what will happen	Pupils are asked as a result of their work whether what happened was what was expected	Pupils are asked if what happened was expected and to give some reasons
Variables	Teacher helps to select variables, e.g. type of material, amount of water	Teacher and pupils select variables together. e.g. type of material, amount of water, type of liquid. They work in simple tests and find patterns and observe over time	Teacher and pupils brainstorm variables then pupils choose, e.g., types of material, amount of water, type of liquid, amount of material

Aspects	Reception	Year 1	Year 2
Range and interval	Range selected by teacher and activities are influenced by the resources they provide	Simple range discussed by pupils and teachers. Interval set by teacher	Range developed by the pupils, e.g. three materials chosen. Interval discussed where relevant, e.g. 0 ml water, 50 ml water, 100 ml water
Choosing and using equipment	Everyday objects used, provided by teacher. Used with some support	Some everyday objects and simple equipment, sand timers, straws (non-standard measure) selected with limited support	Independent usage of simple equipment provided by teacher, e.g. metre sticks, scales, tape measure
Observations and measurements	Simple observations made, e.g. wet/dry	Beginning to use non-standard measurements and to talk about their observations	Some use of standard units to measure length, mass. More than one reading beginning to be made. Observations used to make comparisons
Oral communication	Pupils respond to questions about their work. They are able to talk in sentences relating two events together	Pupils begin to talk about whether what happened was what they expected	Pupils make comparisons, e.g. this cloth was more absorbent than that one. Some simple reasons are given
Written communication	No written feedback expected. Emergent writing or Q&A by adult represents work	Simple writing to convey meaning used to communicate findings, e.g. a letter to Alex's mum	Writing used to describe what happened. Scientific knowledge and understanding is developed through simple conclusions
Graphical representation	Charts modelled by teacher begin to be drawn by pupils	Tables (two columns) and charts produced by pupils with limited support. Bar charts are modelled by adult	Tables with space for a repeat reading introduced. Pupils draw bar charts. Adult helps with scale if appropriate. Patterns and trends are discussed as a class
Scientific vocabulary	Simple words. Adult models correct vocabulary, e.g. hard, soft, smooth	Vocabulary extended. Adults are still modelling. Displays provide important reinforcement. Pupils should read and spell scientific vocabulary at a level consistent with their increasing word-reading and spelling knowledge	Pupils use simple vocabulary to explain results. Adult modelling and displays still very important. Pupils should read and spell scientific vocabulary at a level consistent with their increasing word-reading and spelling knowledge. Concept maps/KWHL grids develop vocabulary
Health & Safety	Follow simple instructions when carrying out activities	Follow instructions when using equipment	Increasing knowledge of safe and careful working. Following instructions

TABLE 5.2   Progression of procedural understanding KS2 (ages 7–11)

Aspects	Year 3	Year 4	Year 5	Year 6
Methods of working	Individual work within a group with some supported by adult	Teacher supports occasionally when needed. Pupils work in groups	Group working mainly unsupported	No support for groups in normal situations. Scaffolds removed
Question formation	After class brainstorms of global question, pupils start to raise own questions	Questions selected by pupils. Global question starts process	Opportunities are given for pupil questions to be followed as a result of an initial investigation	A range of questions is tested as a result of their own ideas that arise from work. Not just of fair test variety
Prediction	Predictions are made with encouragement. Predictions include a reason	Level 3 predictions beginning to include knowledge and understanding	Predictions draw on past experience. Simple knowledge and understanding is used	Predictions are developed and explanations of these use sound understanding of area covered
Variables	Pupils with support, identify a range of variables that could be tested, e.g. height, weight, material, size, way it is dropped, length of wing. Standard units are introduced	Pupils identify variables with limited support, e.g. amount of soil, type of soil, amount of water, temperature of water	Scaffold used independently and a wide range of variables are identified, e.g. type of substance, amount of liquid, size of container, amount of sugar, temperature of water, type of liquid, stir or not	Variables are identified by pupils and are chosen and manipulated ensuring a fair test if appropriate
Range and interval	Pupils begin to understand the need for range. Range chosen suits investigations, e.g. 3 helicopters. Interval developed with help of teacher but is still non-standard, e.g. small, medium and large	Range understood. Numbers used varies according to context but a minimum of 4, e.g. 4 types of soil, materials. Interval identified by pupils but still non-standard, e.g. coarse, fine, thin materials	Range used independently and 5 or more are used routinely. The interval contains standard measurements and is systematically selected with some limited support from peers and teacher	Pupils use appropriate range to enable patterns and trends to be identified (6 as minimum). Pupils use K&U (Knowledge and Understanding) to identify appropriate intervals in a systematic way. Standard units are selected

Aspects	Year 3	Year 4	Year 5	Year 6
Choosing and using equipment	Using simple equipment with some support, e.g. thermometer, Newton meter, stop watch	Using equipment confidently with limited support to nearest whole number	Know what equipment to use, selecting it themselves. Careful and correct usage: 1 N, 1 g, 1 mm, 1 cm^3	Self-selecting using past experience. Range of equipment selected for a range of tasks. Repeated measurements taken which are precise
Observations and measurements	Simple observations used and measurements (3) accompany these. SI units of measurement for temperature, time, force	Three or more measurements taken routinely. SI units used with care. Scanning for unusual readings introduced	Dependent on context multiple readings become part of procedure. Unusual readings are discussed and repeated if time allows	Multiple measurements taken (6+). These are accurate. Unusual results are repeated automatically
Oral communication	Teachers use feedback session to develop oral skills. Events described in order	Pupils report back with limited support. Teacher questioning used to develop explanations	Teacher's role is to prompt when descriptions not explanations are given. Teachers and pupils ask questions to develop K&U. Systematic concise style encouraged	Pupils report back including all relevant details. Explain what they found out and how they could improve their investigations. Teacher's role is as audience
Written communication	Teacher models appropriate responses. Simple writing frame supports simple conclusions. Patterns and trends are written about. 'What does it mean?' is more important than 'What I did.'	Explanations encouraged through written work. Patterns and trends developed. Questions: Did the evidence support the prediction? What do I know now that was not known before?	Method, apparatus conclusions are NOT recommended. Explanations are given, patterns and trends are discussed. Generalisations are included. Scaffolding is reduced	Scaffolding is reduced/removed. Conclusions draw on scientific K&U, the predictions and the evidence

(Continued)

TABLE 5.2 (Continued)

Aspects	Year 3	Year 4	Year 5	Year 6
Graphical representation	Tables – 3 measurements and * (star) columns are drawn unaided. Total or median used. Bar charts produced unaided. Teacher helps pupils to identify the patterns and trends	Tables constructed unaided. Pupils check for unusual results with adults. Median used. Bar graphs constructed unaided. Patterns and trends discussed with limited support	Tables are sophisticated. Averages used. Unusual results discussed. Line graphs are drawn which have a few points and whole number scales. Decisions about line/bar graph or scatter graph made in consultation with teacher	Tables are clearly presented. Average used where appropriate. Consolidation of line graphs, bar charts and scatter graphs. These have more points and complex scales. IT is used effectively. These graphical representations are used to draw results
Scientific vocabulary	Vocabulary used to develop concepts. Correct vocabulary used to explain observations. Comparisons used effectively. KWHL grids/concept maps start process off	Correct vocabulary, e.g. dissolving, melting, evaporating is used by teacher in course of work. Differences between the definitions of scientific words developed. Scientific vocabulary used as matter of course	Simple generalisation explained using correct vocabulary. Definitions of words used given by pupils, e.g. gravity. Questioned by adults/peers. KWHL grids/concept maps still used as starting point	Scientific vocabulary used effectively to develop generalisations. KWHL grids/concept maps compared by pupils and definitions for words explained. Terms used effectively, e.g. melting, dissolving, evaporating, condensing and in a range of contexts
Health & Safety	Know terms hazard and risk. Begin to use terms while assessing 'dangers' in practical work	Develop idea of recognising hazards and risks in investigative work. Can respond to questions	Begin to assess hazards and risks in their own work without prompts. Beginning to take action to control risks	Control hazards and risks. Demonstrate in their work that they understand concept of hazard and risk

Communication by learners at various stages of a fair test activity on bouncing balls in a Year 2 class (Figure 5.5).

Selecting the equipment and showing what to change. Ellie changed the surfaces but kept the purple ball throughout. She selected a metre stick to measure the outcome (Figure 5.6).

Lucy drew a table and was able to record her readings using standard measurements. She changed the types of balls (Figure 5.5).

Bubble writing encouraged Luke to explain what he found out, why he thought this was and then what if anything he would change (Figure 5.7). He changed the surface and thought the foam provided was too small!

Whatever type of investigation is planned it is helpful to identify in advance:

- What type of investigation will be undertaken.
- The variables and approaches that are suitable.
- Proposals for how and what data collection methods might be used.

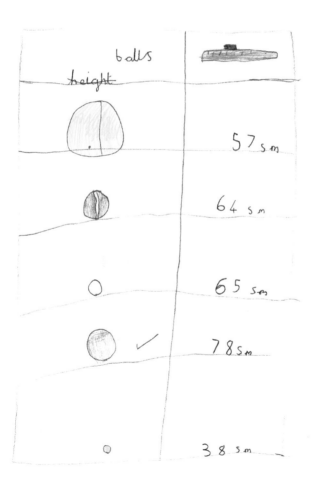

FIGURE 5.5
Bouncing ball results chart

FIGURE 5.6
Child's
drawing,
bouncing ball
experiment

FIGURE 5.7
Bouncing
ball results,
dialogue
bubbles

As already stated in Chapter 2, trying to 'shoehorn' a fair test into a survey will result in strange results and confuse teachers and learners.

QUESTION FORMULATION

In order to begin to investigate, an event, an idea or a question is needed to stimulate thinking. With younger learners this process of asking questions is part of their approach to the world. However, getting a question into a format that can be investigated often requires the adult to scaffold and support the process for many learners. Selecting a simple global question that results in few variables, where there are clear outcomes (results) and the context is related to real life, is central to success. In Early Years classrooms the opportunity to try simple tests or look at changes over time enables many different type of investigations to be introduced. Learners can help to solve problems, sort and group objects and begin to find out from secondary sources the answers to questions about their world. It does require an adult who is able to follow their lead, so when it hailed outside one Reception classroom and the learners noticed that the hail melted quicker on the grass than on the playground, the teacher planned an over time activity with ice balls to see if their observations could be tested. By the age of seven, learners will have tried many types of questions, be able to respond to the global question and begin to identify variables themselves. The teacher will at this stage still be supporting the process. However, by the age of 11, most learners can think of their own questions as a result of ideas developed from illustrative tasks.

SETTING THE CONTEXT

In the initial stages it may be necessary to introduce the learners to the problem they will have to help solve. Whilst some learners are able to ask questions the teacher needs to plan some events to cover all of the Programme of Study. This setting of the context is what Gagne (1972) called 'getting attention' where the learners were placed in 'an expectant state'. This has also been called a 'hook' as an analogy for pulling learners like fish into science. A range of new resources have been developed to target this area with many scenarios used as a starting point for comparative and fair tests, including Rapunzel (testing friction) or Cinderella (testing materials) (BBC Education Resources – www.bbc.co.uk/schools/0). These new resources all have a common feature: to present the problem or global question in a situation that will engage the learners. What they do not always do is reflect the diversity of the learners who will be undertaking these tasks. Science has an image that is in need of transformation and Culturally Relevant Science Teaching (Johnson, 2011), where science concepts are not presented in an isolated manner from only one cultural perspective, is proposed, along with high expectations of all learners. Aikenhead (2001) noted that for many learners their life outside school and the science within were not related and this disconnect he referred to as 'border crossing'. Introducing contexts that reflect the interests and experiences of the learners is an important starting point.

PLANNING INVESTIGATIONS

If a fair test activity is selected, then the use of a planning format can support both teachers and learners. This modelling is necessary because it makes explicit that which is implicit in the process of investigating an idea. A range of types of scaffolds should be used, which increase in complexity throughout the primary years and many are based upon an original idea by Goldsworthy and Feasey (1997).

Pictorial clues, pictures of objects to change or measure, rather than only written words, should be used with young learners wherever possible as a way of communicating effectively. With experience the learners can identify a range of variables. Figure 5.8 demonstrates variables identified

FIGURE 5.8
Which tea bag makes the darkest dye?

by a class of Year 2 learners investigating the global question 'Which tea bag makes the darkest dye?' The learners were introduced to different types of tea bags. They had not taken part in a complete investigation prior to this lesson, but were able to brainstorm all the factors in less than five minutes. They had, however, been introduced to an illustrative activity with one type of material, and three different tea bags, so they had some experience to draw upon. Although this activity was of a fair test type, learners should also be introduced from an early age to sorting and classifying, surveying, problem-solving and investigating change over time.

CASE STUDY

Torches

A group of Year 1 learners were investigating which of their torches was the brightest. They were provided with a range of torches, some plastic cups of different colours and samples of different materials. They were asked to think about how to find out which was the brightest torch. Their responses were recorded as a floor book where every-thing they said was recorded in writing so that they could look at it later. When asked how they could find out which was the brightest torch,

> Boy A said, 'The biggest one will be best, the blue one.'
> Girl A said, 'Shine it on the floor and see which one shows up.'
> Boy B said, 'Shine it on the board and see which one you can see.'

Learners were put into groups of three, and were encouraged to think about how they would find out which was the brightest torch. They talked and then their ideas were shared. They began to see which torch shone through one cup, and then two and then three, etc. Some children saw the size of the light beam. They recorded their work by drawing around the torches and ranking them, using a star system, with ***** being very bright and * being not very bright. The lesson finished with children sharing their findings, which were recorded in words and pictures. The children's work and their thoughts were then made into a book for the learners to look at again and again. It was an investigation because each of the groups selected what they wanted to change and measure, they worked independently and were able to talk about what their group had found out. Although for this activity all groups worked at the same time, it would have been just as effective for groups to work at different times throughout the week.

GROUP WORK

Learners should be encouraged to work in small group situations from the Early Years onwards. However, in the Early Years the activity is likely to be tackled by the learners individually taking turns, rather than as a co-operative working group. What is important is the opportunity for learners to be introduced to practices that will be refined throughout their education. There is no requirement that all groups should work at the same time, and the investigation could be a teacher-directed small group task, if this suits the learning needs of the learners or overall plans. Blatchford et al. (1999) found that whilst 34% of the teaching of science involved pupils working together, this was only 6% for mathematics. However, the size and composition of the group is important for effective working. If the groups are too large then each learner will not have enough to 'do', resulting in opportunities to be 'off task'. Few schools have enough equipment for pupils to work individually, but group work has been repeatedly found to be of value in developing children's understanding of science concepts (Howe and Tolmie, 2003). In many activities in classrooms where the examples for this book come from it was found that when the learners were of a similar ability they did not want to listen to each other's ideas, whilst less able pupils often lacked the skills to speak and listen with confidence and when placed in a group together seemed to wait for an adult to come and tell them what to do. If the groups were too large then it was more problematic for the learners to reach an agreement about the task to be undertaken. Groups of three seem to be most effective for whole investigations where learners are planning and carrying out their own ideas. It can be effective to give these learners labels to help them with their group work

FIGURE 5.9
Learners
adopting
roles within an
investigation

TEACHING SCIENCE IN THE PRIMARY CLASSROOM

skills (Figure 5.9). One can be the 'observer' whose role is to record or watch what happens. Another can be the 'communicator' whose role is to record the results and be ready to report back to the class. The final role is the 'experimenter', the learner who will undertake the task. In most investigations these roles can be changed so that each learner undertakes each role, and the activity is replicated three times, which will enhance the reliability of the work. On some occasions it is just as effective to change the roles in the group for each lesson. Some learners do find it very hard to work with others regardless of their age; however, the skills of co-operation are ones which will be needed in later life so all should be encouraged to take part.

CASE STUDY

Exploring space

Always starting an investigation with a question may not enable learners to develop all their scientific skills. Frequently, lessons are not long enough for a whole investigation and as a result more directed work can occur. This often results in limited opportunities for children to take ownership of their learning and to work co-operatively. Providing learners with a number of open-ended challenges is one way of starting investigative science activities and putting the learners in control of their learning, within carefully decided boundaries.

Learners were provided with a letter from an alien who wanted to know about their planet and what they understood about various scientific topics. Within the letter the alien posed questions that covered the main misconceptions that primary children hold about the area under study (SPACE, 1990–1998). The letter was accompanied by a decorated box of science equipment, which the learners could use to answer the questions posed by the alien. Included with the box was a range of everyday materials and some specialised science equipment. Learners had to decide what the equipment was for and how they could use it to answer the questions posed within the letter. Initially they undertook a period of exploration, then started to suggest simple experiments, investigations and problem-solving activities. They reported their work back to the alien as a series of postcards, posters or PowerPoint productions which each answered the alien's questions. In total 10 boxes were used with learners in a number of schools across one local authority. The advantage of this approach was that it provided challenges for the learners and ensured they had to think for themselves. There was no right answer to find and they did not need to prove anything. The need to find out the answers to the questions posed by the letter ensured the work stayed within the requirements of the National Curriculum and an added advantage was that, by explaining to an alien, the learners were explaining and using scientific vocabulary continually.

TABLES, CHARTS AND GRAPHS

While it is important to provide interesting and open-ended contexts, learners also need to be supported with some basic skills such as tables and graphs.

Even the youngest learners are capable of creating a simple chart with help. Drawing the chart is a skill and thus can be modelled to the whole class, and then additional support can be provided for those learners who have difficulty with this form of representation; interestingly, such

Chart

Change	Observe
	✓
	✓
	✗

Real objects. Standard measurements, median and mode used

Simple 2 C table

Change	Observe/ Measure
	3
	3
	1

Pictorial representation of objects. Non-standard measurement and ranking

4 C table

Change	Measure	*

Pictorial and written objects. Standard measurements, adding totals

5 C table

Change	Measure	*
Brown		
Caster		
Granulated		
Coffee		

Written objects. Standard measurements, median and mode used

6 C table

Change	Measure	*
10 cm		
12 cm		
14 cm		
16 cm		
18 cm		

Standard measurements, median, mode used. Identification of unusual results expected

7 C table

Change	Observations	Measure	*
10			
20			
30			
40			
50			
60			
70			

Range of results over time, with accuracy of readings. Selection of all responsibility of pupils. Use of mean, mode or median

FIGURE 5.10 Table development scaffolds

learners often have difficulties later with drawing graphs. At these early stages it is important that the charts are very simple and directly related to the activity. For example, if the activity is to find a material suitable for an umbrella, a sample of each of the materials to be tested can be stuck into the chart, because drawings and other representations are too difficult for many learners at this stage.

While it is important for the adults to understand the progression of the skills of working scientifically, this can also be communicated to the learners by changing the scaffolds that are in use. An example is provided for constructing tables (Figure 5.10). This shows progression from simple charts to two-column tables (2 C tables) and eventually to tables that can include a range of measurements and observations.

There is no expectation that young learners will construct their own graphs. It is important to note that time spent with young learners constructing pictograms can sometimes be part of problems with graphs at a later stage, i.e. numbers drawn in the boxes, rather than on the lines. By the age of seven, learners should be able to draw their own simple bar graph with limited support relating to the selection of scale. By the age of 11, learners are often confident enough to draw line and scatter graphs. It is important that these skills are initially developed outside the framework of investigations. Many investigations falter at this point because without graphs, learners are unable to complete the process, as they cannot identify clear patterns and trends from which to draw conclusions.

COMMUNICATING RESULTS AND CONCLUDING

When communicating findings, learners need to be provided with many opportunities and styles. How the results are communicated should vary according to the age of the learners as well as the enquiry type, as discussed in Chapter 2. While young learners are developing their ability to use written language, an approach focused completely upon this mode will be unsuccessful. When the observational part of an activity is completed, the work should be discussed orally and the outcomes shared visually; making a wall display or putting some outcomes into a class 'scrap book' celebrates this work.

In complete investigations learners should be enabled to demonstrate their skills. Learners who find written responses difficult should be supported and provided with prompts to help their writing. However, providing the same scaffold at the end of each investigation limits motivation and creativity. Creativity occurs when time and choice are provided.

This was demonstrated by a Year 1 child (aged five or six) investigating the global question 'How to keep teddy dry'. She used all the materials she had tested to make a collage of the teddy, with the umbrella made of foil, the material that she had found to be waterproof. In addition, she had stuck a flap on her work, which when lifted had the word 'foil' written underneath. Her response took no longer than any other child's but was even more outstanding as this was the first lesson in the term where she completed a lesson in an appropriate manner.

Writing a letter to explain results is effective, especially if the letters are posted and responses are received. Survey investigations such as 'Which washing-up liquid produces the most bubbles?', 'Are all kitchen towels as strong?', 'Which is the most effective toothpaste?' or 'Which is the most environmentally friendly washing powder?' offer great opportunities for letter writing. Not all conclusions have to be written; pictures can convey meaning and adults can ask questions and transcribe responses for future reference. News reports and role-play enable learners to demonstrate their understanding, which is the main point of concluding and explaining the results. Picture boards and story boards also make excellent communication strategies.

SUMMARY

There are many different ways to investigate ideas in science and working scientifically involves many types of activities. A framework was presented to help with continuity and progression throughout the primary age range. As scientists tackle different questions in different ways, so learners need opportunities to carry out 'fair tests', surveys, sorting and comparisons, problem-solving and to investigate changes over time. These opportunities can be introduced from an early age, and such activities encourage learners to use literacy and numeracy skills across the curriculum.

FURTHER READING

BBC (2008) *An Investigation of Friction*. Available from: www.bbc.co.uk/education/clips/zht2tfr (accessed 18 August 2015).

CBI (2015) *Tomorrow's World*. Available from: www.cbi.org.uk/tomorrows-world/story.html (accessed 18 August 2015).

Howe, C. and Tolmie, A. (2003) 'Group work in primary school science: Discussion, consensus and guidance from experts', *International Journal of Educational Research*, 39: 51–72.

Watson, J.R., Goldsworthy, A. and Wood-Robinson, V. (1999) *Second Interim Report to the QCA from the ASE/King's College Science Investigations in Schools (AKSIS) Project*. London: King's College.

6

ASSESSING LEARNING

Hellen Ward and Keith Remnant

Assessment is an integral part of teaching and, as such, is all the processes used to facilitate optimum learning. Effective assessment ensures learners achieve to the best of their ability. Assessment is much more than merely recording and reporting. This chapter will explore the whole area of assessing science in the primary classroom.

ASSESSING LEARNERS' LEARNING IN SCIENCE

A reminder of why assessment is important and of its role in education is useful at any time, but particularly in England with the introduction of the new National Curriculum in 2014 and the introduction of assessment without levels. At this time of curriculum change it is worth looking back to the original assessment task group where levels were first suggested. Assessment was defined by the Task Group on Assessment and Testing (TGAT) as:

> A general term enhancing all methods customarily used to appraise performance of an individual pupil or a group. It may refer to a broad appraisal including many sources of evidence and many aspects of a pupil's knowledge, understanding, skills and attitudes; or to a particular occasion or instrument. (TGAT, 1988: 3)

Assessment is part of teaching and should help learners know how well they are doing and where they are meeting the expectations of their teachers. Whether this then needs to be given a level or a number is a debated point. Black and Wiliam (1998) state that understanding what learners know is vital, particularly in science, because their prior ideas form a framework which influences what else is learnt. So a constructivist view of learning focuses on what the child already knows and these ideas are used by the teacher and learner to plan the next steps in learning. Assessment is also the mechanism by which teachers tell parents and carers about progress and what help can be provided to support learning at home. There is also the role of assessment in evaluating the class and the school.

TYPES OF ASSESSMENT

There are different types of assessment:

Ipsative assessment measures what one learner can do with reference solely to their past performance. This is a powerful form of assessment and is focused only on the progress of this one learner.

Criterion-referenced assessment is based on each learner's performance against a set of criteria regardless of the performance of others. Here if every learner is successful against the known criteria then all reach the known position.

Norm-referencing is where the expectation of the average learner is known and used. The problem with norm-referenced assessment is that it labels pupils. By the nature of norm-referencing there will always be 50% of learners above average and 50% below, regardless of ability to complete the task or test.

Diagnostic assessment is used to identify or diagnose areas of strength or weakness.

A SHORT HISTORY OF ASSESSMENT FOR TEACHING

The original assessment using levels, in the first National Curriculum for England and Wales, was built on a system of criterion referencing that was to be used to record each pupil's learning, *only at the end of each key stage* and this was a statutory requirement. But as Dylan Wiliam (2015) says, it was not the system of levels which caused problems but how it was corrupted:

> then schools started reporting levels every year, and then every term, and then on individual pieces of work, which makes no sense at all since the levels had been designed to be a summary of the totality of achievement across a key stage. And then Ofsted inspectors insisted students should make a certain number of levels of progress each year and started asking students what level they were working at, in response to which schools started training students to answer appropriately. And don't get me started on sub-levels...

The division of levels into sub-levels was a major problem but this became worse when learners were labelled and indeed some children, knowing they were at a certain sub-level, referred to themselves as such, for example, 'I am a Level 3b'! Broadfoot (1996) suggested that much of the data that was produced about learner's attainment was merely a set of numbers and was really dead data. The focus on a very narrow range of competencies that are easily tested and with judgements based only on these had been recognised as a danger and was originally identified by TGAT in 1988:

> some kinds of tasks are easier and cheaper to set and mark than others. Use of only one kind of assessment instrument in the interests of economy can lead to undue emphasis on some targets at the expense of others, threatening distortion of curriculum coverage. (p. 22)

The creation of a sub-level system where all learners were expected to make two sub-levels of progress each year, when viewed from outside the classroom, had an 'emperor's new clothes' feel about it! But it became more challenging when first teachers' performance and pay was linked to this system and then a decision about whether a school was successful or failing depended on the overall level pupils reached, and the progress, in levels, made by each cohort was the defining judgement in the school inspection system. As a result it should be no surprise that teaching, particularly in Year 6, focused more upon the subject areas to be tested. In English, speaking and listening is a key part of the statutory Programme of Study and deemed equal in importance to reading and writing but because under the current system it is not tested nationally teachers do not give it high regard. Indeed, because it is reading and writing that are tested nationally, the Department for Education only records a score for pupils' achievement in English at 11 years of age in the form of teacher assessments. Much greater importance is placed upon test results, achieved by these same pupils, in reading, writing and in mathematics. Indeed these are the results that are published nationally, not teacher assessments, and in current inspections schools can be, and are, judged to be successful or not on the performance of cohorts of pupils in these tests.

The overall result therefore has been a narrowing focus on learning and on recording attainment and measuring achievement in those specific aspects that were tested, rather than planning for learning across whole subjects and indeed all subjects. Too much summing up of assessment often results in a loss of teaching time and certainly not enough time on learning for the wider curriculum.

Whilst formative assessment and summative assessment are common terms, Pollard et al. (1994) identified these two types of assessment in a different way. One they called *overt*, where the aim was to monitor the acquisition of knowledge and assessment. Others have termed this summative assessment or assessment of learning. The other form Pollard et al. termed *covert* – its role was to support the acquisition of knowledge (1994: 190). This is often called formative assessment or assessment for learning. The assessment for learning (AFL) initiatives began in earnest as a result of the publication of research by Black and Wiliam with the results summarised in *Inside the Black Box* (1998). This research had been commissioned by the Assessment Reform Group (ARG). The process was later hijacked by the national strategies and although intentions were worthy and indeed some of the materials produced useful, the initiatives resulted in perhaps making all assessment *overt*.

The power of formative assessment, or assessment for learning, was not about adopting the strategies but instead lay in the involvement of learners who become active participants in their learning. Marshall and

Drummond (2006) found formative assessment was being implemented in the 'letter' rather than the 'spirit'. They defined this as teachers adopting strategies which looked like formative assessment but instead led to instrumental learning. In many primary schools there has been a focus on the pupils reaching levels and on using Assessing Pupils Progress (APP) materials and therefore 'up-levelling' work in a mechanistic way. Up-levelling requires the learners to look at the assessment criteria and then add elements of these to make the work more advanced. Other mechanistic assessment strategies focus around: teachers writing the learning intention on the board, which learners then copy, or stick a pre-printed copy, into their books but do not necessarily engage with or even understand; or the provision of feedback that focuses on the assessment outcomes not the learner and their needs; and other didactic techniques that do not allow learners to construct knowledge (Black et al., 2006). When teaching instead becomes coaching, and classroom practice focuses on the processes and procedures of assessment related to a very small number of criteria, the result is an over reliance on the teacher. This in turn emphasises 'What is needed for a level X?', and the curriculum becomes distorted. This is a problem, as it is often seen as teachers having a very clear idea of what they want their pupils to learn; however, the 'opportunities for originality, creativity and validity in assessment methods diminish as student learning becomes rote, short-term and narrow' (Hume and Coll, 2009: 270). Torrance (2007) termed this *assessment for teaching* rather than *assessment for learning*, with Sadler going further and suggesting that assessment was masquerading as, or was, a substitute for learning itself (Sadler, 2007: 388).

This is problematic, as the learning that could be gained from true formative assessment is substantial (Black and Wiliam, 1998). However, for formative assessment or assessment for learning to be successful, the learner must be fully engaged in the process and indeed doing much of the work. In reality, some of the practices that focus on teachers training learners to undertake tasks in a narrow set of ways, in order to try to achieve high test results, may not lead to long-term benefits in learning. The outcome is surface learning rather than deep learning and a narrowing of the curriculum.

Scientific enquiry, like speaking and listening, was a casualty of the national tests, often referred to as SATs. This worried educationalists, who felt that teaching just knowledge was not improving pupils' attitudes to science. The Royal Society (2010) made a causal link between attitudes to science and learners' future attainment in science. The reason for this concentration on attitudes appears to be because of a belief that attitudes, in the primary phase, influence pupils' involvement in the subject in the later phases of education. This is another common belief, but research has proven that attitudes do not directly link with pupil attainment; research by Fraser (1982, cited in the Royal Society report, 2010: 67) concluded that the relationship between positive attitude and higher attainment was very weak and that teachers should focus on improving attainment. Throughout the Royal Society report (2010) there is little mention of the knowledge of science and a greater focus on the practical approaches.

> Science needs to be enquiry-based at all levels of education, but teaching to the test together with its associated fact based approach to learning misrepresents how science works, and conflicts with children's natural curiosity and exploratory instincts. (2010: 89)

A research project in 2008, funded by the Wellcome Trust and the Association for Science Education (ASE), asked primary school teachers how they taught children, ahead of the science tests in Year 6, and concluded:

> There was a tendency for Y6 teachers to focus on aspects of science likely to be tested and this resulted in a narrow curriculum for science and fewer opportunities for pupils to undertake science investigations or other practical activities in science in Y6. (Wellcome Trust, 2008)

Yet, whilst teachers and educationalists were generally pleased by the removal of the primary school science tests, because of a belief that more time would now be spent on teaching and learning that was enquiry based, a CBI report has said this change was a contributory factor in some schools changing their curriculum emphasis with many teachers reporting a noticeable reduction in the importance of science (CBI, 2015); without the SATs there was no longer a test to teach to. In the report *Tomorrow's World*, 53% of the teachers surveyed by 'YouGov' for the CBI said science teaching had become less of a priority over the past five years, and 36% of responses from Key Stage 2 (ages 7–11) schools indicated that they were not providing the minimum recommended two hours each week for science teaching and learning. Indeed as the science testing was removed, the stakes were raised for tests in reading, writing and mathematics.

A further study carried out by the Wellcome Trust in 2010 sought the views of children and parents and found that:

> The majority of children in English schools *did not* agree with the abolition of science SATs. Their reasons included a concern that they would not learn as much science, they would not know their levels in science, that SATs are a good preparation for secondary school and that science will become less important in school without SATs.

Although testing did not provide information on scientific enquiry, the abolition of tests was supposed to encourage access to the full science curriculum and a greater range of teaching opportunities. However, the outcome appears to be that too many learners are now not being given the opportunities to learn science in primary school and 11-year-old pupils were able to predict this outcome. It must be noted however that some schools that took part in the CBI survey indicated that more science was now being taught than before; so it would appear the effect is restricted to some schools in some areas. Interview evidence from science consultants suggests that it is in the schools where the lowest levels of attainment in literacy and numeracy are recorded where the curriculum is narrow, and that possibly this is because there is an attempt to boost outcomes in these high-stake areas of learning. One science consultant reported, 'Those schools have a massive focus or tunnel vision so you have to do literacy and numeracy only' (science consultant, London). He went on to note that those schools, even with such a limited view of education, were not actually achieving in literacy and numeracy either.

Assessment in the classroom

There are only three ways of gaining evidence about how learners are learning:

- by observation;
- through discussion;
- by marking work/looking at completed tasks.

In order to be useful assessment needs to measure clearly defined criteria and the teacher needs to be aware that there are always compromises to be made. It is not possible to listen to every conversation or to observe every learner in every situation; planning for assessment is thus needed. Even if the focus is solely on the completed task the outcomes will often be influenced by how well a learner reads and writes, and there are many skills which cannot be fully assessed by a completed task, such as investigative work. Science is focused on learners using their senses to discover more about their world. Whether they are discussing what happens when they drop different objects, taking measurements about the time things take to fall or deciding whether Aristotle or Galileo had the right idea about how objects behave when falling on the earth, science is about a way of working as well as a body of knowledge. Assessment should focus on making judgements about what is known and the next steps for all learners. Black and Harrison (2004: 4) identified four principles for assessment in primary science, and these were:

1. Start from where the learners are, as learners have to be active in reconstructing their ideas.
2. Learning has to be done by the learners and cannot be done for them.
3. In order to learn the learners must understand the learning target.
4. Learners need to talk about their learning.

It is possible that an additional principle could be added, that of making sure the learners are a resource for each other.

The key principles in all aspects of constructivist learning theory state:

> that students are far from being 'empty vessels' waiting to be filled with new knowledge. And, the knowledge they already have is difficult to change. (Colburn, 2000: 10)

Whilst the four principles seem common sense, in a culture of levels, lip service could be paid to them rather than the necessary full adoption. Finding out learners' ideas takes time, and evidence suggests that science in primary school is less important now than five years ago (CBI, 2015). The second principle, that learning has to be done by the learners, is true, but in order for this to happen open-ended challenges must be provided, so that learners can identify where their ideas do not match those of the science being learned. However, if science is a set of pre-planned, 'hands-on' activities, then learners do not have to use their own ideas, and so they remain undeveloped. If learners are to be successful they need to have a very clear understanding of the learning target, but often this can be problematic, especially if the teacher is not very clear about this them-self. Too often the learning intention is described as something the learners will do rather than something they will learn; for example, 'I can make a complete circuit' is a 'doing' learning intention, which could be achieved by watching and copying others. However, if the learning inten-tion is presented as, 'I can explain what is needed in a circuit for electricity to flow' then for a learner to be successful there is a require-ment to access knowledge and understanding as well as skills. There are also issues when the learning intention gives away what the learner is meant to have found out; for example, 'I know a complete circuit is needed for the circuit to work'.

Ensuring that learners talk to each other is important, because through these discussions they will have opportunities to identify where others hold different ideas to their own. In most classrooms, learners engage with 'talking partners' but the quality of learning is most successful when the conversation relates to a rich question posed by the teacher rather than merely a request to talk to the person next to you 'about what we did last week'.

CASE STUDY

Aristotle and Galileo

The learners in this case study were in Years 5 and 6 (so aged 9–11) and the aspect of working scientifically being taught was that 'ideas have changed'. The class was asked to decide whose ideas, Aristotle's or Galileo's, were correct when it came to describing 'how things fall'. The basic ideas of each scientist were presented: Aristotle believed in *levitas*, i.e. that things had a natural place and therefore heavy things fell to the ground as this was where they were meant to be; Galileo identified that it was not the mass but the surface area that was important. Learners were also told that in their work they had to make a series of accurate measurements and use these in an explanation to support which scientist was right.

The lesson started with simple annotated diagrams, 'draw what will happen when simultaneously you drop from the same height two film canisters, one with Plasticine in it and the other empty'. The learners were told to discuss this around their table and give reasons. Some learners benefit from asking their classmates rather than the teacher (Bell and Cowie, 2001; Hume and Coll, 2009), and group work enables this to occur. Unsurprisingly, most of the learners decided the heaviest object would fall quickest. After they had discussed the ideas, drawn and annotated their drawings, they were then given two simple tasks to undertake, one where they changed the surface area of paper but kept the mass the same and one where they changed the mass of an object whilst keeping the surface area the same. They had to plan and make a record of this activity, making sure they repeated and kept records of the activity more than once. The learners were engaged and enthusiastically involved in testing and, because they had to decide which scientist's ideas they agreed with, the activity had greater purpose. The outcomes, when they tested in a scientific way, did not match their everyday observations, and this caused considerable debate. Discussions were often heated, with some learners stating that heavy things did fall quickest, and others in their group arguing that they did not. However, after many, many tests a consensus was found. The final discussions and explanations focused on how light things floated to the ground and that it was surface area that was important. The learners were able to discuss their findings and it was agreed, by a class vote at the end of the session, there was overwhelming support for Galileo's ideas. Assessment opportunities were presented throughout the activity: by observing how learners were working; by talking to them as they worked and discussing what they were finding out; and by listening to, and reading, their final explanations about what they had found.

Why was the case study activity successful?

The activity covered the four assessment principles identified by Black and Harrison (2004); it included the learners' ideas, they were not treated as if they had no ideas or the wrong ideas, and the notion that scientific ideas can change was included in the activity. It involved discussion and active processes and although it was set up and planned by the adult, the learning was undertaken by the learners themselves. The learners had a clear purpose, although no learning intention was written up, nor was it written in their books before the lesson. It involved talking, to each other, about what they were doing and for the activity to be successful they had to work together co-operatively and be a resource for each other.

The Aristotle and Galileo challenge was an example of criterion-referenced assessment. However, a teacher could use this activity as a starting point to assess one learner's performance in the task, and as an outcome would have information about the areas of learning for supporting the learner in the future.

Whilst the focus on the history of science assessment might seem counterproductive, it is only by looking at past mistakes that learning can happen. The idea is not to repeat the same mistakes. Moving forward into an era of no levels, Dylan Wiliam (2015) suggests schools should focus on the following: the big ideas of learning, the progression in learning, having checkpoints, knowing where evidence will come from, deciding how much evidence is required and setting careful targets. Working with a primary school and attempting to tease out these big ideas, the approach in the Case Study below was taken. It should be noted here that this approach worked for this school and appears to be working in other schools, but the big ideas selected should not be used as a blueprint that will work for all schools. It is the process of discussion and agreement that is important and different schools may end up with a different but equally important focus to their science curriculum.

CASE STUDY

Identifying the big ideas

The teachers in the school decided to create an assessment system that was in line with their new curriculum. Many of their local schools have stayed with the level system even though it does not match the new curriculum. The starting point was the 2014 Programme of Study, as this is statutory and lists what has to be taught. Through discussion it was decided which 10 ideas were the most important for each year group. The teachers identified that within the curriculum some ideas are more central to an understanding of science than others and these foundation blocks should form

(Continued)

(Continued)

the basis of the learning. For example 'Knowing what scientific vocabulary is associated with the parts of the plant and being able to name a leaf, stem and root' was identified as a central part of learning for Year 1 pupils (aged 5–6) and therefore this became a *must*. The teachers identified that future learning should build to include the functions these parts of the plant are responsible for. In this way it was decided how knowledge could be built up through the school. Thus, in the example, knowing the parts of the plant leads to the functions these parts play, which in turn leads to further knowledge of adaptation where changes have taken place to ensure the plant is suited to its environment. This then leads finally to the process of evolution and even how some random mutations might provide a difference in a plant which makes it able to survive. Some teachers immediately said some children in Reception can already name the parts of the plant but, as a result of discussions, it was agreed that in reality this often only related to one type of plant and just involved the labelling of a diagram. It was decided that there was a need to provide more authentic learning and a greater range of opportunities. So in this school the planning now has an emphasis on widening the opportunities; for example, to make sure learners are provided with many types of leaves, different stems (trunks), flowers and roots. In the same way that learners extend reading by being given experiences that widen their vocabulary, so too in science there needs to be exposure to more examples of plants and their constituent parts thus increasing understanding.

Each year group identified the 10 important things for their children as the building blocks for future learning, identifying the key ideas which would be built upon later in this school or the next one. This process resulted in a changed mindset in these teachers. They said that 10 key things were manageable and therefore it is their responsibility to provide many opportunities to allow learning to happen. The mindset here is that all learners can achieve rather than having an impression that some children might not achieve and thus be labelled as 'working towards'. So instead of teaching a specific idealised plant the teachers planned to widen the opportunities and experiences to provide greater learning experiences. The identification of the important aspects meant it was possible to think of revisiting these 10 aspects many times and in a range of contexts because they were the building blocks for future learning. The discussion and planning also resulted in teachers knowing what it would mean when the children achieved each aspect. In Table 6.1 the big ideas for each year group in the school are shown.

LEARNING PROGRESSION

It is unlikely that all learners will reach the same outcome in the same way. Sometimes learners get ideas more quickly whilst at other times it appears that some may never 'get it'. By taking an approach which

TABLE 6.1 Suggested big ideas for each year group for the school

	Year 1	Year 2	Year 3	Year 4	Year 5	Year 6
1	Naming common plants and knowing about types of trees	Describe how seeds and bulbs grow into plants	Know the functions of stems, roots leaves, roots, etc.	Know that living things can be grouped in different ways – use keys	Describe how humans change as they age	Know about the circulation system in humans – incl. pulse rate, heart veins, etc.
2	Describe basic structure of plants, incl. trees – stem, roots, leaves, flowers, etc.	Know what plants need to grow healthily – water, temperature and light	Know the requirements for growth and how they change from plant to plant	Know about digestion, including role of teeth	Identify differences between life cycles of different animals, birds, mammals, insects, etc.	Know about the impact of diet, drugs and exercise for humans
3	Know animal groups such as fish, amphibians, birds, etc.	Know that animals have offspring like themselves	Know the role of flowers in pollination, seed production and dispersal	Know about types of teeth and predator–prey relationships	Describe reproduction in plants and animals	Describe how nutrients and water are transported within animals and humans
4	Know about carnivores, omnivores and herbivores	Know what animals need to survive	Know that humans need a balanced diet	Know sounds are made by vibrations, how to change pitch and loudness and how sounds change with distance	Know about the effects of gravity, air resistance, water resistance and friction (contact and non-contact forces)	Know how classification works and give reasons for classification based on specific criteria
5	Name parts of the human body	Know about the importance of diet and exercise for humans	Know the role of the skeleton and muscles	Know how to construct a simple electrical circuit and know a complete circuit is needed	Know the effects of levers, pulleys and gears	Know that living things change over time and are adapted to their environment

(Continued)

TABLE 6.1 (Continued)

	Year 1	Year 2	Year 3	Year 4	Year 5	Year 6
6	Compare structure of common animals with humans (legs, etc.)	Know what is living, dead and has never lived	Know that darkness is the absence of light and light is needed to see things	Know that some materials conduct and others are insulators	Know the movement of the planets, the moon in relationship to the earth, and explain day and night	Know that offspring are not identical to their parents and that this leads to variation
7	Know about the seasons	Name animals and plants in the local habitat	Know how shadows are formed and how to change these	Know the properties of solids, liquids and gases and use this to compare and group materials	Understand properties of materials such as solubility, conductivity, magnetic, transparency, etc. Know uses of simple materials	Know that changes in the environment and the population can lead to evolution
8	Observe weather and know that day length changes	Use simple food chain to explain how animals and plants get food	Know about contact forces and how they affect movement on different surfaces	Know some materials change when heated and cooled	Know some materials will dissolve to form solutions, know how to recover the substance	Know the effect of changing components within a circuit
9	Name common materials and their properties	Know that properties of materials are related to their uses	Know about magnets – poles, attraction, etc.	Know the temperature at which some materials change state	Use knowledge of SLG to decide how to separate materials	Know and use electrical symbols
10	Compare and group materials according to properties	Know that materials change shape when squashed, bent, etc.	Know about simple rocks, soils and how fossils are formed	Be able to explain the water cycle with relationship to evaporation and condensation	Know that some new materials are formed and these cannot be reversed, such as acids with bicarb, and burning	Know that fossils provide information about living things that inhabited the earth millions of years ago

focuses on a range of contexts, everything is not 'lost' if a learner is absent, or not 'on form' when an idea is covered. The suggestion to have only 10 important aspects of science each year allows progress to be more easily monitored and it will be possible to revisit various aspects. Those struggling with the initial learning might be presented with a different context or activity, while those who were absent or not 'on form' might work with another learner who can support the teacher and 'teach' this individual or group thus deepening their own knowledge at the same time. Using these approaches every learner benefits.

Establishing checkpoints

When thinking about checkpoints, Wiliam (2015) identified both external demands, such as parents and end-of-year reporting arrange-ments, and internal demands of the school, and the internal demands of the subject itself. External demands are easier to deal with as the progress has to be reported at set times. Internal demands of the sub-ject focus around the things that are known to be difficult but which are fundamental for future learning. Not all of the 10 outcomes in each year will be as challenging as others. Yet some things, for example 'why things float or sink', the 'speed that things fall', the 'phases of the moon', 'invisible forces', 'seasonal change', 'dissolving', 'electrical circuits' and the ability to decide on a approach to take to answer a question, are examples of internal demands which need to be checked a number of times.

WHAT TYPE OF EVIDENCE?

If teachers are using authentic activities and deep questioning techniques, where learners record their own outcomes rather than using videos, worksheets and comprehension questions, evidence of what learners know and can do will be in their science books. If learners are drawing their own ideas, using scientific labelled diagrams throughout the lesson, this will provide dependable evidence. Teachers annotating the books can provide evidence of thinking and discussion as long as the question is included alongside the answer. It provides a record of that moment in time. Evidence will also come from marking work and observing learning in action (Figure 6.1).

FIGURE 6.1

Child's anatomy
drawing

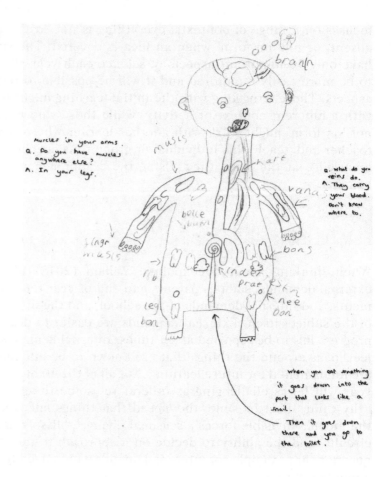

HOW MUCH EVIDENCE?

How many times should learners demonstrate their knowledge, skill or ability before they can be assessed as having achieved an aspect is a question that is often posed. If the same or similar activity is repeated three times that might not be as helpful as showing that element of learning in three separate settings. Different settings would indicate that the learning was able to be transferred and applied to the new contexts, which some call mastery. However, completing three photocopied sheets will not illustrate the learner has knowledge of the parts of a plant as effectively as involving them in an activity, such as 'Do the tallest weeds have the longest roots?' In this activity learners are faced with many different types of plants, they have to compare, measure and draw the different plants in order to answer the question. More able learners may use standard units of measurement and be able to compare and contrast a greater number of plants than someone with fewer skills. However, they are all involved in an authentic science activity which will provide real evidence of what they know and can do. Teachers can observe and talk to them, identifying what they know, understand and can do. Scientifically, there are no such things as weeds, just plants growing where gardeners do not want them.

Moderating, in staff meetings, the evidence in learners' work books helps to confirm teacher judgements as well as providing opportunities to share good practice and ensure there is progress in learning across the school. Engaging in this activity also provides an opportunity to develop professional practice. In a recent staff meeting in a primary school, this sharing of practice allowed teachers to identify that some types of activities and methods of recording only illustrated that the children had been present, because the work in the books provided no possibility for an assessment of what the individual learner knew or could do. Teachers were also able

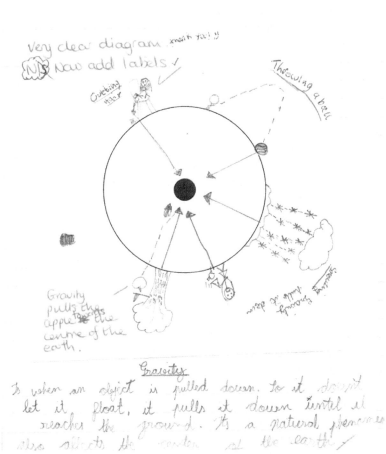

FIGURE 6.2
Diagram showing what one learner knew about gravity

to identify the activities and recording approaches that made it very clear what had been learnt (Figure 6.2). Inter-school moderation allows work and achievement in one school to be compared with the judgements in another and thus develops consistency as well as contributing to continuing professional development for teachers.

TARGET SETTING

The long tail of underachievement in science learning is not a new phenomenon (Hart, 1998) and while the mindset of some teachers revolves around the idea of fixed abilities (fixed mindset) and beliefs that some learners will never achieve, this tail is unlikely to change; indeed if teachers believe in a fixed mindset then this is easily transmitted to learners. This is not an issue that is only found in England (Elle and Grudnoff, 2013). Therefore, a change to a growth mindset, a belief that all can learn and achieve, alongside a focus on what is crucial in science should allow time to provide opportunities to ensure that all learners can achieve. If the teacher's assessment suggests that some learners are not there yet, a change in the way the learning is presented or an opportunity later in the year to revisit the element would be best. What should not happen is that a summative statement is recorded in October which says in effect that the learners do not know or have not achieved. An approach that focused on all learners achieving was seen as unrealistic in practice because there was too much 'stuff' to be taught, learned and assessed. Science had moved on to a new topic and new things to be learnt. There will be some readers who are already challenging this notion that the age-related targets can be achieved by all learners is unrealistic. Yet if this is so it will perpetuate the fixed mindset view of learning where not every learner can succeed, and the associated underlying belief in innate ability. Unfortunately, this ability issue is prevalent in many classrooms and as a result some learners do sit in the 'bottom group', and what is worse is that these learners then develop a view of themselves as failures and as having a fixed mindset (Dweck, 2008). A question that should be asked of all assessment systems is: do they promote a fundamental view of education that only some will achieve? Even a criterion-based system is underwritten by normative assessment beliefs.

Good assessment practice comes from good teaching which involves learners in thinking about, planning and completing their own learning. It involves a growth mindset and active learning approaches. Some key features of this approach involve deep questions; observed events; comparing, sorting and grouping; and a range of ways to communicate what has been discovered or learned.

Target setting within the new curriculum is simple: all learners should achieve the age-related expectations. Some may do this earlier than others, but now there is *not* the expectation that these learners will move on with different targets. Instead the intention should be that they should deepen their knowledge and understanding of these same aspects of learning. One way of achieving this could be to use these learners as an additional resource to support their peers' learning and in this way they are also extending their ability to explain and communicate their own learning.

DEEP QUESTIONS

Activities that enable learners to see flaws in their thinking and thus make them more ready to accept other alternative explanations are important in science learning. Open-ended rich questions are a key to good assessment as they will enable teachers to understand what learners are thinking. However, these deep questions require 'wait' and 'talk' time so that the learners can reflect and formulate their ideas. So asking a question and then providing time for 'partner talk' will give opportunities for more engagement in learning. Asking 'How many wires do you need to light the light bulb?' is a good question to promote thinking and discussion. This can then be followed up by asking learners to draw their ideas and the equipment they would need to test their ideas. In turn they can share these drawings with the class, and so the full range of the ideas generated by the class can be assessed. From this starting point all learners will have demonstrated their knowledge and ideas although often only three distinct ideas will emerge, as many learners will have the same or similar thoughts. These three ideas can be then tested out practically by all the class in their pairs. This approach provides a clear way to move learning forward, and in a short time it will be clear to everyone which idea works best, that a complete circuit is needed, and all should be able to set one up. If by any chance no one draws a complete circuit then the teacher can add one as their alternative idea, perhaps having engaged with one child without a 'talk partner'.

Some other examples of 'deep questions' which can support reflection and thinking are:

- Which is heavier, a balloon filled with air, or an empty balloon?
- Are all plants green?
- Where are the tallest plants found?
- Do heavy things fall quicker than light things?

- Are all gases poisonous?
- What is inside a seed? (Leading to 'Are seeds alive?')
- Why is it hotter in the summer? (Show your answer as a series of annotated pictures.)
- Why does the moon appear to change shape? (Drawing the idea is recommended.)
- Are some materials only found as a gas? (List examples.)
- Does everything living start as a seed?

These questions focus on some of the misconceptions that learners hold about science and have been identified through research by various authors (Bell, 1981; Driver et al., 1985; Nussbaum, 1985). Learners' alternative ideas are an excellent starting place for more examples of deep questions.

OBSERVED EVENTS

What will happen if a lemon and a lime are placed into water? They are about the same size and shape so learners might expect the same thing to happen with each. Figure 6.3 illustrates what will usually be the outcome (unless the lime is old).

Activities that do not do what one would expect are called discrepant events. These will provide a good starting point for assessment of

FIGURE 6.3
What will happen if a lemon and a lime are placed into water?

learners' ideas, challenging their thinking and becoming a basis for investigative work. Pea pods will float whilst an individual pea outside the pod will often sink. A horse chestnut seed (a conker) in its shell will float but take it out of the green case and it will sink. The heaviness for size element of whether something floats or sinks is a difficult concept for learners. An orange in its skin will float but without its 'life jacket' a different thing occurs. These examples of discrepant events provide an opportunity for learners to share their ideas and reasoning, test them and explain what happened. In the process they are engaging with aspects of 'Working Scientifically': testing out ideas, making observations, measuring and trying to find generalisations. Within this aspect of learning a further problem-solving challenge can be set by asking learners the question, 'Can you make an object that sinks, float?'

The balancing cola can activity is another discrepant event that supports learning of forces (Figure 6.4). It also links science with everyday

FIGURE 6.4
The balancing
cola can

life and is something that can then be tried at home. It is the amount of liquid in the can that affects the balance. The teacher could either have a can of cola with just the right amount of liquid left in it (about a third), so that when it is tilted on the bottom rim it balances; even better, if it is then gently pushed it will turn in a circle on its rim. To be really 'magical' the teacher could open the can of cola and drink just the right amount and then balance the can on the table. After this demonstration learners take part in discussion and communicate their ideas in scientific labelled drawings. Then they are set the problem of finding out the amount of liquid needed for the can to balance on its bottom rim. The learners are provided with empty cans to which they can add water. The reason for water and not cola at the start is because there is likely to be spillage and water is easier to clean up than 'sticky' cola. Balancing a can is harder on some surfaces than others, and for an extension task different types of cans could be made available. As too much or too little water will affect the result, the challenge is to find out how much or little will work. The understanding of capacity, measuring and forces that comes from this starting point are excellent but the 'it must be magic' first response from the learners is the reason why it is a great learning task. For assessment, the ideas at the start of the activity provide a clear insight into the learners' starting points and their language acquisition. The ability to observe them at work on an open-ended task provides opportunities to assess their true knowledge understanding and skills. These types of events do not have to be provided only at the start of a unit of work and there are many to select from.

SORTING AND GROUPING

Providing some true and false cards to start a teaching unit of work affords an understanding for the teacher of where to concentrate their future teaching – What do the learners know? What do they need more time on? This assessment task should include some ideas that are very easy; it is just as important to find out what learners already know about a subject as it is to learn about the alternative ideas they hold. Also, providing time to talk about their ideas and allowing them to find out how they could discover the answer to the questions they have raised will be a more powerful learning opportunity than the teacher telling them the answer. Coming back to this at the end is also a good way to help them see how much they have learned.

Other sorting and grouping activities include comparing objects, for example, two twigs. Try to ensure there are a range of different objects

FIGURE 6.5
Comparing
pictures of
two different
tree barks;
notice the
horizontal
(a) and
vertical
(b) lines

(a)   (b)

and look to include a greater range of items from the natural world. For example, look at the pictures of two tree barks in Figure 6.5. A comparison is a good way to provoke questions and also to start investigative work.

BEFORE AND AFTER

Free mind maps before and after a topic is a good way to assess what language skills and ideas learners hold. This is an example of ipsative assessment, what the learner knew before and what they now know. Writing a 'what I still want to know' question at the bottom can show learning is ongoing.

MARKING AND FEEDBACK

For very young children, on-the-spot, or at-the-side marking makes more sense. Providing a question or a prompt might also help consolidate some learning experiences and provide extra information. The omnivores and herbivores activity from a Year 1 class shows how Charlotte the teacher is promoting learning (Figure 6.6).

FIGURE 6.6
Feedback
marking

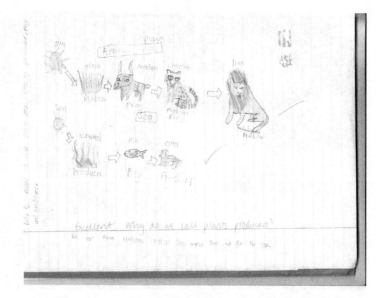

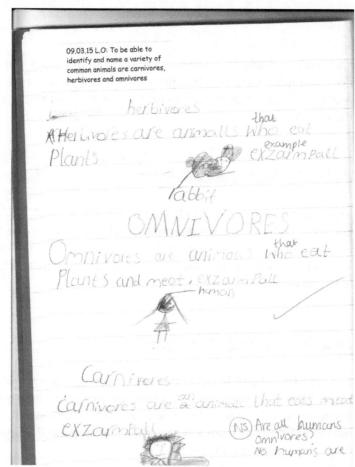

On its own it does not prove the child knows what omnivore or herbivore means, but as the next activity involved making a mobile using the characters from a Disney film *Finding Nemo* as a way to extend learning, the key concept of 'what eats what' is covered again in a different context and thus leads to mastery.

RECORDING PROGRESS

A simple formative system for recording progress could be up arrows demonstrating attainment above the expected (a more challenging task now needs to be set), dots meaning the learners achieved appropriately, and down arrows indicating learners that did not meet the learning intentions (and therefore need further support). The next lesson should be amended in light of this and a series of assessments will provide information on attainment and indicate changes in overall performance for a particular learner. For example, if a learner who had been achieving highly starts to perform less well, this should be investigated. It could be the aspect of science that is a problem, or that they missed a lesson where a key skill was taught, or that there are issues at home. This type of assessment is only formative if it is acted upon by the teacher and/or learner (Black and Wiliam, 1998).

SUMMARY

This chapter has suggested that assessment is only a key part of teaching if it involves learners and encourages open-ended tasks which prompt them to think about what they know. If assessment becomes a set of procedures, such as copying the learning intention into the books, but not checking whether this is a clear learning target, then this is assessment camouflaged as teaching which results in limited learning for all. Narrowing of the curriculum reduces creativity and if learners are not asked to think about what they know, their ideas are not challenged. Through planning open-ended tasks and deep questions teachers can find out what learners know and can then plan the next steps in their learning. Focusing on the 10 foundations of future learning makes the process simpler and should enable a growth mindset approach to teaching, learning and assessment.

(Continued)

(Continued)

FURTHER READING

Dweck, C. (2008) *Mindset: The New Psychology of Success*. New York: Ballantine Books.

Elle, F. and Grudnoff, L. (2013) 'The politics of responsibility: Teacher education and "persistent underachievement" in New Zealand', *The Educational Forum*, 77(1): 73–86.

Hart, S. (1998) 'A sorry tail: Ability, pedagogy and educational reform', *British Journal of Educational Studies*, 46(2): 153–68.

McNess, E., Triggs, P., Broadfoot, P., Osborn, M. and Pollard, A. (2001) 'The changing nature of assessment in English primary classrooms: Findings from the PACE project 1989–1997', *Education 3–13*, 29(3): 9–16.

Swaffield, S. (ed.) (2008) *Unlocking Assessment*. London: Taylor & Francis.

Warwick, P., Sparks Linfield, R. and Stephenson, P. (1999) 'A comparison of primary school pupils' ability to express procedural understanding in science through speech and writing', *International Journal of Science Education*, 21(8): 823–38.

7

SCIENCE FROM STORIES

Claire Hewlett

Stories, both true and imaginary, can offer a rich source of learning opportunities for learners of all ages. The traditional folk tales, myths and legends and modern stories that deal with the world in which people live can all be used as a stimulus for supporting learning across a range of curriculum subjects, including scientific investigation, as well as to provide an everyday starting point for science. This chapter considers why stories should be used as a resource and how fiction can be used to develop scientific understanding, with a particular emphasis on the 7–11 age range (Key Stage 2). A range of practical investigations is suggested as a starting point to illustrate how scientific investigation might be linked to a selection of popular learners' literature.

WHY USE FICTION?

Fiction, which also includes poetry, provides learners with opportunities to make connections between scientific concepts, which can be abstract and challenging in nature, and their own life experiences by providing a frame of reference on which to base their learning. Stories provide a vehicle to link previously learnt concepts with new ideas. Good stories have the potential to motivate learners by making them feel involved through the linking of their own understanding of the world to the characters within the book.

People learn in different ways and for different reasons. Using fiction provides the teacher with a resource that can encourage, support and develop a range of different learning styles. It could also be argued that teachers who consciously plan lessons or topics around the use of stories are more likely to adopt a range of different creative teaching styles themselves in order to meet the needs of the class. The stories chosen in this chapter provide examples of how to interpret the curriculum in different ways and provide learners with a stimulating and varied range of lessons that will involve them in their own learning.

Teachers involved in teaching Key Stage 1 regularly use stories both as a starting point and as a stimulus for teaching a range of curriculum subjects, including science. An impressive range of texts, often beautifully and imaginatively illustrated, that explore the world of the child are widely available. Classic texts such as *The Hungry Caterpillar* by Eric Carle, or *Tadpole's Promise* by Jeanne Willis and Tony Ross, are standard texts found in the book corners of many infant classrooms, and learners have opportunities to enjoy these stories on many levels.

This good practice tends largely to disappear in the Key Stage 2 (KS2) classroom, where teachers are less likely to utilise fiction as a resource within their science teaching. There are possibly several reasons for this; stories are longer and more complex, so finding a story that suits a particular teaching need may be difficult. For the same reason it may be problematic to find a story that appeals to all the learners in the class, or one which allows for continuity and progression within a topic area. With pressure on teachers to deliver a broad and balanced curriculum, they may feel there is not the time to spend reading a story as well as completing a scheme of work, and that getting too involved in the story might result in losing the science. However, as the science content at Key Stage 2 becomes more challenging, some of these concepts can be far removed from learners' own experiences and understanding. By providing a context that learners can relate to it is possible to make the learning more meaningful.

There are obvious solutions. It is not always necessary to read a complete text. Initially a story could be retold in a summarised form to provide the overall context, with relevant chapters then selected to provide the stimulus for further investigation. Another possibility would be to use a text that has been read before that the learners are familiar with, perhaps from another lesson, literacy being the obvious example. Also, it is not always necessary to be tied by the constraints of age-appropriate texts. Many picture books aimed at the younger reader introduce scientific ideas very simply but the underlying concepts are, in fact, quite complex and therefore the material is also relevant for older learners. For example, a story such as *Mommy Laid an Egg* by Babette Cole introduces the concept of reproduction in an accessible way to younger learners but could also be used for teaching about aspects of 'Animals, including humans' in KS2, as outlined in the 2013 National Curriculum. One of the characteristics of stories for this younger age range is that they are often very humorous, and this can be an added advantage when teaching older learners, helping them to feel more at ease when discussing issues they may find embarrassing.

When thinking about selecting a suitable text, it is important to consider that fiction can be used in different ways and for different purposes. Think about the intention. It may be that the aim is to draw out the learners' interest in a story to stimulate and develop lines of enquiry to do with a particular area of study, for example electricity or forces. Alternatively, the aim could be to encourage the learners to solve scientific problems within the story setting that certain characters have encountered; for example, 'Can we make a periscope to help the hero see what is over the wall?' The story may come first with the science developing from it, or vice versa with the science prompting the selection of a relevant text. There are also excellent texts available that tell the life stories of famous scientists, providing a further context for scientific discovery. A text such as *What Mr Darwin Saw* by Mick Manning and Brita Granstrom follows the voyages of *HMS Beagle* and tells how Darwin's theory of evolution was formed. Some stories may lend themselves to a range of ways in which they can be used while others are very specific. A text such as *Danny the Champion of the World* by Roald Dahl provides plenty of opportunity for problem-solving activities to be undertaken in the classroom, while also lending itself to supporting more particular areas of study such as the examination of materials or forces. *Old Bear* by Jane Hissey, on the other hand, tends to focus on one thing and therefore could be used specifically as a starting point for an investigation, in this case looking at parachutes.

DEVELOPING SCIENCE FROM STORIES

Whichever story is chosen, and for whatever reason, it is important to remember not to get overly involved in the text and carried away. Research has found that teachers plan for far more than they ever teach, so they should make sure it is clear how the story is to be used and how it will be integrated into the science teaching. Think about how progression and continuity will be planned for. Read the story and decide whether it covers concepts, skills or attitudes. Then read the story, or the relevant part of the story, with the learners and explore their areas of interest. From these initial 'idea showers' decide upon the investigations and focus upon particular targets.

The following points should help when focusing on planning:

- What exactly will the learners be learning?
- How will they be doing it (the activity)?
- Why do it? (What skills, concepts or attitudes are you hoping to develop?)
- Is the activity appropriate? (Matching needs, abilities, previous learning.)
- What organisation will be needed?
- What resources, materials, equipment will be needed?
- Safety awareness.

SELECTING STORIES FOR STARTING SCIENCE

The following classic texts illustrate how texts can be used to support the teaching of science by providing interesting starting points for investigative science. Many of the activities are aimed at Key Stage 2 in order to demonstrate how abstract concepts might be supported, but several of these activities, and indeed the texts themselves, could be adapted for learners younger than this.

Stig of the Dump by Clive King (1963), Puffin Books

This modern classic about a cave boy transported into the modern world encompasses many areas of the science curriculum, including the overarching requirements of the nature of scientific ideas. This story has great potential for investigating concepts within the science curriculum and also for developing cross-curricular links to other subjects, in particular design and technology, art and music. The suggestions included here address several areas of the Programmes of Study so this story could be used to teach any one of these.

MATERIALS AND THEIR PROPERTIES – SEE PP. 2–3   Taken as a stimulus for work on materials, a suitable starting point might be studying rocks and soils in Year 3, or looking at changing and separating materials, Year 5. Activities could include:

- Starting with some careful observational work: adopt a rock or pebble; memorise the characteristics of the pebble by observation of the size, shape, mass, texture, colour. Can learners identify their own rock when all the rocks are grouped together? Rocks and soils can be investigated further by testing the hardness of different rocks – scratch test – and testing for permeability. Can the learners devise their own investigations to do this?

- What is soil? Can the class make soil? Design and make a wormery (Design and Technology links). Learners could consider how Stig might filter his drinking water.

- Changing materials can be investigated by undertaking activities such as making fossils. Use Plasticine to make casts from shells, fossils or leaves then pour in a plaster of Paris mix. This activity could be a starting point for investigating reversible and non-reversible changes.

Children could also look at pictures of cave paintings: is it possible to produce rock paintings using different soils or by extracting colour from fruit or vegetables? Or, consider how charcoal is made; draw with chalk and charcoal.

FORCES AND MOTION – SEE PP. 152–4   This section really lends itself to the investigation of forces, in particular studying levers, pulleys and gears, and exploring concepts such as friction and gravity that is part of the upper KS2 Programme of Study. There is great potential for problem-solving here. By providing some open-ended questions that relate to the characters in the story learners have opportunities to take charge of planning investigations independently and explore a wide range of investigative work, for example:

- What happens when more stones have to be pulled up a slope?
- What happens to the force needed as the mass increases?
- What happens when the slope is steeper?
- Where would most force be needed if moving a stone up a slope: in front or behind?
- Which surface makes moving the stones easiest?
- What is the best way to lift or lever a stone off the ground?

This sort of questioning encourages learners to plan fair test investiga-tions and think about how they will record their results in a systematic manner (a planning format could work very well here). Practical work on pulling and lifting, using stones, containers, slopes, different surface materials and Newton meters, will help to develop conceptual under-standing of friction and gravity. Learners could start by investigating what happens when the weight of the stones in a container is increased when the container is pulled along a flat surface. Are there any patterns in their results? What can they conclude? Learners could then progress to investigate the effect of slopes by pulling a fixed mass up different gra-dients. Can they first predict what might happen? Can they explain their reasoning? Still using the same basic equipment, they could move on to explore the concept of friction and look at how different surfaces affect the pulling force.

This type of investigation is well within the capabilities of upper junior learners. How might a very simple lever mechanism help to move a stone or help stand a stone upright? A simple way of demonstrating this princi-ple is by using a wooden ruler balanced over a pencil, like a see-saw, and placing a heavy object on one end. By exerting pressure with a finger on the other end, learners can explore what happens when the pencil, or ful-crum, is moved nearer to or further away from finger or object. The story ends with the characters at Stonehenge. Learners could then develop their ideas further to investigate how they might move or lift stones to create a small-scale Stonehenge in the school grounds.

LIGHT AND SOUND: THE EARTH AND BEYOND – SEE P. 156   This part of the story provides an opportunity to tie this work in with earth and beyond, particularly looking at day and night. The small-scale model of Stonehenge could be used to investigate shadow formation, to track the movement of the sun during a school day and to look at how shadows can be used to tell the time.

The Iron Man by Ted Hughes (1968), Faber and Faber

This dramatic story lends itself in particular to topic work on electric-ity and magnetism, and the exploration of metallic materials and their properties.

MATERIALS AND THEIR PROPERTIES: PHYSICAL PROCESSES – ELECTRICITY, FORCES AND MOTION – SEE PP. 17–18   The links to metal and magnetic properties tie this activity into science in everyday life. Learners could begin by exploring the properties of different metals and considering the different uses of metals. They could then test different metals for their magnetic qualities and record their findings in simple charts or tables. Questions such as 'Are metals with magnetic properties still attracted to magnets through different materials such as card, water or fabric?' could be answered. Get the learners to plan different ways of testing the strength of a range of magnets. Is strength related to size? Results could be recorded in a variety of charts or tables devised by the learners on the computer.

What would be the best metal for the Iron Man to have been made of? What happens to iron when exposed to salt water? Technically, looking at rusting is not in the National Curriculum but it could be included as part of the breadth of study requirements and it does provide opportunities for learners to plan their own fair test investigations if they explore what makes iron nails rust. Rusting represents a major economic cost to the industrialised world. Is it possible to prevent rusting? Here would be a good opportunity to place primary school science within the bigger picture and consider science in the future.

Stories can often give rise to misconceptions regarding scientific concepts, as the need for dramatic effect, through the use of language and illustration, often takes precedence over scientific fact. During this story the Iron Man's rusty exterior turns back to shiny rust-free metal. Is this possible in the manner in which it is told? These kinds of misrepresentations in stories could be the basis of investigative work and used to challenge learners' knowledge and understanding. By presenting learners with challenging thinking questions it is possible to raise their awareness of misconceptions; they could then try to solve the problem of the characters either from the Iron Man's point of view or from that of the villagers. As a teacher it is important to be aware at all times of how scientific facts and concepts are being represented in fictional texts.

The changing colours of the Iron Man's eyes are referred to several times throughout the story. Besides looking at how to construct simple circuits and switches, learners always find experimenting with flashing light bulbs in circuits fascinating. What makes the bulb flash? What will happen to another bulb in a series circuit when a flashing bulb is included? Again, open-ended questioning can be used to get the learners exploring for themselves and coming up with hypotheses about the flow of electricity around a circuit. Make either a two-dimensional or three-dimensional model of the Iron Man's head, or look further at robots and make a whole iron man from construction kits or from suitable materials. Can the learners make a model where the eyes flash different colours or flash on and off for a fixed period of time? Can they make the eyes flash alternately or alter the brightness of the eyes?

Upper Key Stage 2 learners could investigate simple variable resistors in order to do this.

Dr Dog by Babette Cole (1997), Sagebrush

ANIMALS, INCLUDING HUMANS   This book, aimed at Key Stage 1 (children aged 6–7), uses a medical pretext to indulge the reader in a range of outrageous scatological jokes. As with many of her other books there is some serious teaching underpinning the humorous and somewhat ridiculous storyline, in this instance the dangers of smoking and unhealthy eating and the importance of washing hands to prevent germs spreading. Again, it is a story that could be enjoyed by earlier learners in Key Stage 2 (children aged 7–8) as well as by younger learners. This is a funny and entertaining resource to support the teaching of 'Animals, including humans' – about the danger of drugs and unhealthy living and about life processes. Learners are often confused about life processes and what these involve, even at the end of Key Stage 2, and stories can help to make these more explicit when studying either plants or animals.

The danger of drugs is included in the Programme of Study in Year 6 (Animals, including humans). The effect of smoking on the lungs could link to other work on life processes, in particular the importance of exercise and the role of the lungs within the circulatory system, and there are plenty of opportunities for practical work, for example comparing lung capacity. Comparison questions that encourage looking for and interpreting patterns in data could be investigated, questions such as 'Do taller learners have a bigger lung capacity?' or 'Do learners with longer legs jump further, run faster?'

Grandpa's rather distasteful eating habits could provide a starting point for work on nutrition and the need for a healthy and varied diet. Learners can survey the ingredients in school dinners and create a school menu for a week that provides a balanced diet. It is important to be sensitive to the diets of the children in your class as this can cause upset, therefore surveying lunchboxes is not advocated as an activity. Alternatively, plan a healthy meal for the Grandpa character in the story. Investigate complex and simple carbohydrates by looking into sugars in food and drink, and how much hidden sugar is in food by reading the ingredients on packaging. With older juniors, studying packaging can also be a helpful way of learning about microorganisms. Investigate fortified iron in cereal; some cereals contain iron fillings as the source of iron. Further universal issues could be considered, for example how foods are preserved and stored, how different foods are grown and transported around the world. www.nationalstem centre.org.uk is an excellent website for teaching resources such as these suggested here.

Understanding the digestive system is part of the Programme of Study for lower KS2. Learners are egocentric and fascinated about learning about themselves, including the journey of their food through the body. Taking basic scientific information as a stimulus for creative writing, or just as a means to record what has been learnt, can be very productive. The digestive process is an exciting story in its own right and lends itself to imaginative 'adventure' story writing (Figure 7.1). Getting learners to write their own science stories and poems provides opportunities for self-expression and an interesting diversion from the more formal formats often used for writing up a science investigation. The digestion story also makes an exciting starting point for drama and the story could be acted out and presented to other learners. Posters and health warnings can also be used to convert the findings of an investigation and be displayed in the classroom or around the school. These are particularly effective when used to support

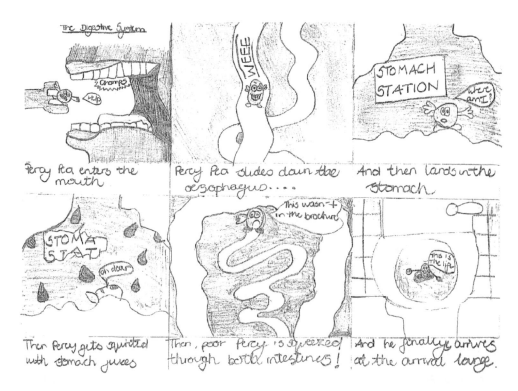

FIGURE 7.1   The digestive process

work on life processes; for example, personal hygiene to prevent the spreading of germs, or healthy diet to promote growth or healthy teeth and bones.

Other texts

Tables 7.1A and B and 7.2A and B provide further suggestions for how a range of fictional texts might be used as starting points, or for developing topic work. Both tables include many activities or investigations that can be adapted across the 5–11 age range, though some are specifically targeted at an appropriate age range. The stories selected represent a very small sample of the wide range of fiction available to support science teaching. Texts aimed at the 5–8 age range are also generally suited to the teaching of concepts with older junior-aged learners.

TABLE 7.1A   Further suggestions for use of fiction as a starting point in science (living things and their habitats, animals, including humans, plants)

Over the Steamy Swamp by Paul Geraghty	A hungry mosquito starts a food chain in a steamy swamp as each hungry animal both preys and is preyed upon. Introduces the concepts of food chains or habitats
Flotsam by David Wiesner	A science-minded boy goes to the beach equipped to collect and examine anything floating that has been washed ashore. A wordless story leaving lots of room for the imagination and the use of talk
Tadpole's Promise by Jeanne Willis and Tony Ross	Embodies life cycles of frogs and butterflies as a tadpole and a caterpillar fall in love with dire consequences
One Smart Fish by Christopher Wormell	Follows the journey of one fish from sea to land and introduces the concept of evolution in a clear and concise way
What Mr Darwin Saw by Mick Manning and Brita Granstrom	The book follows the journey of *HMS Beagle* and the reader is able to follow the steps which led to Darwin's inspired theory of evolution. Because of the careful balancing of differing points of view, the book could also be effectively used to introduce the work of Darwin in KS2
The World Came to My Place Today by Jo Redman	The story follows George's day as he discovers the wonder of plants and how they affect his daily life
The Secret Garden by Frances Hodgson Burnett	A secret garden, walled, locked and forgotten. Can it be brought back to life? A children's classic

TABLE 7.1B Further suggestions for use of fiction as a starting point in science (living things in the environment, food chains and evolution)

Careful observation of the environment The 2013 curriculum has a far greater emphasis on identifying and classifying plants and animals. Take young children on nature walks and mini safaris to look for things, e.g. flowers with 3/4/5/6 petals, plants that match colours on a paint palette, leaves with different textures, shapes, etc. Older children could plan or design their own nature walks. Foster Darwin's spirit of enquiry by encouraging all ages to carefully observe and record local plant and animal species and how they interact. Make cross-sections or transects of a chosen area to enable children to observe very carefully what is living in different areas, e.g. under a tree, by a path, near a hedge, in the middle of the field. Use viewfinders to focus on the micro, take digital photographs and share on the *interactive whiteboard*. Older learners can record random sampling using hoops or ropes to mark a small area. What is living within? What conclusions can be drawn?

Adopt a tree. What lives in your tree? How tall is your tree? Measure the girth with non-standard measurements, how does it change throughout the year?

Classify plants and animals by their different features by recording observations in table form. The 7–9 age range can identify locally occurring plants and animals and assign them to groups using simple keys, older juniors can make their own dichotomous keys. Grow fast-growing plants – beans in jam jars against blotting paper allows children to see the root system develop. Create seed packets with information about growing conditions. Invent (and make) your own plant or animal, name it and create its habitat

Design a small wildlife area for your school, what conditions could you provide for plants and animals? Consider the life processes, what is necessary for plants and animals to survive. Undertake a survey to establish living conditions of snails, woodlice or earthworms. Use secondary sources to answer questions that arise when observing living things. Design a home for some woodlice so they can be kept in the classroom

Identify simple food chains in an ecosystem Food chain game – children get to be something (e.g. sun, grass, cow, man) and have to put themselves in order. Record food intake from yesterday. All food comes from plants or animals, find out where your food comes from to develop simple food chains (links with geography). Write a dramatic food chain story or act it out as a drama

Upper juniors should develop the concept of food chains Some animals eat different things, e.g. herons will eat other things besides fish. Use secondary sources to develop ideas about ecosystems, contrast food webs from Britain with webs from other habitats/ecosystems (*Over the Steamy Swamp*, though aimed at the 5–7 age range is an excellent resource for older pupils). Link children together with string to show these complex links. Look at a food chain starting with a mosquito and ending with man, what are the implications? What happens when disease wipes out something in the food chain?

Evolution and adaption Teach about Darwin's theory of evolution through games such as 'The Evolution Experience' playing the role of a young bird trying to survive winter long enough to reproduce. Or 'Game of Survival' - can you live for a million years? (both accessed at www.darwinslandscape. co.uk). Darwin noticed that on each of the Galapagos Islands the finches had different shaped beaks, adapted for different food sources. Which are the best-shaped beaks for picking up seeds? Test the theory by seeing how many seeds can be collected using blunt and pointed tweezers. Research and compare the story of Darwin with modern-day naturalists such as David Attenborough, look at new species that have been discovered and their habitats. Become palaeontologists and investigate fossils and how they were formed. Create moulds and cast fossils for digging up around the school grounds

TABLE 7.2A Further suggestions for using fiction as a starting point for use in science (forces, earth and space)

Man on the Moon by Simon Bartram	Bob is the man on the moon, and he has a very special job, looking after the moon, cleaning it up, showing visitors around and selling souvenirs
Flat Stanley by Jeff Brown	Stanley Lambchop awakes one day to find he has been flattened. Various adventures follow, including being flown like a kite
Danny, Champion of the World by Roald Dahl	Much-loved tale about a boy and the relationship he has with his father. Making a hot air balloon and flying kites are included in two chapters
Black Holes and Uncle Albert by Russell Stannard	Second book in a series of three. An adventure story set in deepest space that introduces and explains many phenomena, such as how is it that you are made of stardust? The main character is also a female!

TABLE 7.2B Further suggestions for use of fiction as a starting point in science (gravity, air resistance, water resistance and earth in space)

Investigating gravity Drop a weight from different heights into a sand tray. Predict what will happen first. Will there be any difference in the depth of the imprint? What will happen if the height of the drop is altered? Younger children could investigate this and observe what happens, older junior age children could hypothesise before testing. Drop items that are made of the same materials but different shapes, what happens?

Air resistance/gravity Make kites, paper planes, spinners or parachutes. Investigate which stay in the air the longest, travel the furthest, are the most aerodynamic, etc. (adapt the following investigations). Again, younger children could observe what happens whilst older juniors can develop their own investigations by raising their own questions, identifying variables, thinking about how they might record their results. Explore questions such as:

- Are some materials better than others for making parachutes/spinners/kites/planes?
- How can you keep something in the air for the longest time or travel the farthest?
- What happens when variables are changed, size, materials, shape, etc.?
- Look for patterns in results
- Record in pictures showing direction of the forces with arrows

Make links to birds and other living things that fly, including aeroplanes. Link to mathematics, e.g. find out how much fuel an aeroplane consumes in a given journey

Water resistance Use the same approach to investigate water resistance by considering different materials that float/sink. What happens to an orange and a lemon when put into water, or a can of coke and a can of diet coke? Present learners with visual puzzles to develop thinking skills. Investigate changing the shape of an object or the density of a liquid

Earth and space Simulations and models can be used to explain abstract concepts. Make an orrery to show the position and orbits of the planets. Investigate the sun – why does it appear to be small? Again, link to maths by measuring out the positions of the sun and planets in the playground, to scale (1 m = 1 million km). Make a shoe box solar water heater and record temperature over time. Use real NASA data (www.nasawavelength.org) to plot and record a variety of data about earth and space in real time, such as how the sun heats up air, land and water

Own a piece of the moon – samples of real moon rock can be borrowed from Jodrell Bank and observed under a digital microscope and compared with rocks found on earth. Links can be made to literacy, create brochures for holidays on the moon for a travel company

Use video clips to demonstrate force and motion in space, e.g. the hammer and the feather demonstration to make further links to work on forces (both these topics are in Year 5) www.national stemcentre.org.uk/elibrary/resource/1356/the-hammer-and-the-feather-on-the-moon

SUMMARY

This chapter has considered how fiction can be used as a vehicle to support learning in science. By linking previously learnt concepts with new ideas, fiction can provide a frame of reference on which to base future learning. Fiction provides opportunities for making connections between scientific concepts and learners' own life experiences. Making only small changes to existing planning and practice, to include more use of a wide range of fiction, can enable teachers actively to promote learners' creativity and respond to their creative ideas and actions. Fiction is a powerful and readily available resource to support and engage learners with their own scientific understanding. Good stories have the potential to motivate learners by involving them through linking their own understanding of the world to the characters within the book. Specific examples from well-known learners' literature have been presented to illustrate ways in which fiction might be used as a science resource to support a range of teaching and learning styles. The chapter has also briefly explored how learners might develop their own self-expression through writing about their science understanding in a variety of ways.

FURTHER READING

Dunne, I. (2006) 'Bring the story alive', *Primary Science Review*, Issue 92: 22–4.

Ovens, P. (2004) 'A "SANE" way to encourage creativity', *Primary Science Review*, 81: 17–20.

Turner, J. and Bage, G. (2006) 'Real stories, real science', *Primary Science Review*, Issue 92: 4–6.

(Continued)

(Continued)

Useful websites

www.darwinslandscape.co.uk
www.edenproject.com
www.jodrellbank.net
www.nasawavelength.org
www.nhm.ac.uk
www.nationalstemcentre.org.uk

8

USING ROLE-PLAY TO STIMULATE AND DEVELOP LEARNERS' UNDERSTANDING OF SCIENTIFIC CONCEPTS

Maria Elsam and Julie Foreman

This chapter will include a brief overview of the theory underlying the use of the active approach of physical modelling, to promote learners' learning in science. Role-play will then be explored as a pedagogical approach to promote primary school learners' understanding of abstract scientific concepts. Throughout the chapter the importance of teachers modelling this approach (Dodwell, 2009; cited in Kambouri and Michaelidas, 2015) will be emphasised, along with the importance of providing opportunities for learners to practise role-play as a valuable tool of learning. Incorporating role-play with relevant talk will ensure that learners' understanding is developed effectively. Practical suggestions for work in the classroom will follow. Finally, to raise awareness and to avoid misrepresentation, the limitations of the use of role-play will be highlighted.

TEACHING APPROACHES IN THE NATIONAL CURRICULUM

The Science National Curriculum (DfE, 2013b: 3) encourages teachers to develop students' curiosity when teaching science, it states that 'pupils should be encouraged to recognise the power of rational explanation and develop a sense of excitement and curiosity about natural phenomena'. This view is echoed in the recent survey *Maintaining Curiosity* (Ofsted, 2013, Introductory Page) into science education in schools, the purpose of which is to 'support schools in implementing the new National Curriculum'. One of the key points identified by this survey (Ofsted, 2013: 5) is that the best-performing schools 'set out to sustain pupils' natural curiosity, so that they were eager to learn the subject content as well as develop the necessary investigative skills'.

Some would argue that imagination, rather than knowing facts, is the most important factor needed to learn science and, therefore, the use of imagination should be reflected in its teaching. This line of thought is endorsed by Newton and Newton (2009: 46) when they state that 'creativity in school science means taking opportunities in science contexts which foster empowering, imaginative thought in the children'. Without doubt, science is an integral part of modern culture and must aim to stretch the imagination and creativity of young people. Harlen (2010: 6) identifies how a positive emotional response that motivates further learning is evoked by 'both the process and product of scientific activity', thus enhancing 'learners' curiosity, wonder and questioning, building on their natural inclination to seek meaning and understanding of the world around'. Therefore, learners should be given the opportunity to respond to aspects of science in an imaginative and a creative way that is driven by their own curiosity. This is especially important if it is to nurture future scientists, since both creativity (Newton and Newton, 2009) and an ability to communicate ideas clearly to others (Smith et al., 2012) are important attributes of successful scientists.

The implications of this for primary science teaching are huge. Recent Ofsted reports have highlighted that teachers must challenge learners of all abilities (Ofsted, 2008a), particularly the most able (Ofsted, 2011; Ofsted, 2013), much further than at present, and that learners need to experience more complex forms of learning. After all, it is generally accepted that learners can achieve more if they are challenged in a non-threatening, motivating way.

While it might be that traditional approaches to teaching science may not stifle creativity in some learners, it is well known that many people have been put off science in the past by their own experience of science in school. Osborne and Collins (2000) and Osborne et al. (1996; cited in

Osborne et al., 2003: 694) argue that 'science education is science's own worst enemy leaving far too many students with a confused sense of the significance of what they have learned, an ambivalent or negative attitude to the subject itself'. However, it is easy to accept that the development of an individual's creativity in science may well be dependent upon the quality and diversity of the learning opportunities provided in the classroom. In terms of developing scientific literacy, Smith et al. (2012: 129) acknowledge that it is 'about how new ideas resonate and work effectively within a range of diverse classroom contexts and cultures and how teachers' thinking and experiences shape ideas in and through practice'. In fact, Harlen (2010) identifies that the linking of new experiences to existing knowledge, via a process that includes talk and questioning, enables learners to learn more quickly, as they are motivated by curiosity to answer questions. Hence, if too few opportunities are provided for learners to show curiosity, then their motivation to engage in creative behaviour can easily be dampened. So, it is important to approach activities in a creative way, ensuring that risk and exploration are encouraged.

The cognitive development required to understand scientific concepts is in itself reliant on what Barnes (2011) describes as the need to develop connections within the brain. The former will allow for intelligence to be applied to other situations, therefore allowing intelligence to be modified (Adey and Serret, 2010; Muijs and Reynolds, 2011). So, there is a need for the provision of diverse teaching and learning strategies, strategies that provide different representations of the same concept, through different 'multi-modal' forms (Prain and Waldrip, 2006: 1844). Learners learn in different ways all the time, and there is no one 'right' way for all; teachers therefore need to draw upon a variety of pedagogical approaches in their teaching to cater for the variety of learners.

Research suggests that drama is often identified by educators as an 'active approach to learning' (O'Loughlin, 1992; cited in Braund, 2015: 104). Role-play is just one aspect of drama (others include dance, mime, scripted drama/plays) that is perceived as enabling children to develop their understanding in the form of 'acted out simulations' (Braund, 2015: 104), whilst also increasing learners' interest and motivation (Cakici and Bayir, 2012). The self-perpetuating saying 'I hear and I forget; I see and I remember; I do and I understand', shows the importance of practical activities. Role-play is in essence a form of physical modelling; when it is a new experience for the learner it is described by Barnes (2011: 219) as an example of 'performance for understanding', a new opportunity that can help learners to visualise and understand, what are in this instance, abstract scientific concepts. Yet, when referring to drama, Braund (2015: 103) identifies how 'it is alarming to note how little attention it often receives'. This is further explained as the possible 'lower status attributed to the arts in both the curriculum and research compared with other subjects' (Anderson, 2004; cited in Braund, 2015: 103).

Role-play has been shown to build upon learners' natural enjoyment of play and can provide much fun and real interest, 'the key to role-play is that it is based on play' (Cakici and Bayir, 2012: 1076). Role-play can be considered to be a very natural learning medium from which children gain a lot of enjoyment and satisfaction (McSharry and Jones; cited in Cakici and Bayir, 2012). One only has to consider how much time very young learners spend in engaging in undirected, imaginative, fantasy play both in their own play outside school and, when given the opportunity, in the nursery and Early Years classroom. The Statutory Framework for the Early Years Foundation Stage (DfE, 2014) also identifies how 'planned purposeful play' led by both children and adults is essential for child development. This natural tendency to engage in role-play (DfE, 2014) can be harnessed by the teacher in a more structured way to encourage learning about aspects of science across the primary curriculum. What is more, role-play is motivational not only because it involves activity, but also because it provides a break from established classroom routines. Cakici and Bayir (2012: 1075) reflect on the work of Marianne Ødegaard, and identify how she has completed an 'extensive review of the literature on drama activities in science education'. Ødegaard (2003: 75) herself claims that 'There is evidence that the use of drama in a well considered manner, guided by reflective science teachers, may provide empowering learning environments for students'.

It is also important to consider that 'when words fail there are other routes for expression of an idea' (Dorion, 2009: 2266). Role-play involves physical movement, it can be used to help to explain abstract or complex concepts, that can be re-enacted in a fraction of the time compared with other pedagogical approaches (Braund, 2015). This is complemented by Alexander's (2010; cited in Barnes, 2015: 263) account of neuroscientific research where it is identified that 'learning is strengthened not only in relation to how many neurons fire in a neural network, but also how they are distributed across different domains, such as the motor and sensory cortices'. However, role-play can also demand more than just bodily movement; understanding can come not only through the participants' high level of physical involvement, but also through exposure to ideas, discussion and collaboration with other learners. Exposure to ideas, discussion and collaboration, situated within an appropriate context (Loxley, 2009) are aspects that could be included in various drama activities, whilst also being highlighted as constituents of the social constructivist paradigm. Loxley (2009: 1608) places an emphasis on the 'the use of language and context as key pedagogical tools for meaning making' and identifies that they are grounded in 'social-cultural theory'. Added to this notion, creative activities such as role-play allow learners not only to communicate using familiar language codes, but may encourage learners to communicate using scientific language that is used by scientists. This use could be perceived as not only increasing the learners' use of scientific vocabulary, but also allowing for the learners to negotiate the meaning of the word(s) (Adey and Serret, 2010; Ma, 2012) and to 'construct new meanings from such a language' (Evagorou and Osborne, 2010: 136). It should be acknowledged that whilst the final outcome may be that of a role-play, as opposed to a scripted drama (Ødegaard, 2003), the process of arriving at the role-play will have included discussion and collaboration, set within a given context.

In order for role-play to be effective in giving an insight into a scientific way of thinking, it is important that the teacher models an idea before it is practised by the learners, a technique known as 'teacher in role' (Dodwell, 2009; cited in Kambouri and Michaelidas, 2015: 10). To achieve maximum benefit, role-play should be used regularly in science from the earliest days in formal education and throughout the school. In this way, learners become familiar with this strategy and therefore will develop their confidence in participation – confidence being an important aspect in both teaching (Braund, 2015) and learning (Ødegaard, 2003). Familiarisation has also been shown to develop learners' ability to use role-play more effectively to show their learning and so provide a possible form of assessment (Braund, 2015). The assessment can be completed by the teacher and/or peers (Dorion, 2009) to provide information about the knowledge gained.

ROLE-PLAY IN THE PRIMARY SCHOOL

Role-play is already an important strategy in the Early Years of schooling, though not necessarily for the development of scientific knowledge and understanding. It is very common for very young learners in school to 'act-out', for example, an extract from books or traditional tales and to engage in more informal role-play in the 'home corner'. It is easy, therefore, to extend this idea to simple scientific ideas at the Early Years Foundation Stage. It is straightforward to link literacy to science in this way. The use of 'props' can also play an important part in role-play. Braund (2015: 114) identifies how the use of props, along with the learners' physical involvement, 'make a sometimes hard to visualise process "come alive"'. Older learners may benefit from the use of labels and pictures during the delivery of their role-play. Younger learners may well 'dress-up', wear masks or dress models to help to communicate scientific ideas.

One difficult concept for younger learners to understand relates to forces, i.e. pushes and pulls. For this, following the reading of *The*

Enormous Turnip, small groups of learners can role-play parts of the story to pull the enormous turnip from the ground. In doing so, their understanding of forces will be developed. Similarly, many scientific concepts can be explored through role-play, starting with a story, or observation. Older learners can often approach the representation of ideas in a very creative, imaginative way if they are given the opportunity to put forward their own ideas after brief instruction.

Table 8.1 illustrates how other topics can be developed through the use of role-play throughout the school. However, it is important to appreciate that many of the same ideas can be approached at different ages and abilities. Here, it is the role of the teacher to choose the level of the idea to be explored and to decide how much help to give to learners in formulating the role-play. For example, within the topic of electricity, while initially learners may only be asked to represent the flow of electricity in an electric circuit using a skipping rope, more experienced learners could be expected to role-play, for example, the flow of the electrons, the learners themselves acting as the electrons in a circuit. Concepts such as resistance, series and parallel circuits could then be developed in this way.

TABLE 8.1 Aspects of role-play that could develop from different starting points

Topic	Age group	Aspects of role-play
Shoes (scientific aspect: materials and their properties)	Early Years Foundation Stage	Pupils think about the properties of the materials used for different kinds of footwear, e.g. soft warm fabric for slippers, stiff leather for boots and some shoes, flexible materials for beach 'flip-flops' and 'jelly' shoes. Pupils then to act out one of these to demonstrate the properties
Mini-beasts	Foundation Stage	Following observation of mini-beasts, pupils could pretend to move like different creatures: props could include, e.g., additional limbs to enable pupils to become spiders or insects. A small sleeping bag can make a good 'prop' for the skin of a caterpillar
Waterproofing	5–6 years	Ideas related to the properties of materials: some materials can let through water others cannot. Pupils enacting the particles of water and different materials
Life cycle of a butterfly	6–7 years	Following revision of the seven life processes, children consider the different stages of their lives and when they change. Discuss and draw comparisons with various life cycles, e.g. plants and trees, frogs and lions. Present key stages of the life cycle of a butterfly and ask children to re-enact the stages through a carousel of activities representing each stage

Topic	Age group	Aspects of role-play
Shadows	7–8 years	Ideas related to how light travels: some materials allow light to pass through whilst others do not, i.e. exploring opaque, translucent and transparent materials. Pupils enacting the path of the light and how it may be reflected passed through or absorbed by the material in its path
Food chains/webs	8–9 years	Pupils acting as the sun, plants and animals in a number of food chains using string to link them appropriately. Cross-link food chains to show a food web with the sun at the centre
Electricity	8–9 years	Push the push: pupils to stand in a circle holding a rope and pass it through their hands to illustrate the flow of electricity. One pupil could act as the light bulb and slow the movement of the rope
Sound	8–9 years	Ideas related to vibrations that are acknowledged as not being readily visible. Pupils stand in a single row with their arms on the shoulders of the person in front of them and re-enact the sound wave by rocking backwards and forwards. Changing how far they move backwards and forwards represents amplitude, and changing the rate at which they move backwards and forwards represents the frequency
Thermal insulation	9–10 years	Ideas related to heat transfer: why ice cream does not melt when wrapped in newspaper and why newspaper keeps chips hot. Pupils representing the heat transfer and the newspaper, i.e. the heat is prevented from passing through the newspaper either from the outside, or the inside of the package
Day and night	9–10 years	Ideas relating to the movement of the earth in relation to the moon and the sun. Pupils enacting the spin of the earth in relation to the sun to show how day and night occur
Dissolving	9–10 years	Ideas about solubility: that some things will dissolve in a liquid, whilst others will not. That there is a limit to the amount of substance that will dissolve in a liquid. Pupils acting as the particles of a liquid and the material to be dissolved
Filtering	9–10 years	Ideas about particle size: that some particles are too big to pass through a filter, whilst others are not. Some pupils acting as the filter letting some particles through, other pupils acting as the particles trying to get through the filter
Evaporation	9–10 years	Ideas about movement of particles: puddles evaporating. Pupils acting as the particles of a liquid changing to a gas – without boiling
Sun, moon and stars	9–10 years	Ideas relating to the position and movement of planets around the sun

(Continued)

TABLE 8.1 (Continued)

Topic	Age group	Aspects of role-play
Sun, moon and earth	9–10 years	Ideas relating to the position and movement of the earth around the sun, and the moon around the earth. Pupils to act as the sun, earth and moon to show the orbits of the earth and moon. The same side of the moon facing its orbit can be enacted and the length of one complete spin of the earth explained
Sexual reproduction in plants: pollination	9–10 years	Pupils can take the role of the sex organs of flowering plants such as the stamens and the stigma. One pupil then acts as a pollinator (e.g. a bee) flying from flower to flower
Making a classification key	9–10 and 10–11 years	All pupils in the class to line up and discuss/develop questions with yes/no answers to group/classify the pupils as in a branching key, e.g. 'Does the child have blue eyes?'
Heart and circulation	10–11 years	See Case Study

CASE STUDY

The circulatory system

This case study comes from a three-form-entry primary school situated in the centre of a small town in the south east of England. The class contained a wide range of abilities with a high proportion of learners with special educational needs. Learners in Year 6 had been undertaking a topic on health and fitness, including learning about the circulatory system. The teacher realised that many learners in the class were confused about this process and she felt that many in the class found the diagrams in the available non-fiction books were difficult to interpret. The teacher decided to involve the learners in a role-play as a way to develop their understanding of the circulatory system. The role-play consisted of the journey of the blood between the lungs and heart. This was used to explain how oxygen and carbon dioxide are transferred to the organs of the body by the blood.

The school, like many others, had a tradition of each class taking turns, each week, to present a class assembly which parents were invited to attend. The class in question, when it was their turn, decided that they would like to present their role-play from earlier in the term. The class were accustomed to making their own decisions about what and how to present their assemblies, so, after initial discussion, the class were left alone to plan for themselves. What resulted was an extended version of their original role-play, expanded into a scripted drama that included actions, expressions and dialogue. The narrator, electing to wear a white laboratory coat, goggles and a red wig, and armed with a clipboard and pointing stick, proceeded to act out the role of 'mad scientist'. Whilst explaining the journey of the blood around the body, some of the learners were organs strategically placed around the hall, while the remainder of the learners took the role of the corpuscles. The corpuscles moved around the hall filling up with oxygen in the lungs and slowly running out of oxygen as they moved around the body feeding the organs.

When the class were preparing their 'leavers' service the following year they were asked to write about their favourite memories. The narrator wrote about their play and could still recall the main teaching points he had learned the year before.

THE USE OF ROLE-PLAY IN TWO AREAS OF THE NATIONAL CURRICULUM

The remainder of this chapter will look at the use of role-play in two areas of the National Curriculum based upon work with classes of Year 4 and Year 2 learners respectively, i.e:

• solids, liquids and gases – Year 4,
• life cycle – Year 2.

In each example, the National Curriculum references covered by the role-play within the Programmes of Study will be highlighted. Guidance will be provided to show how role-play can be used to physically model these scientific concepts. Photographs will be included for illustration. Suggestions will be made for points to emphasise during the role-play in order to challenge learners' possible misconceptions. Additionally, this section will outline possible group extension activities to enable learners to use role-play to show their conceptual understanding. Finally, this section will present examples of possible outcomes of using these approaches in the primary science classroom.

In the solids, liquids and gases activity, it is important, before undertaking any role-play activities, that the issue of scale and analogy in relation to learners acting as the particles is clearly explained to them, as we are dealing here with a highly abstract concept. In the role-play example presented here, it was stressed that only the movement of the particles was being represented, not appearance or size.

MAKING A SOLID

What are you trying to show?

Solids, liquids and gases form part of States of Matter (Year 4) within the National Curriculum. It is expected that 8–9-year-old learners should be taught to recognise differences between solids, liquids and gases, in terms of ease of flow and maintenance of shape and volume. Non-statutory notes for States of Matter: 'Pupils should explore a variety of everyday materials and develop simple descriptions of the states of matter [in that] solids hold their shape'.

Learners are to represent the motion of particles (atoms and molecules) in the role-play.

Teaching points

- The particles in a solid can only vibrate in fixed positions, they cannot move around because the particles are tightly bound – ask the learners to simulate this by wobbling.
- The solid has a fixed shape and volume. It can change its shape only when another external force is applied – this can also be simulated.

What do you need?

Examples of solids for learners to examine their properties. Learners could also bring into school lists of solids investigated at home or on the internet. They could be encouraged to make a written list or bring in a pictorial representation of solids that are in, e.g., their shopping trolley, their sports bag, their lunch box, etc.

How do you prepare the class?

Learners to investigate a range of solids and establish the properties of a solid.

Running the role-play

Select nine learners to form a solid. Arrange them in rows of three, as shown in Figure 8.1.

Questions to ask

Before the role-play
If we were to become the particles in a solid (explanation of scale would be needed here), how do you think we could show the properties of a solid?

FIGURE 8.1
Learners role-playing a solid

During the role-play

How can we show that the particles in a solid can only vibrate in fixed positions and cannot move around?

Could we show that the particles are tightly bound and a solid has a fixed shape and volume?

After the role-play

Discussion to reinforce the properties of a solid referring to the role-play.

Follow-up work

Learners to record the properties of a solid referring to the role-play using a method of their choice, such as:

- a cartoon strip,
- a newspaper article,
- a poster,
- a diagram,
- a story on the life of a solid,
- a poem.

Further role-plays on liquids, gases and change of state to be covered next.

MAKING A LIQUID

What are you trying to show?

Solids, liquids and gases form part of States of Matter (Year 4) within the National Curriculum. It is expected that 8–9-year-old learners should be taught to recognise differences between solids, liquids and gases, in terms of ease of flow and maintenance of shape and volume. Non-statutory notes for States of Matter: 'Pupils should explore a variety of everyday materials and develop simple descriptions of the states of matter [in that] liquids form a pool not a pile'.

Learners are to represent the motion of the particles (atoms and molecules) in the role-play.

Teaching points

- The particles are still closely bound, but they can 'slide' around each other in a liquid.
- Liquids can change their shape to fit the container they are in or form a pool.
- Liquids cannot be reduced or increased in volume, they therefore keep the same volume when they are poured from one container to another or allowed to pool. Keeping the same number of children as in Figure 8.1, they could be rearranged to form any order, including a single line.

What do you need?

Examples of liquids. Pupils could bring lists of liquids from investigation at home, on the internet, etc. They could be encouraged to make a written list or bring in a pictorial representation of liquids that are in, e.g., their shopping trolley, their sports bag, their lunch box, etc.

How do you prepare the class?

Pupils to investigate a range of liquids to establish the properties of a liquid.

Running the role-play

Select another nine pupils to make a solid again and explain that as heat is absorbed a change will be observed. The absorption of heat could be re-enacted by the modelling of the application of a heat source.

In a solid, as it melts, the particles begin to vibrate/wobble faster and the material gradually becomes a liquid, a temperature is reached that causes the particles to vibrate/wobble so fast that they break free of their fixed arrangement and begin to flow.

Ask the pupils to 'slide' around each other and rearrange themselves in a less ordered manner.

Questions to ask

Before the role-play

How can we change a solid to a liquid? Can you think of any examples where this happens in everyday life? For example, heat energy transfers from the sun, or a man-made heat source, such as a candle. How does a liquid differ from a solid?

If we were to become the particles in a liquid, how could we show the properties of a liquid?

During the role-play

How can we show that particles in a liquid are still close together, but can slide around each other?

How could we show that liquids can change their shape to fit the container they are in or pool on a surface, but keep the same volume?

After the role-play

Discussion to reinforce the properties of a liquid referring to the role-play. Further comparison of the properties of a solid and liquid.

Follow-up work

Pupils to record the properties of a liquid referring to the role-play using a method of their choice, such as:

- a cartoon strip of how a solid changes to a liquid,
- a story to describe the journey of a liquid,
- a flow diagram of what happens to the particles in a solid as it changes to a liquid,
- a poster to compare the properties of a solid and a liquid,
- a diary in the life of a solid and how it changes to a liquid.

Further role-plays on gases and changes of state to be covered next.

MAKING A GAS

What are you trying to show?

Solids, liquids and gases form part of States of Matter (Year 4) within the National Curriculum. It is expected that 8–9-year-old learners should be taught to recognise differences between solids, liquids and gases, in terms of ease of flow and maintenance of shape and volume. Non-statutory notes for States of Matter: 'Pupils should explore a variety of everyday materials and develop simple descriptions of the states of matter [in that] gases escape from an unsealed container'.

Pupils are to represent the motion of the particles (atoms and molecules) in the role-play.

Teaching points

- Gases have no fixed shape or volume and they can spread out to fill any space or container – the pupils running around to the extremities of the room space can show this.
- The particles are spread out with nothing between them, moving fast and in all directions – the pupils as particles may occasionally bump into each other and change direction to simulate the gas.
- The particles of a gas can be squeezed into a smaller space – pupils moving from the playground space to the classroom for example can simulate this.
- Warming a gas makes its particles move even faster and further apart, causing them to press harder on the sides of a container or space.

What do you need?

Examples of gases. Pupils could bring lists of gases from investigation at home, from the internet, etc. They could be encouraged to make a written list or bring in a pictorial representation of gases that are in, e.g., their shopping trolley, their sports bag, their lunch box, etc. This is much more conceptual than for the solid or liquid, e.g., 'bubbles in an Aero', a carbonated drink, 'air' in a spongey material, etc.

How do you prepare the class?

Pupils to observe and discuss where gases are found to establish the properties of gases.

Running the role-play

Select another nine pupils to make a solid, then a liquid again and explain that as heat is absorbed a change will once again be observed. The absorption of heat could be re-enacted by the modelling of the application of a heat source.

This time, by more heat being absorbed, the particles move around each other more easily until they move so quickly that they escape from the surface of the liquid.

Ask the pupils to move very quickly around each other and then one by one leave the 'liquid' and move quickly in random directions around the room space as shown in Figure 8.2.

Questions to ask

Before the role-play

How can we change a solid to a liquid, to a gas? How does a gas differ from a solid and a liquid?

If we were to become the particles in a gas, how could we show the properties of a gas?

During the role-play

How can we show that particles of a gas can spread out to fill any space or container and have no fixed shape or volume?

How could we show that particles of gas move very fast and in all directions? How can we show that the particles move even faster when warmed?

How can we show that particles of a gas can be squeezed into a smaller space?

After the role-play

Ask questions to elicit from the pupils what they have learned about the properties of a gas – referring to the role-play in order to reinforce the concepts.

Further comparison of the properties of a solid, liquid and gas.

Follow-up work

Pupils to record the properties of a gas referring to the role-play using a method of their choice, such as:

- a cartoon strip of how a solid changes to a liquid to a gas,
- a story of life as a gas particle,
- a poster showing a range of gases in everyday life incorporating the properties,
- a newspaper article on what happens when a solid changes to a liquid to a gas.

Further role-plays, changes of state in everyday life to be covered next,
Possible group extension activities to enable learners to use role-play to show their conceptual understanding.
After these illustrative role-play activities learners can be grouped to show through role-play the concepts for assessment purposes and to provide opportunities for presentation and whole-class discussion to clarify any misconceptions arising.

(Continued)

(Continued)

FIGURE 8.2
Learners role-playing a gas

TABLE 8.2 How to manage role-plays

Possible role-plays	Links to National Curriculum	Instructions on how this can be managed relevant to any one of the scenarios provided
Evaporation What happens to the water particles in wet hair/washing as a hairdryer/circulating air is drying it?	• Properties of materials • Changes in materials • Reversible changes • The water cycle	Establish with the pupils the change of state taking place Consider the motion of the particles in each state of matter
Evaporation What happens to water particles when water evaporates from a puddle?	• Properties of materials • Changes in materials • Reversible changes • The water cycle	Ask pupils what happens in the change of state in question – refer to the previously explored role-plays
Condensation What happens to water vapour in the air as it hits a cold glass of water?	• Properties of materials • Changes in materials • Reversible changes • The water cycle	Identify in chosen groups who is to act as one of the particles, who is to be the narrator and any other props, e.g. the hairdryer
Melting What happens when chocolate melts?	• Properties of materials • Changes in materials • Reversible changes	Groups of pupils then prepare their identified change of state role-play for presentation to the rest of the class
Freezing What happens to water in an ice cube tray placed in the freezer?	• Properties of materials • Changes in materials • Reversible changes	
Boiling What happens to a pan of water as it is boiled on the cooker hob?	• Properties of materials • Changes in materials • Reversible changes	

Note: It is important to make clear that most substances demonstrate a very minor contraction when they change from a liquid to a solid. Water is an exception, as it expands and this expansion is quite noticeable. Think along the lines of the expansion you observe when you freeze a bottle of water. The learners could be challenged to show this in the freezing role-play, by rearranging themselves at arms' length from one another, thus forming a more open structure.

Outcomes of using these approaches in the primary science classroom

Knowledge and understanding that matter is made up of particles and their arrangement and movement in solids, liquids and gases is not identified in the Key Stage 2 Science National Curriculum (DfE, 2013b) – this concept is identified at Level 6 Understanding in Key Stage 3 Science National Curriculum (DfE, 2013c), although modelling is identified at Level 5. However, research has shown that even secondary and post-secondary students 'have identified a variety of cognitive and pedagogical factors that make the particulate worldview challenging' (Gustafson et al., 2010: 104). Other research has shown that learners modelling the intrinsic motion of particles can enhance the understanding of the properties of solids, liquids and gases (Johnson and Papageorgiou, 2010: 143). Below are some of the responses of a Year 4 class interviewed after taking part in the role-play of solids, liquids and gases:

> I think when I look at solids, liquids and gases I will think of what is going on inside them. (Boy aged 8 years)
>
> I learned that molecules actually move round, before I didn't know I thought they just stayed still and then if you move them and then they move. (Boy aged 9 years)
>
> Because we got to do what they [particles] were doing and if you had to write it down you wouldn't know what they would be doing and what it would be like to be them. (Girl aged 8 years)

The learners' class teacher stated that the use of role-play:

> Helped to explain concepts that are very hard to understand. I think that really took them that stage further and also consolidated what they already knew ... it stretched them to the limit of what they could assimilate.

These learners were also able to retain the knowledge and understanding attained through the role-play, when questioned at the end of the school year, with responses as follows:

> We went into groups and showed how solids, liquids and gases move and we were the molecules. When the molecules were tightly bound they were a solid, when they were free and filled all the space they were a gas and when they slide over and around each together they were a liquid. (Girl aged 9 years)
>
> My group's role-play was when you had washed your hair and you are drying it with the hairdryer. The water started off as a liquid and finished as a gas because the hair was dried. We moved slowly at first but got faster as the hair dried. (Girl aged 9 years)
>
> We could actually do what we felt but when you are writing you can't really do it ... Sometimes I find it hard to put my ideas down. It made it clearer than just normal speaking, because we could actually do it and it would make us understand more. (Boy aged 9 years)

LIFE CYCLE

What are you trying to show?

Life cycles features in 'Animals, including humans' (Year 2) in the National Curriculum. It is expected that 6–7-year-old learners should be taught to notice that animals, including humans, have offspring which grow into adults, and to find out about and describe the basic needs of animals, including humans, for survival (water, food and air).

Non-statutory notes for 'Animals, including humans': 'They should also be introduced to the processes of reproduction and growth in animals. The focus at this stage should be on questions that help pupils to recognise growth; they should not be expected to understand how reproduction occurs'. The following examples might be used: egg, chick, chicken; egg, caterpillar, pupa, butterfly; spawn, tadpole, frog; lamb, sheep. Growing into adults can include reference to baby, toddler, child, teenager, adult.

Learners are to represent the four stages of the life cycle of a butterfly in the role-play.

Teaching points

- There are various/other life cycles that the learners should be made aware of.
- The life cycle of a butterfly has four stages and this is a cyclical process.
- None of the four stages can exist in isolation, hence the terminology 'life cycle'.

What do you need?

A sheet with the title of each stage as follows: Stage 1 Eggs and Larvae, Stage 2 Caterpillars, Stage 3 Pupas and Stage 4 Butterflies.

A book or short pictorial/written account of the details for each stage to place at each stage.

Large green painted leaves (Stage 1).

Large sheets (Stage 3).

Large painted flowers (Stage 4).

How do you prepare the class?

Learners should investigate and observe using secondary sources that different animals have different life cycles.

Learners can share observations about the life cycle of a butterfly and identify that there are four stages to the life cycle of a butterfly.

Stage 1: Eggs and caterpillars (young larvae) hatching

Use the teacher to model the role-play first, so that the learners have the experience of observing and questioning the teacher prior to enacting and 'feeling' the role-play for themselves. The role-play demonstrates that as an egg, they are attached to the underside of a 'leaf' and that they have to hatch into 'wiggly' young caterpillars (young larvae).

Teaching points

- Can the learners explain who laid and attached the eggs to the underside of the leaf?
- Can the learners explain why the eggs are laid on a leaf?

Stage 2: Caterpillars (maturing larvae)

Use the same arrangement as before with the teacher modelling the role-play first, so that the learners have the experience of observing and questioning the teacher prior to enacting and 'feeling' the role-play for themselves. The role-play demonstrates that as a caterpillar they wiggle around whilst continually feeding.

Teaching points

- Can the learners explain the consequence of the continual eating in terms of the growth of the caterpillar?

(Continued)

(Continued)

FIGURE 8.3
Learners
role-playing
the caterpillar's
continuous
feeding

Stage 3: Pupa (chrysalis)

Use the same arrangement as before with the teacher modelling the role-play first, so that the learners have the experience of observing and questioning the teacher prior to enacting and 'feeling' the role-play for themselves. The role-play demonstrates that as a caterpillar, they are transformed into the pupa (chrysalis) by being wrapped in a sheet from head to toe. For this part of the role-play, it might be easier to nominate one learner from each half of the class to transform into the pupa, with two or three other learners wrapping the cloth round the designated 'pupa'.

Teaching points

- Are the children aware that the pupa is still alive?
- Can the learners identify/describe what is happening inside the pupa (chrysalis)?

Stage 4: Butterfly

Use the same arrangement as before with the teacher modelling the role-play first, so that the learners have the experience of observing and questioning the teacher prior to enacting and 'feeling' the role-play for themselves. The role-play demonstrates that as a butterfly they are able to move and collect their food from a selected source by flying to and feeding from it.

Teaching points

- Are the learners aware of how the butterfly is able to move in order to obtain its food?
- Can the learners identify what the butterfly feeds on?

FIGURE 8.4
Learners role-
playing the
butterfly

Questions to ask

Before the role-play

What do you think are the basic needs (water, food and air) of all animals?

Do you think there is any stage in the life cycle of the butterfly, when it is not alive?

If we were to become an egg/caterpillar/pupa/butterfly how could we show this through role-play? What would we be doing?

During the role-play

Can you explain to the person next to you/your talk partner what you are going to be doing in the next stage of the role-play?

Which stage of the life cycle do you think is the beginning and/or end?

After the role-play
Referring to role-play:

Can you place the stages of the role-play in the correct order of the cycle?

Can you re-enact all of the stages one after the other, in the correct order?

Follow-up work

- Recap on how all animals have the same basic needs.
- Revisit and explore the life cycle of another animal, using appropriate secondary sources.
- Possible group extension activities to enable learners to use role-play to show their conceptual understanding.
- Re-enact all of the stages one after the other, in the correct order.

(Continued)

(Continued)

- Ask a small group to re-enact the finer detail of the change (growth) that occurs in Stage 2: Caterpillar.
- Challenge the learners to make suggestions as to how, or if, they think they could re-enact the various stages of the life cycle of another animal.

Learners will need to draw upon their knowledge of the role-playing of the life cycle of a butterfly to identify how the life cycle is continuous and that the animal is always alive.

Outcomes of using these approaches in the primary science classroom

Almost all the learners who were interviewed after being involved in the life cycle role-plays were able to visualise the four stages of the life cycle of a butterfly, which they considered enhanced their learning. Comments made by the learners included:

> It is easier to remember the life cycle of a butterfly in the role-play, easier than writing it down. (Boy aged 7 years)

The observation of the role-play was also beneficial for those who could not visualise the re-enactment of the life cycle in the role-play:

> I wasn't really sure of what to do, but I could really see this when I watched the others doing the role-play. (Boy aged 7 years)

Similar to the outcomes discussed earlier, it was also shown that learners were able to retain the knowledge and understanding attained through the life cycle role-play, when questioned later in the school year, with responses as follows:

> I learnt that the stages go round in a circle, in order. (Girl aged 6 years)
>
> I learnt that the pupa is not dead. (Girl aged 7 years)

During their associated presentations the following comment was made:

> I want to know how long it takes in real life for each stage to happen. (Boy aged 7 years)

When questioned later on in the year the following expression was recorded:

 Everything has a life cycle and although there is a sort of a beginning and end, it will keep going as new animals are made or die. (Girl aged 7 years)

SUMMARY

This chapter has considered why role-play is an important and appropriate teaching strategy for use in primary science and has explored a number of ideas for use in the classroom. The following provides a number of issues to think about and guidance points to consider when planning to use role-play in the classroom:

Issues

- Role-play and drama can provide a break from established classroom routines, something learners enjoy.
- Role-play can provide a fun way to focus learners on specific aspects of value in learning.
- The physical modelling as a form of active learning enables learners to understand abstract concepts.
- Role-play is a form of learning of that is accessible by all learners irrespective of ability and learning style.
- Learners are very aware of their own learning and are able to retain scientific concepts through the physical involvement.

Guidance

- Initially there is a need for the teacher to model and intervene to support learners' development of independence, confidence and proficiency in using role-play as a tool to show understanding.
- Grouping learners to devise their own role-plays to show conceptual understanding challenges them through cognitive conflict to develop thinking.
- Learners prefer to use role-play as the method to show their understanding as opposed to writing it down.
- Presentation of the role-play can provide a class with an opportunity to consolidate their own learning and the teacher with an opportunity for assessment.

(Continued)

(Continued)

It is hoped that the examples of role-plays discussed within this chapter and the evidence presented will inspire you to use role-play across the science curriculum to illustrate scientific concepts. What is most important is to consider learners' creativity in devising their own role-plays. Your learners may never cease to amaze you with their imagination and ingenuity!

FURTHER READING

Braund, M. (2015) 'Drama and learning science: An empty space?', *British Educational Research Journal*, 41(1): 102–21.

Kambouri, M. and Michaelidas, A. (2015) 'Dramatic water: Using a drama-based approach to science in the early years', *Primary Science*, 136: 10–12.

Littledyke, M. (2004) 'Drama and science', *Primary Science*, 84: 14–16.

Ødegaard, M. (2003) 'Dramatic science: A critical review of drama in science education', *Studies in Science Education*, 39: 75–101.

Smith, K., Loughran, J., Berry, A. and Dimitrakopoulos, C. (2012) 'Developing scientific literacy in a primary school', *International Journal of Science Education*, 34(1): 127–52.

Ward, H. (2007a) Chapter 4 'Moving and learning', in *Using Their Brains in Science: Ideas for Children Aged 5 to 14*. London: Sage.

9

SCIENCE FROM GAMES

Hellen Ward

Learners need to be able to use the complex language of science and without this language they may fail to make progress. Games offer opportunities for learners to learn both knowledge of science and associated vocabulary in a motivating way. Games also enable repetition of learning without becoming boring, and this repetition of scientific concepts is vital for future learning of science. Language acquisition and enjoyment can be promoted effectively through the use of scientific games.

HOW CAN THE USE OF GAMES ENRICH THE PRIMARY SCIENCE CURRICULUM?

Playing games of different types provides a wealth of learning opportunities. Play can be a powerful mediator for learning throughout a person's life. Learners select different types of games outside the classroom and they thrive on learning that is challenging:

> Did you ever hear a game advertised as being easy? What is worst about school curriculum is the fragmentation of knowledge into little pieces. This is supposed to make learning easy, but often ends up depriving knowledge of personal meaning and making it boring. Ask a few kids: the reason most don't like school is not that the work is too hard, but that it is utterly boring. (Papert, 1998)

This view is one that chimes with many observations of learners who exhibit behaviour problems in the classroom. This is because 'challenge', 'play' or 'personal relevance' to learners do not feature as elements of learning in some classrooms – 'They go on and on and when they have finished you do not have enough time to do the work' (Year 3 boy, large rural local authority). However, science should be stimulating and memorable and support the development of both vocabulary and concepts. Most of the games suggested in this chapter focus on the development of scientific language and associated concepts.

A study conducted by Braisby et al. (1999) established that 4–7-year-old children struggled to acquire novel science terms from single, incidental exposures which were presented in a science lesson delivered by videotape. Best et al. (2006) though, showed that learning words and concepts was effective when linked to meaningful contexts. Chapter 8 puts forward a convincing argument that play and its associated teaching strategies can be used effectively to enhance learning and provide the motivation and long-term development of positive attitudes towards science.

The benefits of using games in the classroom as an appropriate teaching strategy can be enormous. Kirikkaya et al. (2010) tested a board game about space and the solar system and found it was thought to be useful by both teachers and learners. When pupils were asked if more games should be introduced into other units of work, 25% of the learners suggested that games should be introduced into Physics as 'Physics is already boring; it will be more enjoyable. It can be applied all of the lessons' (2010: 9). They identified that games taught learners much more than language.

> Children's abilities such as memorizing remembering, naming, matching and classifying develop while playing a game. They learn reasoning, relating cause and effect. Also they learn focusing, directing

themselves to an aim, realizing the problems that appear in the game and finding solutions to these problems. (Dağbaşı, 2007; cited by Kirikkaya et al., 2010: 1)

Whilst the idea that learners have different learning styles is discussed in many schools and has become central to some schools' ways of working, with teachers planning visual, auditory and kinaesthetic (VAK) activities there is no evidence that these are of value. Scott (2010: 5) notes that:

Among the currently most popular means for discerning and classifying individual difference are theories of 'learning styles'. 'Learning styles' as a concept is widely endorsed, geographically, across educational sectors and in many other domains of human activity.

However, while 'brain gym' and VAK have become popular, scientific evidence to support their use has not been published. Coffield (2005) identified 71 different theories of learning style in use in the UK.

Hattie (2009) in a meta-analysis of 141 learning styles studies argued that learning styles are noted for their lack of impact, he identified that effective learning was concerned with

the power of using multiple and appropriate teaching strategies with a particular emphasis on the presence of feedback focussed at the right level of instruction (acquisition or proficiencies); seeing learning and teaching from the students' perspective; and placing reliance on teaching study skills and strategies of learning. Hattie (2009: 199)

Games are a way to increase the number of teaching strategies within a classroom as well as seeing learning from the learners' perspective, as games are aspects enjoyed by many. In *Talking Science*, Lemke (1990) claimed that a large part of learning the conceptual content of science is learning to talk its specialised language and use that language in meaningful ways. Too often scientific language use is included in science lessons without consideration of what the learners comprehend. Games are a way of helping learners have access to complex language 'Games made foreign languages easy to learn and students enjoyed the lessons because of the games' (Fırat, 2007; cited by Kirikkaya et al., 2010: 1).

To increase positive participation, depending on the games chosen, an element of competition could be introduced. Having a reason or an audience for the activity can enhance motivation. Team games in science are more motivating for all learners, particularly when the teams are made of learners of mixed ability. Baines (2012) identified that ability grouping exacerbated inequalities, so games are an opportunity to use mixed ability grouping which will promote the use of collaboration, explanation and elaboration. Games provide an opportunity for all to participate together and reduce the opportunity for lack of challenge:

> If we assume that the bottom set cannot cope with difficult ideas and keep everything simple for them to manage with little effort we are robbing them of the opportunity to grow intellectually. (Adey, 2012: 202)

If the game is designed in a way that encourages learners to improve on past performance then they will be keen to learn vocabulary or concepts and may not even think of it as 'work'. This type of play is a 'win–win' situation, where all learners work together to improve the class time or score rather than one group winning at the expense of the rest of the class (Pan and Tang, 2004) in a study involving the teaching of statistics suggested games could reduce anxiety towards the subject matter, which might result in increased transfer of knowledge and better future application and success. Games can also be good for helping learners with the hard-to-learn facts such as the life cycle of plants. Chow et al. (2011) in a study that used the TV show *Deal or no Deal* as a format for learning statistics found that

> By repeatedly playing a game with which the students are familiar, students benefit from the repetitive aspects of the method, without the tedium of traditional paper and pencil worksheets or exercises. (2010: 263)

Games are also a good way to bring up complex issues such as drugs or smoking as they involve active learning methods. Active learning involves the conjecture that learners who actively engage with material will find recall of the information easier (Bruner, 1961).They also suit different ages, with Klappa (2009) having success with a pub quiz approach with undergraduate bioscience students.

DEVELOPING SCIENTIFIC LANGUAGE THROUGH GAMES: LINKS TO LITERACY

As scientific language development is central to learning science, games that help with this should be encouraged. Bingo, chain (or link) games and matching words and definitions are all easy, fun and enjoyable. Bingo and chain games (Figure 9.1) are most effective if played in mixed ability teams to begin with, rather than all learners having their own cards. These activities can later be used as individual games when confidence and understanding of vocabulary are raised.

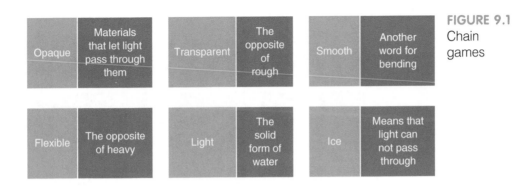

FIGURE 9.1
Chain games

Opaque	Materials that let light pass through them	Transparent	The opposite of rough	Smooth	Another word for bending
Flexible	The opposite of heavy	Light	The solid form of water	Ice	Means that light can not pass through

Chain games start with one learner or the teacher reading the first question, the answer being provided on a card somewhere else in the room. The person with the correct answer then reads their question and so the chain (or link) is made. It is important that the words used are discussed with the class since learners may suggest more than one answer and the precision of word usage is one of the most difficult aspects of science for learners to develop.

Subject-specific bingo (Figure 9.2), for example, on forces, helps learners to be exposed to scientific vocabulary and promotes learning by immersion. Vocabulary development is always an area where learners need help, and regular immersion for short periods of time is more beneficial to learning than exposure only once a week. Lemke (1990: 24) suggested that learning science was like learning a foreign language, where immersion and regular involvement enhance understanding and proficiency. Usually in bingo gaining a 'full house' is the target, but here, because of time constraints, learners could play just for one line. In this case, the teacher selects words according to the scientific topic under study and reads the definitions to the learners. Although many games of this type are commercially produced, these can be made easily and cheaply using index cards. In this way, the game can be tailored to the different needs of specific learners and can make these ideas accessible to all.

Scientific 'hangman' can develop learners' visual vocabulary. When the word is guessed the learners can gain extra marks from the teacher if they can define the term accurately. Here, there is room for further discussion and exploration of the meaning of terms and so, in the long term, learners will become more able to define terms accurately.

'I can think of three' is a quick and easy game to encourage learners to use their thinking skills; for example, 'Name three solids that are opaque'. To increase the demand, older learners in groups could be asked to think of as many opaque solids as they can in three minutes. At the end of the time the group that has been able to think of the greatest number can be selected to share their ideas first. This enables common answers to be discussed.

FIGURE 9.2
Bingo

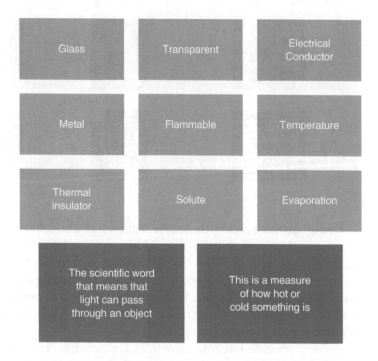

Other groups can then add any additional examples that the first group has not included. This discussion develops the links in the learners' brains and will remind them of things that they already know (Ward, 2007). The fact that there is not one answer also makes the learners think creatively. The debate and discussion that follow these activities are as important as the list generated, as discourse is found to improve learners' national test scores (Mant et al., 2007). An example of this was provided by a group of Year 6 learners who had a very lively debate on the state of matter of toothpaste as a result of the above challenge.

Crosswords and word searches have always been used extensively in science, along with cloze procedures. When churned out in worksheet format the focus of the lesson can easily be lost and so can the fun. This does not have to be the case. If crosswords are produced on an interactive whiteboard, an effective lesson starter can be created. Learners can then work together; for example, some groups solving the across clues whilst others focus upon the down clues. This is an easy way to introduce differentiation and helps learners not only with the development of vocabulary, but also with the spelling of scientific words, i.e. if the words are spelt incorrectly they will not fit into the gaps.

Spelling of scientific vocabulary should be linked to literacy with older learners, and links should be made with the technical vocabulary requirements of literacy. The use of a small notebook for the collection of scientific words can be helpful. Better still, if this personal scientific dictionary is then carried by a learner through a key stage it can become very useful for long-term reference. The use of crosswords can be further developed by providing a completed crossword, but without clues. Learners can then be challenged to produce the clues (definitions). These definitions can then also be added to the learners' own scientific dictionaries.

Starting from the answer and developing the question provides learners with the opportunity to think in more detail. For example, provided with the answer 'Space', many questions could be asked, from '*Star Trek* calls this the final frontier', to 'Sounds will not travel in this medium' and many more besides. A focus on possible questions can lead to discussion with learners about the quality of and categorisation of the questions asked, for example those that are truly questions, and those responses that are really definitions. This categorisation of questions is a skill that can be developed from this type of activity which links very well to other aspects of question-raising discussed elsewhere in this book. Even teachers have found this to be a challenging activity, but challenge brings rewards and enjoyment for the teacher too.

Removing the common term 'forces' from the centre box on a challenge sheet provides a good starting point to enable learners to link these ideas together.

All these ideas provide the opportunity for learners to develop their communication skills and their ability to work co-operatively in a group while simultaneously developing their scientific knowledge and understanding. The outcomes from this work can be linked to literacy lessons related to question-raising. These activities can promote thinking by learners and should be encouraged. Thinking skills can also be developed using the 'impossible question' idea; for example, 'What material cannot be washed?' Science and creativity go hand in hand and the teaching skills and ideas used today in primary schools could help pave the way for promoting and encouraging creative thinkers of the future.

VISUAL MEMORY GAMES

Using memory games can enhance visual memory and the ability to make links. The memory is not found in one place in the brain but throughout, and can be enhanced with practice (Ward, 2007) which promotes the development of memory and observation skills. 'Kim's game' is a party game played by many learners in the days prior to the video and computer age. Provide the learners with a range of scientific equipment suitable for the topic being studied and allow them to look at the selection for some time. Then remove the items from view and ask the learners to name all the equipment that was provided and give its use. This causes discussions about the types of equipment as well as what they are used

FIGURE 9.3
Bundles of three

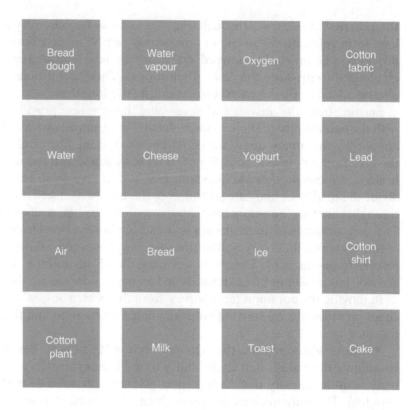

for. The development of observation skills is occurring as well as language skills; these functions are situated in different parts of the brain and are being made to work at the same time. Removing only one item could change this activity, requiring the learners to identify what is missing.

Talk about

'Talk about' questions or cards help learners with difficult science concepts or ideas that relate to their everyday lives. They can be used to challenge common misconceptions. Start by providing the learners with a question on the board to spark discussion: 'Why would a scientist think it is strange that your mother tells you to turn the volume on the television down?' or 'What would an unhealthy person do?'

It is also effective to provide a range of true and false statements or ideas about one topic, such as smoking or drugs, to challenge a viewpoint. For example, 'All people who smoke die', 'Smoking makes you slim', 'Smoking makes your teeth go brown', 'Smoking makes you one of the gang'. Learners should debate and evaluate the ideas provided to refine their views and opinions, ensuring that they can use evidence to support their views. This is a good starting point for fact and opinion work in other subjects and can stimulate the need to use research skills. It also allows some difficult topics to be discussed by learners without it appearing that the teacher is judging what happens at home.

GAMES TO HELP LEARNERS MAKE LINKS

Games like 'finding bundles of three' (Figure 9.3) help learners to make links. Making links and identifying why things are part of a pattern are important scientific skills. This type of learning is active and requires the learners to be engaged in their learning. In Figure 9.3 there are a number of threes that are easy to spot and are about where materials come from. The 'finding bundles of three' activity helps to expose misconceptions; for example, some learners are not aware that cotton comes from a plant and in fact suggest that 'Cotton comes from a cotton wool, it is like a sheep but it does not live here' (Year 2 learner in an urban school). The solid, liquid and gas state of water is easy to spot. To provide more of a challenge, learners could be asked to spot other gases or to identify three solids. Learners' talking in science lessons is often an underrated activity that needs a higher profile in many classrooms.

Learners can also make links by playing 'odd one out'. It is important to start with a number of real objects (for example, a small sample of metal, a wooden brick, some butter and a chocolate button) with young learners so that the pattern can be found, increasing the number of items with older learners. There is often more than one answer; this is important as it prevents the learners seeing science as a series of questions in which their role is to find out what the teacher is expecting as the answer. This is also an effective assessment activity. Science in real life is not cut and dried and there may be many answers, some of which are not yet known. Using real objects or pictures and words until the learners' sight vocabulary is developed enough just to provide the words has been found to be effective. Learners of different ages and abilities tend to choose different objects as the 'odd one out'. The object chosen by learners of course will depend on their previous knowledge and understanding of the properties of materials. For example, some younger learners may select metal 'because it made the light bounce', whilst most primary-aged learners are likely to select wood 'as the rest will change state'. Metal might be selected 'because it will conduct electricity', and 'because it is magnetic'. An adult learner might select metal, as 'it is not made of more than one type of element', whilst another might suggest metal as the odd one out because 'the rest have carbon in them'.

While games can be made from everyday resources, it is important to ensure that knowledge learnt through games is scientifically correct, as learners will remember both the activity and the learning. It is also important to remember that some questions in science can have more than one answer. This is important and should be encouraged; it is through such discussions that a clearer understanding of the correct meaning of scientific terms can be developed.

While it is possible to teach information by rote, for many learners this will only last in the short-term memory. Learning by rote does not enable a link to previous experiences and the learners make little sense of the learning. As a result they may know less and be more confused than they were before the lesson.

FIVE-MINUTE SCIENCE

There are times when it is helpful to provide questions where the learners select the answer from a range of answers provided. Five-minute science is also available in an interactive whiteboard format (www.tts-group.co.uk). When selecting questions it is important to include some of the common misconceptions. The answer to the question 'What are the incisors for?' had some learners suggesting B from the following:

A – to cut the food.

B – to stop the food from falling out of the mouth.

C – to tear the food.

D – to grind the food.

Again, in science it is not just the right answer that is important, but *why* it is the right answer. Questions could be posed about why the learners selected this answer and why the other answers are not right. In mathematics there has been an emphasis on asking learners to explain how they worked out the answer, so that the answer itself was not the only outcome of the learning but the strategies adopted for solving the problem were also important. Meta-cognition is also important in science, so that learners are not just asked to learn the right answer and accept ideas without being asked to articulate why they are right. Later in a learner's science education this ability to justify beliefs will be even more important, and fundamentally this is what science is all about. The nature of scientific ideas is central to science learning. The famous scientists who struggled to develop the immense body of knowledge that is known today had to be able to justify and convince an often sceptical public that their ideas were correct.

While challenges are an effective learning approach – they relate to the idea of 'hard fun' proposed by Papert (1998) – so is presenting information in different formats to ensure that learners are able to transfer knowledge and understanding from one context into another. One example of a challenge would be the life cycle of a plant that has gaps that need to be completed. Other cycles in science could also be used to challenge learners' understanding. Just turning the arrows the other way round has dramatic effects with some learners, as does presenting the same information as a linear flow chart. Altering the format of all work is strongly recommended, as learners need to be made to think.

Playing the game 'twenty questions' can provide challenge as well as help learners to ask effective questions. The challenge could be that the learners have to identify the questions that will identify an object selected by the teacher as quickly as possible. To play 'twenty questions' learners have to ask questions to which the answer can be only 'yes' or 'no', but if they state an object (guess) and it is not the right answer they lose a life. Lives are also lost if the question is one to which the answer cannot be 'yes' or 'no'. Learners who play this game regularly, and start by 'losing lives', stop thinking about trying to guess the item, e.g. 'Is it a pencil?' and start to think of key questions that will help in all circumstances, e.g. 'Is it alive?' or 'Does it breathe?' The more experiences the learners have, the more the focus shifts towards scientific words and questions. These skills are vital if learners are really to understand sorting, grouping and classification, all of which are key scientific skills. They are also used when making dichotomous keys, a skill that some learners find difficult.

GAMES TO CONSOLIDATE LEARNING

Using a beach ball with scientific vocabulary written on the sides provides a quick and easy way of recapping language. The ball is thrown or rolled to a learner who has to explain what the word near their right thumb means or give a definition of the word so that the other learners in the class guess what they are referring to. Other language games include ideas from television programmes including games where the learners have to pass from one side of the board to the other answering scientific questions whose initials are given on the board (Figure 9.4).

There are many commercially produced board games and true/false games, as well as activities that enable learners to act out elements of science. The possibilities are endless. Whilst not all lessons should be game related, elements of the games discussed in this chapter will promote learning and some games-related activities could be built into the science teaching in each topic. The most important criterion as to whether a game should be used at all relates to the learning intention of the lessons. If the learning

FIGURE 9.4
Blockbuster
game

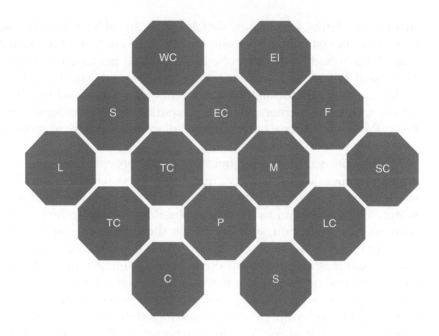

intention can be met through a game approach, then deciding which game is the next decision, along with knowing what the learners will learn as a result of this game. Games are not a panacea for poor science teaching and should only be used in appropriate amounts to develop skills and understanding. The starter games can have the greatest impact as they get learners motivated to learn, while in the plenary they enable learning to be consolidated. Some games are ideal during the main teaching section of the lesson for groups or specific individuals. However, games might occur in the odd five minutes at any time of the day or week.

SUMMARY

This chapter has shown the positive role that games can play within a well-planned scheme of work. Not only can such games be motivating and enjoyable for learners and their teacher, but they can also effectively reinforce important aspects of learning. More specifically, the games presented have been justified in terms of how they can help in the development of scientific vocabulary alongside knowledge and understanding of science. Importantly, the chapter has shown how games can be used to expose and deal with learners' ideas and provide an opportunity for assessment.

One important aspect running through this chapter is the importance of learners being provided with regular opportunities for discussion and collaboration. The learners of today will be growing up to work in a world where, if knowledge is needed, the internet will provide it, but group working and collaboration will be the skills most used on a day-to-day basis.

The final word on games is that there are many still to be invented, modified or rediscovered that will improve science teaching and learners' learning.

FURTHER READING

Adey, P. and Dillon, J. (2012) *Bad Education: Debunking Myths in Education*. Maidenhead: McGraw Hill/Open University Press.

Davies, G. (2005) 'Stories, fun and games: Teaching genetics in primary school', *Journal of Biological Education*, 40(1): 31.

Mercer, N., Dawes, L. and Kleine Staarman, J. (2009) 'Dialogic teaching in the primary science classroom', *Language and Education*, 23(4): 353–69.

10

USING COMPUTERS IN SCIENCE

Manette Carroll and Hellen Ward

Computing has huge potential for supporting learning in science but is often not used effectively for a number of reasons. Teachers are often not aware of available packages or not familiar with the opportunities their use could provide for learning. They may find difficulty in the use of the equipment or with the organisation and management of equipment for learning. This chapter begins with a brief overview of computing and then looks at the uses and abuses from a classroom perspective. It aims to provide an insight into new ever-advancing technology, with the introduction of 'Digital Tool Kits' as an everyday teaching resource. The ownership of the tool kits is placed with the child who is encouraged to select the correct hardware for the task. Throughout, the focus will be on the wider teaching issues associated with the use of computing in the classroom rather than on how computing equipment can be set up and used. Undoubtedly, practical difficulties arise with the use of computing equipment, which many teachers find frustrating.

Some aspects of computing such as databases and spreadsheets do not feature here because although programs such as 'flexi tree' are easy to use they are constantly being updated and changed. Specific examples are selected to highlight their innovative nature, ease of use or widespread availability. Details of programs that support writing, such as 'clicker', and are modifications to screens or keyboards for special educational needs, are also not discussed as other Information Communications Technology (ICT) publications cover these aspects much more effectively. Instead, the focus of this chapter relates to how computers can be used to help learners learn in science, with links to research and case studies to highlight aspects of current practice.

BACKGROUND

It was in the early 1970s that the first desk top computer was created and this was aimed at scientists and engineers, not businesses or the public. In the late 18th century Charles Babbage created the first machine that worked out calculations, but it was the advent of the Second World War and the need to break enemy codes that led to developments in design and performance. Exactly who invented the first computer is a question that creates great debate in the computing world, but it was probably Alan Turing, whose ideas formed the basis for the machines now known as computers.

Computers and Information Communications Technology are a vital part of everyday life

The European Commission indicated that all learners should have the opportunity to acquire key skills including digital literacy, which in turn involves team work, problem-solving and project management (Voogt, 2010). If learners can acquire these skills in primary schools then it enables these skills to be further developed over the remainder of their education, and provide them with a vital skill for later use not only in the field of science but in all aspects of employment.

Computers have come such a long way since the very first computers, and learners today see the technology as an essential tool of their everyday life. Learners adapt to the changing technology with greater confidence than many of the adults who teach them and see it as a life skill to be able to use the most up-to-date technology. With the information explosion, demands of the work place and easy access to technology, educators need to be constantly updating their skills along with the learners and utilising the technology in classrooms.

RESEARCH EVIDENCE

Until recently the use of computing in science has not been central, with some teachers expressing the view that computers would get in the way and prevent learners from thinking. This attitude to teaching science is changing with the introduction of the new curriculum (DfE, 2013a), as learners now have to be able to use a range of digital devices to reach their goals. It is expected that they will also analyse their findings and that evaluating their analysis is a key to their learning. Learners are now encouraged to see computers in three ways:

- an information tool,
- a learning tool,
- a means to provide basic skills.

Pombo et al. (2011) stress the importance of the use of computers as a tool to enhance the learning process of the learners, and that the learners can achieve their goals more effectively when using computers. With technology being used to enhance communications it should lead to improved teaching and learning.

RULES FOR USING ICT

There are three key rules for using ICT in science, originally developed from ideas presented on the Becta website:

1. The use of ICT must be in line with good practice in science teaching.
2. It must enable the learners to meet the learning intention.
3. ICT should do something that cannot be achieved without its use or enable it to be achieved more effectively.

These have recently been updated by Core Education who produced The Quality Principles for Digital Learning Resources (Core Education, 2006). The newly revised principles contain many important features and include information on each of the following pedagogical issues:

- Inclusion and access.
- Learner engagement.
- Effective learning.
- Assessment to support learning.
- Robust summative assessment.
- Innovative approaches.
- Ease of use.
- Match of the curriculum.

The revised principles provide further depth and are well worth further examination not possible here. However, the three key rules *do* require further examination here as these should always be considered at the planning stage for science activities.

Key rule 1: The use of ICT must be in line with good practice in science teaching

The question here is 'What is good science?' Good science prompts learners to think, to be curious, to observe, to take measurements, to look at patterns and trends, to identify issues and to communicate their findings, and a host of other skills. If a lesson merely enables learners to watch, passively, something on an interactive whiteboard and does not enable or promote the asking of their own questions or the devising of their own ideas, this is not 'good science' or even good learning. Another poor use of ICT would be to encourage learners to look at small living creatures in the environment and then use the internet to identify them. Learning would be far more effective if an identification book or a page of animals with pictures prepared by their teacher was taken outside with the learners on the hunt. This would help in the identification of animals likely to be found and ensure optimum use of time. There are probably few people reading this who have not spent a terrifying amount of time on the internet looking for information.

Another aspect of good science would be to help develop scientific attitudes of co-operation, tolerance of uncertainty and respect for evidence, as well as skills of observing, measuring and communicating. Where used effectively, computing can promote in all learners aspects of 'good' science.

Key rule 2: It must enable the learners to meet the learning intention

This refers to the science learning intention! It is not expected that learners would be taught to use the hardware or software within the science part of the timetable and the focus of the lesson would be firmly rooted in the science and not the computing curriculum. Science lessons should not focus on how to use a spreadsheet program to enter collected data, but rather, should provide an opportunity to use and apply relevant skills learned in computing sessions to move science learning forward.

If the majority of a lesson is spent teaching learners how to use the computer hardware or a software program, then it is not a science lesson but a computer skill-based lesson; for example, learners need to be introduced to data loggers in computing prior to using them, so that they can use a data logger in science lessons to take readings. In this way they can focus on relevant observation, such as how quickly the cups of water cool, or look for patterns by using and applying this technology. Here the computing supports the learners' ability to see what happens to the temperature of the water without having to physically draw the graph themselves, thereby spending more time on the interpretation of the data rather than on manipulating the data itself. In this example, the *learning intention* of the lesson could be 'to be able to identify patterns in data' and the *success criteria* could be:

- to be able to talk about what happened to the temperature using the graph,
- to use the words 'degrees Celsius' and 'temperature change' in your answer, and for some learners,
- to be able to try to explain the graph using these scientific words.

Essentially, the learning intentions and the success criteria are science based, involve a higher-level response from learners and facilitate effective assessment informing subsequent planning at an individual and group level. In this way the computing facilitates the whole process.

Key rule 3: Computing should do something that cannot be achieved without its use or enable it to be achieved more effectively

This is the most important principle. If an old-fashioned book is the quickest and most efficient way of finding the information needed, or if the use of pictures on a screen does not enhance learning, then the computing option should *not* be used. If only one learner is asked to touch the interactive screen whilst the rest of the class passively watches what is happening then the computer is unlikely to enhance learning. If learners were allowed to write their ideas on 'Post-it' notes while they worked instead of having to type up the work later, then the 'Post-it' would win every time.

Questions related to 'how', 'why' and 'when' to use computers need to be asked constantly at the planning stage if they are not to be used in science to reinforce existing computing skills and to fill time. However, if learners are enabled to see why one piece of fabric is more waterproof than another using a digital microscope to look at the structure of the materials, which they would not be able to see without using this hardware, then computers are adding to the science experience offered. The audience provided by another class of learners who can be contacted by email and can comment upon the results and share their own, makes writing a conclusion and communicating the results more authentic, and makes computing worthwhile.

These principles should be adhered to whether computing is used for individual learners, for groups with special educational needs or even by teachers when preparing and using computers for teaching.

FROM SUITE TO STANDALONE TO TABLET

Over recent years there have been many debates on what is the best approach to using computers. As computers became more affordable many schools moved away from standalone computers in the classroom to fully fitted computer suites where every child had access to a computer. This approach was ideal for the direct teaching of computing but it proved impractical to link computers to other curriculum areas, especially science. Some schools progressed to having a computer suite and a portable laptop trolley. This allowed for greater access, however space became limited due to laptops taking up valuable desk space. The next step for schools was a move towards the use of tablet computers; by the end of 2014 68% of UK primary schools had access to tablets (Tablets for Schools, 2014).

The tablet provided wider opportunities for the use of computers in science. It allowed for a number of resources on one device: not only does it provide pupils with access to the internet or use of apps, it also provides pupils with access to cameras, video and voice recording facilities, as many tablets have these as inbuilt features. These can be combined to enhance the teaching and learning of science and allow pupils to present their work using a number of multimedia approaches.

One of the main drawbacks with the use of tablets is the lack of teacher confidence in how to use the software (Bingimlas, 2009), as many learners are more confident than their teachers in using multiple applications at one time. It is important for teachers to understand that learners often use tablets as second nature, and if grouped appropriately they can support each other. An additional concern is that teachers are reluctant to use the tablets in practical investigations in case they get damaged. These concerns will decline over time as both learners and teachers become more confident with their use. It's a matter of reminding them to respect the equipment just as they would with any other resources, and with time and support tablets will become an additional easily accessible resource.

CASE STUDY

Everyday use of tablets

Class of 10–11-year-olds using an iPad as a self-assessment tool

Since the age of eight all the children have had the opportunity to use the iPad as a self-assessment tool. During the lesson the children are encouraged to use the camera facility on the iPad to record any aspect of their learning. Initially it took a few sessions for the children to understand that they don't have to photograph every aspect of the lesson.

Having photographed their learning they select up to six images relating to their learning or lack of understanding. These images are then imported into the PicCollage app (http://pic-collage.com). This app automatically resizes the image. Once the images have been imported the children annotate the images to self-assess their learning (Figure 10.1). Finally they save their work to the library and either print the work and stick it in their exercise book or note in the book which iPad they have worked on.

FIGURE 10.1
Example of a
picture collage

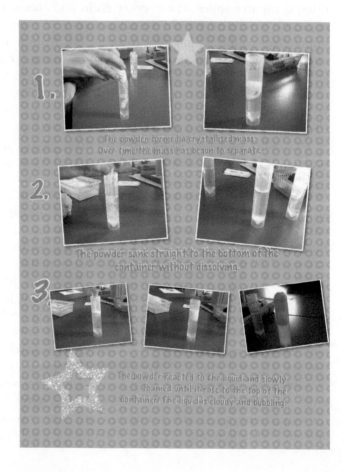

COMPUTING IN SCIENCE

Computing can be used as an effective aid for learning in a number of ways in science (Osbourne and Hennessy, 2006):

- Tools for data capture – processing and interpretation, data logging systems, databases and spreadsheets, graphing tools and modelling environments.
- Multimedia software for simulations.
- Information systems.
- Publishing and presentation tools.
- Data recording equipment.
- Computer projection technology.
- Computer-controlled microscopes.

By making cross-curricular links between science and computing, objectives for both subjects can be achieved whilst putting computing into real-life situations. As the computing Programme of Study states, pupils need to become digitally literate for the future work place (DfE, 2013b). Working scientifically by using data loggers to record accurate measurements and documenting their findings in a number of ways helps to develop these skills.

When learners have the necessary computing skills, they have the freedom to present their findings in a variety of ways, enhancing their learning. By working on a wiki they are able to share information with others in their class and the whole class can contribute. If they are encouraged to combine a range of hardware including voice recorders, videos and cameras, they can make a stimulating and rewarding presentation for all those involved, regardless of their literacy skills.

It is essential that science and computing co-ordinators work alongside each other, to ensure that science and computing skills are taught together and to support teachers, who can then share these skills with their learners. However, the learners are often highly skilled and can support each other.

INTERACTIVE WHITEBOARDS AND DATA PROJECTORS

With the majority of primary classrooms having access to an interactive whiteboard (IWB) there are still vast differences in their use. Some teachers have completed the full circle from using them as fully interactive boards to returning to just using them as a means of displaying text and graphics.

Over time, IWB use could result in learners passively watching moving images whilst waiting for their turn to come to the board. In some classrooms this has been overcome by the use of Apple TV and iPads/iPods; children are encouraged to display their answers or ideas using a tablet and mirroring this on to the screen. The more competitive pupils almost see it as a race to see how quickly they can display their findings.

IWBs have an important contribution to make in science teaching, especially when space is limited. If the IWB is linked to a visualiser this allows the teacher the space to demonstrate safely whilst the children observe on a larger screen. This style of demonstration can be saved and the children can replay it if, at a later date, they need clarification on what they are to achieve.

In schools with more than one form entry the use of IWBs can ensure continuity of provision across the year group; for example, by all classes using the same Smart Slides as a teaching aid with links to specific websites to support the learning, or by having preloaded video clips which allow more time for specific questions and discussions to enhance learning.

One additional advantage of having prepared slides which have the main teaching and learning activities included is that these slides can be used later as a revision tool or to recap on prior learning. They could also allow pre-teaching of some concepts for some learners. They allow the learner to evaluate what they initially knew, what they have learnt and help in evaluation of how their ideas have changed. It can assist learners if their questions are recorded and stored during the lesson and readdressed during the course of the topic as it will keep the questions at the front of the learners' mind and render it easier for the teacher to make links between their ideas and scientific enquiry.

Although not employed extensively, teaching assistants could use prepared slides as a pre-teaching aid for children with specific learning needs. Children with English as a second language could have access to key vocabulary prior to the lesson to ensure they have an understanding of the topic. Slides could also be printed for children who have difficulty in recording and could be adapted to produce a work sheet. They can be used not as a pre-teaching tool, but also to ensure that those pupils who have been absent don't miss out on important learning opportunities.

The use of IWBs is a very effective way of enhancing scientific vocabulary; word banks can be used at the start of the lesson or topic and built up over the course of the unit. The stored scientific words can also be used outside the science curriculum in a variety of ways, e.g. if a child can tell the teacher the definition of a word, their table could leave the classroom first for play time or lunch. Or words could be used in an independent activity whilst the teacher is undertaking guided group work.

Suggested activities could include:

- Making word searches.
- Using dictionaries to find definitions or word origins.
- Exploring sentence structure using scientific words in real-life situations.

SIMULATIONS

The use of simulations has declined over the past decade. They can still be used as an introduction to a practical activity; however, the hands-on approach is more appropriate and ensures learners fully engage in the investigation. Simulations can support investigations over a period of time, although this is also being replaced by time-lapse photography. An area where use of simulations has expanded with the spread of iPads is in the study of planets and astronomy, where children can explore the skies in their exact location by using location settings. The knowledge they gain via the simulation can be used to enhance home–school links, with the learners showing family members where the stars are in the evening. This can increase the awe and wonder of a topic that allows very few practical investigations.

DIGITAL MICROSCOPES

As microscopes have become cheaper, more child-friendly and transportable, schools have moved towards sets of 'Easi-Scope' handheld digital microscopes, also known as 'Egg Microscopes'. Due to their size and shape, all year groups including the Foundation Stage find them very child-friendly and durable for both indoor and outdoor investigations. By using the photo capture option children are able to record an image using a simple one-touch button. Once they have captured a number of images they can be downloaded to a computer using a USB cable. Having stored the downloaded images they can be imported into a number of software packages to enhance presentations of work, or used for class discussions or as evidence of investigations.

'Egg Microscopes' should not be restricted to science lessons and if at all possible it is ideal to have one or two in a 'break time' science resources box, where children are free to explore without the constraints of curriculum objectives. Other science equipment can also be provided in the resources box, for example magnifying glasses to promote independence.

Once the learners have captured images, in one school they are encouraged to take the microscope back to the classroom to act as a stimulus for discussions and talk for writing.

DATA LOGGING EQUIPMENT

Data loggers can provide learners with support in presenting work of a graphical nature. They allow those learners who have not yet become proficient in plotting graphs to evaluate scientific data and evidence in a different format. Data loggers can be set up to record data over a period of time, therefore allowing investigations to continue outside the school day or be extended over lessons and break times. They are also ideal for collecting data outside of the classroom setting due to their portable nature. When introducing children to data loggers, some teachers have a tendency to get the learners to only measure and record temperatures. However, data loggers can also be used as a behaviour management tool by recording sound levels around the school, particularly if these decibel readings are displayed on the IWB and learners know the amount of sound that is acceptable. Data loggers can be used to take readings of sound, light and temperature with inbuilt and detachable sensors. Most systems also offer a heart rate/pulse monitor, however their cost and inefficiency has led to a lack of use.

Due to their cost schools tend to have access to only one or two data loggers, therefore learners have to wait their turns or work in small groups to access the resources. Some schools are linking the collection of data in science with objectives in computing by the introduction of 'Raspberry Pi's'. As they are cheaper and relatively small there are opportunities for schools to obtain more devices. 'Raspberry Pi's' can be used in the same way as data loggers, and can record data over time.

CASE STUDY

Collecting data using data loggers

Upper Key Stage 2
Working scientifically:

- Taking measurements using a range of scientific equipment, with increasing accuracy and precision.
- Reporting and presenting findings from enquiries.
- Using results to make predictions to set up further comparative and fair testing.

Electricity:

- Compare and give reasons for variations in how components function, including the loudness of the buzzers.

This work built on an exploration where the class were previously introduced to energy sticks and encouraged to investigate what the energy sticks could do. It led to complex in-depth discussions on how and where they could use them in a different aspect of the science curriculum. (This was mostly due to the enjoyment they had from using them and a wish to use them more often!)

One group, when they studied electricity, came up with the idea that the more components they added to a circuit the dimmer the bulb or the quieter the sound from the buzzer. They decided if the energy stick was the cell and their peers were the components a good question could be 'How many pupils could you add to affect the brightness of the energy stick?'. The energy stick is a simple electrical circuit. It is used instead of making a simple circuit then adding more components to see the effect more components have on the brightness of the bulb. The energy stick will glow and bleep when the circuit is complete. The more people in the circuit the dimmer/quieter the energy stick. To make this into a comparative study they also looked at the part of the body the energy stick came into contact with. An agreement was made within the group that they would not include the brightness of the energy stick as the daylight and classroom light would have an effect.

FIGURE 10.2
Using data loggers and presenting the findings

(Continued)

(Continued)

Having conducted the investigation they recorded their findings in a simple table and used Excel to present their findings as a graph (Figure 10.2). Their findings could also have been presented in the same form by using the graphing tool on the data loggers. The children are encouraged to present their findings in the most appropriate medium and at this point in the use of data loggers they lacked experience in the graphic tool and felt more confident with Excel.

DIGITAL CAMERAS AND DIGITAL FILMS

Traditionally teachers have used digital images as a means of recording what the learners have achieved during an investigation or as evidence in their books to show what they have done. However, as resources are becoming more affordable and learners and teachers are becoming more digitally minded, more schools are providing more cameras or access to tablets with cameras to enable learners to record their findings. The use of digital imagery allows learners to observe phenomena more carefully and at higher resolution. As the direct observation and immediate display can be captured it also enables additional opportunities to discuss features in more detail once the original opportunity has passed.

Examples of data capture and analysis can be presented in a number of media depending on the desired outcome:

- Windows media.
- Photo Story.
- iMovies.
- PicCollage.
- Prezi.

Voogt (2010) states that all children should have the opportunity to acquire digital skills which will lead to higher-order skills such as team work, problem-solving and project management. These skills can all be seen when learners work as a group to conduct an investigation, and if each learner has a specific role it allows for more effective team work; for example, if during the investigation, one learner is given the specific role of media officer in which they record every aspect of the investigation. These roles change with each investigation.

These types of communication can be used in a variety of ways for recording the equipment and methods the learners use, instead of a formal write up. They also provide an accurate way of recording the findings. When analysing recordings teachers can gain valuable insight into how the group worked, as well as what their scientific understanding is. The opportunity to assess how the learners work as a team to achieve their outcomes is invaluable and allows teachers to regroup learners in subsequent lessons to ensure all are enabled to participate. With the learners recording their conversation during their work, it removes inhibitions of learners worrying they are wrong when the teacher is listening or relying on the teacher to guide their understanding. It also allows the conversation to flow more naturally, and provides a true record of what they knew at any one time.

CASE STUDY

Using video to enhance investigations

Lower Key Stage 2
Working scientifically:

- Identify differences, similarities or changes related to simple scientific ideas and processes.
- Use straightforward scientific evidence to answer questions or to support the findings.

States of Matter:

- Compare and group materials together according to whether they are solids, liquids or gases.

Learners were given a range of clear liquids including water, sparkling water, baby oil, baby shampoo. To each of the clear liquids they added the contents of a blackcurrant tea bag (Figure 10.3). They were asked to make predictions relating to real-life experiences on what they thought would happen in each investigation. Having made their prediction they conducted the investigation and recorded their observations. Before they went on to the next liquid they were encouraged to reassess their original prediction:

C1.   This is our beaker at the side with the sparkling water.
C2.   This is the view from the top.

(Continued)

(Continued)

C2. It's turning a different colour.

C1. I told you that's what happens when you mix blackcurrant and water.

C1. It's turning purple.

C2. Go to the top [*excitedly*] look! What's happening? There's bubbling coming out, there's little like bubbles rising and popping, it's like it's breathing.

C1. It's turning a bit pink.

C1. It's bubbling loads.

C2. The bubbles are rising.

C1. What's the scientific word for bubbling?

C2. It begins with 'ef'.

C1. I can't remember. Is it on the wall?

C2. Effervesces!! That's really hard to say.

C2. Look it looks really cool. That's so cool! It's so different to the tap water.

C1. What do you think will happen with the baby shampoo?

C2. Well when I wash my hair it goes all foamy and white. What do you think?

C1. I think it will smell kind of nice.

FIGURE 10.3
The blackcurrant investigation

VOICE RECORDING MATERIALS

What learners say provides information that is useful for assessing their learning, and there are many options available. 'Talking tins', 'talking pages' and 'talking cards' can be used to record single sentences

FIGURE 10.4
Children using
a floor book

to accompany a photograph of a piece of equipment or to provide the answer to a question that is displayed on a wall or beside an investigation. One excellent use of talking tins for display had a set of questions relating to the solar system. In this activity each group had been given a specific set of questions relating to a planet; these questions included size, gravity, orbit and atmosphere. The learners recorded their findings using talking postcards and attached them to a set of inflatable planets. These were hung in the Foundation Stage and Early Years setting to provide these learners with verbal information. The activity provided a real audience for their science work.

Large floor books are ideal for presentation, group or class work with each page of the book having a few simple sentences relating to the work record (Figure 10.4).

Dictaphones or DragonDicta can be used to support learners with literacy skills in two ways. Firstly, they can be used to record expectations or instructions from the teacher to the learner. Secondly, the learner can use them to provide the teachers with their answers verbally.

iPad apps

Suggested apps available from Apple are listed in Table 10.1, most of them were free downloads. A gentle reminder: apps that you pay for only have a licence for six devices, therefore further devices require additional purchases.

TABLE 10.1 Suggested apps available from Apple

Provider	Title	Review	Topic Area
plasq Ltd	Comic life	Photo package comes with prepared templates enabling you to insert of range of photographs and speech bubbles or text to annotate pictures for the children to produce their own comics to record their observations.	Recording data
Cardinal Blue	PIC Collage	Simple templates to insert photographs and text.	Recording data, self or peer assessment
Tiny Hearts Ltd	Pocket Zoo HD™ with live animal cams	Find out about different animals in your own zoo with animal photographs, videos, sound effects, fun facts and live animal cams.	Animals
Foundation Stage			
Tribal Nova	Seasons and weather	Provides games on what to wear in various weather situations and a calendar to record daily weather.	Seasonal change
Night and Day Studios Ltd.	My very first app	Differentiated including pairs games which are linked to colours, animal homes, animal sounds and food.	Humans and animals
Year 1 and 2			
Rishi Chhibber	Life cycles for kids lite	Very basic app showing what a frog eats during the stages of its development. The more it eats the bigger it grows.	Animals including humans
TabTale Ltd	Four Seasons – an earth day interactive book	Green environment and clean air interactive story book showing seasonal change.	Seasonal change
Apptility Software PVT Ltd	Human body puzzles for kids	Differentiated jigsaw puzzles of body parts, can have 4 to 16 pieces.	Animals including humans
Christopher Duyster	Identify Tree Lite	Enables identification of common trees.	Plants
Mobius for kids	Food chains for kids	Sorting plants and animals into different categories and discovering where they fit into the food chain	All living things and their habitats

Provider	Title	Review	Topic Area
Year 3 and 4			
Nth Fusion LLC	A life cycle app	Fantastic app showing stages of the rock cycle, text can be read or audio version. Also includes life cycle of frog, phases of the moon, parts of plants and many others.	Rocks, plants
Zonkey Interactive	Fun Science Lab	The lab is a toy factory filled with interactive experiments and games, Including an electrical robot and how to use magnets.	Electricity, magnets
Sebit LLC	Building Serial Circuits	Using 3D and 2D electrical symbols, you can assemble different types of series circuits using wires, switches, batteries and bulbs.	Electricity
Year 5 and 6			
Object Enterprise	Video Science	Selection of short video clips showing practical investigations for a whole range of topics.	All topics in upper Key Stage 2
Hanno Rein	Exoplanet	Interactive catalogue of all known exoplanets, planets which are orbiting beyond our solar system.	Earth and space
Nth Fusion LLC	A life cycle app	App shows a wide range of cycles including phases of the moon, rock cycle, life cycle of frog, plants and butterflies.	Living things and their habitats Earth and space
Columbia University	Leafsnap HD	Enables you to photograph a leaf on a white background which identifies the leaf for you and describes the tree and its features.	Plants
Applios Inc	Physic Pad	Use the drawing tools to build your own games and quizzes using rigid bodies, pivots, springs, ropes and gears.	Forces
Go Softworks	GoSky watch Planetarium	Quick and easy identification and location of stars, planets, constellations, galaxies by simply pointing the IPad at the sky.	Earth and space
Pic Pockets Books	Boo! HD	Interactive story with human detectives on how bugs and viruses are transported around the body.	Animals including humans.

SUMMARY

The use of computers in science will continue to develop rapidly over the coming years, as technology advances and equipment becomes more affordable. Schools have to move with the times; this will involve ensuring that teachers' training needs are met and technical support is provided for the teaching and learning. As equipment becomes smaller, more user-friendly and the amount of technology in everyday life continues to increase, it is essential that learners are able to make links between how this equipment works within the school environment and in the world around them, and then how this is linked into industry once they have left formal education. Whilst teachers and learners are adapting to this period of continuous change it is important to remember that technology doesn't always work, and a back-up plan may be needed. In addition, sometimes going with what learners find out and not sticking to the plan because that is what's written down can be important.

FURTHER READING

Caldwell, H. and Bird, J. (2015) *Teaching with Tablets*. London: Sage.

Clark, W. and Luckin, R. (2013) *What the Research Says – iPads in the Classroom: Leading Education and Social Research*. London: Institute of Education, University of London.

Cutting, R. and Kelly, O. (2015) *Creative Teaching in Primary Science*. London: Sage Publications.

Harlen, W. and Qualter, A. (2014) *The Teaching of Science in Primary Schools*. Oxon: Routledge.

Hienrich, P. (2012) *The iPad as a Tool for Education*. NACCE and 9ine Consulting. www.naace.co.uk/get.html?_Action=GetFile&_Key=Data26613&_Id=1965.

11

SCIENCE OUTDOORS

Andrew Berry

This chapter indicates the learning that can take place outside, and provides ideas that can turn outdoor places into areas where all learners will become immersed and engaged in their learning.

When many of us who are involved with science in primary schools first took a look at the National Curriculum of 2014 a few things immediately became apparent. Firstly, the aspects of physics that had once been at Key Stage 1 (ages 5–7), i.e. sound, electricity, light and forces, were no longer there. Secondly, that throughout both key stages there was a greater focus on biology, with new aspects such as evolution appearing for the first time. A consequence of such changes could be that some learners, especially at Key Stage 1, might not encounter as many hands-on learning experiences as they once had as the more manageable activities such as cars on ramps and constructing electrical circuits were no longer a requirement. However, for those of us who have been promoting outdoor learning it was an opportunity to be grabbed with both hands. If ever there was a time to truly embrace the opportunities that lie outside it is now.

The active involvement of the learners in their learning is an essential feature of constructivist theory. By placing the learners in an environment where the natural world surrounds them, they will experience first-hand the wonders of nature throughout the year. As a result of what they observe and measure they will alter and develop their ideas about how the natural world works. Anyone who has supported learners outside the classroom knows how highly motivating the experience of being beyond the classroom is for both the child and teacher, as it helps to stimulate interest, curiosity and passion for 'doing'. Through a range of activities, horizons can be expanded as learners are helped to see aspects of our world that are sometimes separate from the man-made world in which they exist. Simultaneously, being outside also enables them to hone their numerous scientific skills as outlined under Working Scientifically in the Science Programme of Study (DfE, 2013b). From raising questions, to discussing how much trust they can have in data, the outdoors provides the context. In addition to the positive outcomes for the learners and teachers involved, nature itself can also benefit from a greater engagement with the outdoors. By connecting learners with their natural world, positive experiences of nature in childhood are begun, which could have a significant impact on environmental attitudes and behaviours in adulthood.

PREPARING THE OUTDOORS FOR LEARNING

In 2008 Ofsted published its report on the importance of learning outside: *Learning Outside the Classroom: How Far Should You Go?* (Ofsted, 2008b). Among other findings, this survey discovered that when planned and implemented well, learning outside the classroom contributed significantly to raising standards and improving pupils' personal, social and emotional development. It also highlighted how the learning outside the classroom was most successful when it was an integral element of long-term curriculum planning and closely linked to classroom activities. Thus, like other elements of learning within a primary school, the use of the outdoors needs careful planning, in terms of both the activities and the resources that are required. Science is often a subject that relies heavily on resources, and there is no more obvious example when considering how the outdoors should be developed and maintained to enable high-level learning to take place.

To help provide a little structure to this process, one can consider three guiding principles:

1. **Holistic** – From the start, schools will need to consider how to involve the wider community. Not only will this help to embed the school in the community, but it will provide the much needed labour and sometimes some great expertise. Schools should also consider the other subjects within the National Curriculum. Developing the outdoors for all subjects will prevent particular areas being ruined as a result of lack of planning. Finally, schools will need to consider whether the outdoor spaces will be used throughout the day; again planning should ensure that areas are suitably maintained for learning.
2. **Participatory** – Involve the learners from the start. This will provide them with ownership of the spaces, as well as a desire to care for what they have helped to create.
3. **Sustainable** – It is essential to create a process that can be effectively managed over a period of time. This should be a way of learning that is an integral part of a school's philosophy on how learning occurs, and one that does not rely on the passion of just a few people.

Having established the philosophy behind the learning, schools will then need to deal with the more practical issues with supporting learning beyond the classroom. The development and maintenance of the outdoor spaces for learning requires some structure in order for the potential learning to be effective and efficient.

1. **Identify aims** – Establish, with the learners, what the aims are for outside learning.
2. **Site survey** – Find out what it is that you already have outdoors. By creating a map or a model you will establish what it is that you are keeping and where the spaces are for further development.

3. **Planning** – Think 'learning'. Remember that as well as creating environments that will create great habitats for a range of organisms, you must also make all spaces accessible for particular numbers of learners of a range of ages and needs. Consider also the time of year when particular projects should be undertaken. A grounds development and maintenance calendar is essential.

4. **Implementation** – Using your planning as a guide, proceed with help from the whole community to establish zones in which learning can take place.

5. **Maintenance** – Along with the learners other members of the community can ensure that all learning zones are maintained to ensure that they are safe and fit for learning to take place in.

ENGAGING LEARNERS IN OUTDOOR SCIENCE

Although being outside is intrinsically engaging for learning, it is still often the case that teachers need a range of tools to maintain interest and give the learning a purpose. One such strategy can be to support learning by using technology. For instance, using one of the many electronic microscopes that are now easy to purchase, a teacher can help learners to discover a whole new world. Whether it is a woodlouse or a leaf from a hazel tree, learners will be gripped by what they see, and can use this experience to begin to generate questions about what else they would like to find out about the natural world. The Global Positioning System (GPS) is another technological advance that can enhance learning. Along with a digital camera, learners can plan and record a route around an outdoors area and capture images of living things for that time of the year. When downloaded into systems such as Google Maps, this information can then become an electronic diary of what was discovered. Throughout the year this practice can be repeated, so that eventually changes in the natural world across months, seasons and even years can be compared. Another strategy could be to involve the learners in some science that is bigger than the confines of their own school. This could be achieved by participating in one of the many nature surveys that take place throughout the year. The Big Butterfly Count run by the Butterfly Conservation organisation, or the Big Schools' Birdwatch run by the Royal Society for the Protection of Birds (RSPB), are both great projects to become involved in. Not only do they provide opportunities on how to identify different organisms, but learners will also need to consider the needs of these organisms and how their environments can impact on them.

Science outside in an urban school

Even in an urban area there are opportunities for studying living things outside the classroom. A class of learners in an urban school were given a selection of coloured paint swatches and asked to go out into their playground and to try to match the colours of living things to those on the swatches. There was soon a debate about what at first looked like paint on the ground. It was found in three different colours, grey, light green and a rusty colour. It was almost impossible to peel off the playground but when viewed through a magnifying glass became most interesting. After taking photographs and drawing what they saw the learners used the internet to decide on what they had found: it was lichen. The teacher then asked the learners to find the largest patch of lichen they could. Using squared paper that had been photocopied onto transparent sheets learners were able to count each surface area they identified. Back in the classroom they used the identification sheets produced by the Lichen Society and tried to find out as much as possible about these strange things. They found lichens are not a plant, but are able to make their own food because they are a mix of an alga and a fungus. They found also that lichens are a very old form of life and can be used as indicators of clean air. There were no leaf or branching types of lichen found in the school playground but the learners did identify that yellow lichen was found on south-facing walls, whilst north-facing walls had mosses. For more information on lichen visit www.britishlichensociety.org.uk.

RECORDING

The way in which learners' record their science learning is often quite challenging for both them and their teachers. Teachers know that if recording lacks any form of interest for the learners, or is too onerous, then they will become disengaged in their learning. Therefore, when considering how best to use the outdoors for science learning, it is essential that teachers ensure that recording is as engaging as other aspects of the learning. To do this, teachers must first consider why they are asking for a record to be made. There are many meaningful reasons to do so: encouraging closer observation, planning an enquiry, recording findings in order to discover patterns over time, explaining why something has occurred, etc. Secondly, teachers need to encourage learners to begin to understand that there are a range of different methods for recording and that these are suited to whatever it is that one is trying to learn. A tally chart can be used to record the numbers of particular invertebrates, whereas in another situation the learners may choose a photographic diary to record the changes to different species of trees throughout a year. With learners knowing both why and how to record they will view recording as a tool to support their learning, rather than something that they have to do as the teacher asked them to.

LEARNING ZONES

There are numerous potential learning zones that can be established in many school grounds. Each of these can viewed simply as a physical space in which learners will have the required resources to learn about particular aspects from the National Curriculum, and teachers will have the resources to support learning. The design of these areas will obviously be determined by a school's overall aims, the space available to be developed, and a host of other practical constraints such as amount of shade, proximity to buildings, and access to water, etc. However, within each zone some time should be spent planning how the learning will be supported by the teacher. Resources designed for such a purpose could include a mobile board on which the teacher can place magnetic images, graphs, Venn diagrams, etc., or write using a whiteboard marker. The teacher could also have reference books, resources to support closer observation, resources to support children's acquisition of scientific vocabulary and games related to the learning taking place.

When constructing an outdoor learning zone, schools will need to consider how the learners will access it, the type of learning that will take place, and the ways by which the area will be maintained and developed. In this chapter each of the potential learning zones will be considered, with the most relevant practical and resourcing matters covered, and activities linked to the Science Programmes of Study (DfE, 2013b).

Before examining each of the individual zones, it is worth considering how we enable learners to realise the extent of the natural world that may be within the school grounds. Begin by recreating a scene from Charles Darwin's house in Kent. Around a part of his garden Darwin created a 'thinking path', which he would often walk, thinking about nature and our place in it. As a starter activity this will aid observation of the nature around the learners in a calm and peaceful manner. To focus learners onto particular areas of the wildlife area, ask them to become a camera. They could begin by establishing a field of vision by holding up their thumbs and looking between them. The teacher can then use this strategy to hone the aspect of science that is being studied; e.g. 'How many different plants can you see?', 'How can we recognise a plant?', 'Which plant is the tallest/shortest, widest/thinnest?' By increasing the distance between their thumbs you can enable the learners to observe through a 'wide-angled lens'.

Forming your hands into tubes, and placing one above the other can allow learners to zoom in on particular plants or habitats. They could even place different colours of acetate over cardboard rolls and then view the world as it would be seen by various invertebrates. Following on from this activity, they can be challenged to perform a nature scavenger hunt. Without picking anything from trees, learners must collect a range of items that were once alive. They could place their finds in egg boxes. To enhance their observational skills, each pair of slots within the egg boxes can be labelled on the base as opposites, e.g. 'hard' and 'soft'. The learners can then swap egg boxes and work out what the descriptive words on the base could be. This scavenger hunting could be performed in the different seasons; each time the learners could stick their finds on a cardboard cut-out of an artist's pallette. Placed on display in the classroom, these would make a great reminder to the children about changes across the seasons.

FIGURE 11.1
A meadow zone

MEADOW ZONES

Practical matters and resources

Wildflower meadows will provide an incredible range of grasses and wild flowers through spring and summer (Figure 11.1). However, to establish a healthy and sustainable meadow a school will need to consider a few practical issues. Firstly, a school needs to ensure that the area chosen has poor quality of nutrients within the soil in order that the grasses and wild flowers are not competing with other local perennials such as thistles and docks. The easiest way to accomplish this is to simply remove the topsoil from the area in question. Schools will also need to maintain both a spring and summer meadow. By doing so, the summer wild flowers will not have to compete with the spring wild flowers. The cutting times for these meadows will be included in the maintenance plan for the outdoor areas. As with all learning zones, consideration will need to be given to how learners will use this area, as it is a delicate habitat that can be prone to trampling. Some form of a low barrier should encourage children to use a particular path, but also allow them to get close to the plants.

Further advice about creating and maintaining meadow zones can be found on the Bumblebee Conservation Trust website: http://bumblebeeconservation.org/images/uploads/Resources/BBCT_Land_Factsheet_2_Managing_wildflower_meadows.pdf.

In order to identify and name the plethora of organisms that exist in Britain, learners will need access to different types of guides and keys. We need to either purchase or make identification materials that are suited to the ability of the learners we are working with. Home-made identification materials have the advantage of being designed around the plants that you know are in your school grounds. Excellent materials can be purchased from companies such as Gatekeeper or the Field Studies Council. A school also needs to consider how an area of the meadow will be provided to learners for them to focus on. Too often, without a point on which to focus, learners will lose interest as they observe over too large an area. Ways to do this include: providing the learners with a quadrat (purchased or home-made – Figure 11.2), using a PE hoop, or even placing a length of string on the ground to observe along.

From a teaching point of view, a mobile white board can be placed alongside the meadow. Magnetic images of different wild flowers and their names can be placed either on the board, or in a bag attached to the board to be used when required by the teacher or learners.

Conservation note: In Britain it is illegal to dig up wild plants and to pick some wild flowers. Removing any plant or part of a plant without a landowner's permission is illegal.

The learning

To hook the learners into this aspect of learning, they can be informed that they are replicating the work of Charles Darwin at his home, Down House, in Kent. Removing a half square metre of turf from a lawn, they

FIGURE 11.2
A quadrat

can then record over time the type of plants that grow in this place. This is a chance for learners to see what happens when plants are left to their own devices. It also will help them to work out the requirements for a wildflower and grass meadow in order that it does not have to compete with other plants.

A vibrant meadow containing an array of wild flowers and grasses is one of many outdoor learning zones that will provide learners with opportunities to identify different plants through examining their different parts. Using colour charts from DIY stores, learners could try to find many different shades of the colours that appear in the flowers.

Maintaining a plant diary throughout a year enables learners to observe the parts of the plants involved with reproduction. Over the course of the year they can discover the role of the different parts and how they might vary from plant to plant. There is also a great opportunity to press a flower from each of the different plants and, by using sticky-back plastic, place them within a whole-class nature diary.

Due to the number of different animals that can be found living within a meadow, the learners will have plenty to refer to when challenged to think about how these animals have adapted to this habitat.

If you are working in a school without access to a meadow, you might be able to work with a city farm or local garden centre to engage in a similar activity.

CONTAINER ZONES

Practical matters and resources

Whether a school has shop-bought or home-made pots/containers it is important that they are large enough for the plants that will be growing in them, and that there is adequate drainage. Growing plants in containers can have many advantages over permanent raised beds. Firstly, the containers can make it easy for learners to view all parts of the plant; transparent containers will enable the roots to be seen. Secondly, it is easier to move the plants to locations for particular investigations. A basic trolley would be ideal to use for such a purpose.

The learning

Plants in pots could be the easiest way for learners to closely examine all the different parts of the plants. At chosen intervals over a period of time, they could measure and record the length of particular parts of the plants and even look for relationships between them; e.g. 'Do the plants with the longest roots have the longest leaves?' As they are easy to access and easy to move from one location to another, pots allow the learners chances to adjust a range of variables (e.g. light, water, space) to discover whether this impacts on the plants' health and growth. The learners could take photos at reasonable intervals to capture what has happened to their plants.

TREE AND HEDGEROW ZONES

Practical matters and resources

Trees and hedges (Figure 11.3) will need to be properly spaced so that they have the opportunity to grow to the desired height. They will also need some trimming so that they do not have a negative impact on other areas; large branches overhanging meadows might need to be cut back to allow light to reach the plants within the meadows.

Information on planting trees and hedges can be found on the Woodland Trust website: www.woodlandtrust.org.uk/plant-trees.

Information on how to maintain hedgerows can be found on the Bumblebee Conservation Trust website: http://bumblebeeconservation.org/images/uploads/Resources/BBCT_Land_Factsheet_6_Managing_hedges_edges.pdf.

FIGURE 11.3
A tree and
hedge zone

To encourage a greater diversity of organisms within your outdoor learning zones it is better to create hedgerows from native British plants such as hawthorn, blackthorn, hazel, silver birch, beech and holly. These plants not only have a variety of leaves, bark, fruits and seeds for children to examine, but they provide a great habitat and source of food for various birds and mammals.

As with many of the other learning zones, there are a wealth of identification resources to be used to work out the names of the trees that can be found. The Nature Detectives part of the Woodland Trust website provides identification charts based on various parts of the tree: leaves, seeds and fruits, bark, and even buds.

The learning

Using their observational skills, learners can explore the trees in a range of ways. They could begin by placing a plastic mirror on their noses and below their eyes, and then wander under different tree canopies to find out what they look like from a different perspective. Parts of the tree can be labelled by tying labels on the relevant parts. Measurements of some of these parts could be taken at different times over a long period of time. Learners can be encouraged to use their sense of touch to identify particular trees. Blindfolded, the child can be led to different species of trees and asked to describe what the barks feel like. Recording can

TABLE 11.1 Type of fruit and the method of seed dispersal

| Name of tree | Type of fruit | | | | | Means of dispersal | | | |
	Juicy	Winged	Fluffy	Hard case large seeds	Hard case small seeds	Blown by wind	Eaten or carried by animal	Carried by water	Explode from the fruit	Not sure!
Sycamore										
Elder										
Horse chestnut										
Maple										
Hawthorn										

simply be wax crayon rubbings made of each of the different textures. The learners could measure the circumference of various trees. The height of a tree can be measured with a clinometer, or estimated by walking a distance approximating the height of the tree away from the tree, and then by learners turning their back to the tree and looking through their legs to see whether they can just see the top. The leaves of trees in autumn can be collected and sorted using a range of criteria. In Key Stage 2 (ages 7–11) data loggers can be used to find out how much light travels through the canopies of different species of tree.

When studying seed dispersal, the learners could draw a sketch of the area of land that they intend to examine. After they have placed a numbered label on each of the trees on the map, they can begin at the base of one of the trees and then search outwards. If any seeds and/or fruit are found, they can be placed in a food bag and labelled with the number of the tree. The learners can then measure the distance between where the seed was found and the tree from which it originated. By first using a compass to find out where north, east, south and west are in relation to the tree, the children can record their findings on a grid like the one in Table 11.1.

Using Table 11.1, the children could also record which type of fruit came from each tree, and the method of seed dispersal.

As part of their studies of trees and hedges, learners could record significant events in their lives over a period of a year. These could include when the plants begin to bud, when the first leaves are seen, when the plants develop flowers, when seeds are formed, and when leaves fall from the tree. They can then look at data gathered over a set period and try to explain whether the trees were affected by any changes in the environment. As part of this examination, they could look for any significant lichens which could be indicators of particular pollutants. A free identification chart for lichens and the pollutants that they indicate can be found on the OPAL website: www.opalexplorenature.org/sites/default/files/7/file/air-survey-field-guide-2014.pdf.

Finally, learners could examine the trees and hedges as habitats in which invertebrates might be living or feeding. Some of these animals could be collected from the trees by placing a sheet under some branches and then giving them a good shake.

RAISED BEDS, ALLOTMENTS AND HERB GARDENS

Practical matters and resources

Raised beds are ideal for primary schools as they are easy to access. The key to a healthy raised bed or allotment is to plan what is to be grown, when it is to be grown and how it is to be maintained.

Herbs like thyme, chives, parsley, marjoram, rosemary, sage, basil and mints make good choices for the beginner's herb garden. These herbs aren't fussy when it comes to sunlight, fertile soil or water. To simplify garden care for specific herbs, annual herbs (those that need to be replanted every year) and perennial herbs (those that grow back on their own each year) should be planted in separate beds. It's important to till the soil to a depth of about 40 cm using a spade or a fork so that newly planted herbs have lots of room to spread their roots. Spacing between plants will vary according to the plant.

The learning

By rubbing some of the herb leaves learners could try to identify the different plants from their smell, and record the types and numbers of pollinators visiting these plants as well as what they are doing on these visits. As part of a longer-term project, learners could help to research the requirements for a butterfly garden. That is to say, they would need to find out the food sources required for the caterpillars and butterflies that they are intending to live in this habitat. Information about the most appropriate species of plants can be found on the Butterfly Conservation website. Later in the year, children could collect seed-heads from annual plants (e.g. poppies, nasturtiums, pot marigolds and cornflowers) when the flowers have fallen off. After the seeds have been left in a warm place, the learners can sort the seeds from the seed-heads and place them in labelled envelopes. These seeds can then be kept in a dry place ready for planting the following spring.

Learners can be given their own part of an allotment area which they have to tend over time. Through their observations and measurements they will develop a good understanding of the different requirements of the various plants.

POND ZONE

Practical matters and resources

A pond is one of the main features to have in any wildlife area if the aim is to increase the biodiversity (Figure 11.4). Even ponds of a relatively shallow depth will attract an immense number of living things that all learners are fascinated by. However, too often a pond is unsuccessful as a learning zone because there is insufficient thought at the planning stage, and, later on, lack of proper maintenance. *The Pond Book*, published by the Freshwater Habitats Trust, provides a comprehensive guide to the creation and maintenance of a pond.

FIGURE 11.4
A pond zone

The role of the teacher is also crucial to making sure that the pond remains a vibrant home for wildlife as well as somewhere that learners can use. If possible, try to ensure that some of the pond is left undisturbed. This will allow some of the wildlife to remain untouched, which in the long run will help to maintain the wildlife within the pond. Secondly, try to use the correct size nets for the depth of pond (Figure 11.5). There is no need to hook the learners in when learning takes place at the pond; simply finding a newt, frog or tadpoles is engaging in itself. What is challenging is to then focus the learners on the scientific angle that you have in mind. By using a clear container in which to place the finds, you can physically separate the children from the pond. As in other zones, younger learners can begin to learn the names of the animals and plants that they find, as well as describe their parts, and place them in groups. To support learners with classifying their finds they could simply use plastic hoops. In each one a label of an animal group can be placed. They could begin with just two hoops; invertebrates and vertebrates. They could then progress to more hoops: fish, mammals, birds, amphibians, reptiles and invertebrates. A group of learners could be provided with a set of animal pictures, which they then place into one of the hoops.

The learning

Older learners will be able to use their observations to explain how the organisms have adapted to their environments, and how this could be

FIGURE 11.5
Use the correct size net for the depth of pond

evidence of evolution. A useful follow-up activity is to ask them to design their own animal that could live in their pond environment. It could be that you insist that this animal must be an amphibian, and that they have to create its various stages of life by using modelling clay.

If studied throughout a year, the pond can provide many examples of both life cycles and food chains. Through the use of images on the outdoor whiteboard, the children can show which stage they think particular animals are at in their life cycles, as well as what they think they eat, and what eats them.

BIRD AREA ZONES

Practical matters and resources

When positioning bird feeders and bird tables, schools will need to consider the requirements of the birds as well as how learners will view these facilities. Many garden birds such as blue tits and sparrows prefer to fly from hedges (where they have a degree of protection) to the feeders. These feeders will need to be cleaned and food added to them throughout the year, so it is worth considering having different classes responsible for this task for particular months. Bird boxes are a great way to observe certain birds over a period of time. Information about where to place boxes can be found on the RSPB website:

http://bgbw.rspb.org.uk/makeahomeforwildlife/advice/helpingbirds/feeding/index.aspx.

It is now also possible for learners to view what is happening inside bird boxes through the use of cameras attached to computers. However, it is still important to observe birds outside. This could be done from a fixed point in the school playground, or some schools might be able to create a bird hide from which learners, using binoculars, can tally the birds that they see. The size, colour, shape of the bird and the song that it sings are all useful characteristics when trying to identify birds. In the bird hide particular resources could be placed to support the development of these skills. To aid recognition through shape and size, the learners could be provided with four bird silhouette cut-outs: a mallard, a wood pigeon, a blackbird and a robin. They can then compare their sightings relative to these cut-outs. The RSPB website (www.rspb.org.uk/wildlife/birdidentifier) has a section on bird identification that will ask the children for this information in order to help narrow the possibilities. In addition to the cut-outs, learners could have access to either home-made or bought identification charts or keys. This should encourage them to look more carefully at the colours and shapes of the birds.

The learning

Learners should be encouraged to record their findings on a regular basis. This data could then form the starting point for their explanations when they are trying to communicate why there are changes in the number and species of birds across a year. After a few years, schools will then have their own personalised data about their birds which learners can examine and use to explain patterns and differences.

To develop an understanding of what different birds eat, ask learners to design an experiment that they could monitor over time. They could measure the number of visits made to particular foods over a period of time, or they could measure the amount of food at the start and end of a day.

MICRO-HABITATS: LOG PILES, ROCKERIES, WILDLIFE STACKS, LEAF PILES AND COMPOST ZONES

Practical matters and resources

As with other learning zones, consider both the wildlife and how it is to be used for learning. So, use logs that are large enough for a range of invertebrates and amphibians, but not too big that learners cannot move them. Logs at least 100 mm thick with the bark still attached provide the best wood. Hardwood trees such as ash, oak and beech are particularly good. Be careful of freshly cut willow and poplar logs, as these can easily re-sprout if left lying on the ground. Rockeries could be deliberately created using a collection of different types of rocks. Remember that the animals that you are trying to attract require dark and damp spaces, so look for places around your wildlife area that have a good degree of shade. It is also worth cordoning off a particular section of a rockery or log pile in which amphibians might be living throughout the year. A Perspex sheet under a wooden lid can create a good viewing station for many invertebrates such as slugs, woodlice and ants. It is a good idea to build three composters. Each composter can contain organic material at a different stage of decomposing. Ensure that they are made of a height that is low enough for the children to see what is happening. More information about how to compost can be found at www.recyclenow.com/recycle/recycle-school/composting. Wildlife stacks can be constructed with help from the children. By providing plenty of spaces of different sizes you can encourage a variety of animals to live there and possibly hibernate over the winter. Further information can be found on the RSPB website: www.rspb.org.uk/advice/gardening/insects/wildlifestack.aspx.

The learning

The invertebrates found within these habitats can be used by learners to construct their own keys. Each of the animals found can be placed under an electronic microscope and photos taken of them. Learners can then compare the photos and devise the questions that would enable anyone to separate them; e.g. 'Does the animal have six legs?'

These habitats are extremely useful when trying to develop understanding of what it is that animals require in order to survive. To hook the learners in, ask them to imagine that they have been shrunk to animal size, that is the size of a pen cap. Using plastic plant labels as way markers, each learner can plot a journey around the log pile/rockery. This learner then guides another along the journey that 'they' have taken; explaining as they go the requirements of their animal in terms of food, warmth, shelter, moisture and protection from predators.

Invertebrates are some of the easier animals to find when undertaking an animal survey. Rockeries, log piles and compost are a few of many habitats that could be explored, each time noting down the number of each species of animal found. By repeating this survey at different times of the year learners will develop their own bank of data which they can use to explain any differences that occur. It often raises questions such as 'Where are all the slugs?' Answers to such questions can be discovered through researching using secondary sources such as books and websites.

Moving away from animals, the rockery is also a useful resource for learning more about rocks. Labels describing the appearance and the properties of rocks can be given to learners, who must then match these to the correct rock in the rockery. Over time they can monitor the rocks; finding out which ones are permeable, and to what extent they are affected by weathering. Continuing with this aspect of science, learners could be encouraged to carry out some observational work on the compost that has been produced in their composters, and then compare this to the soil found in other areas around the school. Each of these substances can be placed in jars of water, stirred and left to settle. Learners will then be able to study the contents of the different soils and compare them again with the compost. They could also be asked to devise their own test to find out which of the soils is best at absorbing water. Using their findings from this activity they could first predict and then carry out a further test to find out which soil is best for growing plants in.

WEATHER STATION ZONE

Practical matters and resources

'Seasonal change' is an aspect of science that is new to the Programme of Study (DfE, 2013b). Schools now have to consider which types of resources would help to develop the required learning. Although there are many great manufactured resources it could be that schools would prefer to make their own. Measuring devices such as weather vanes, anemometers and rain gauges can be bought, or, although maybe not as permanent, learners can construct their own. Weather boards where learners can turn wheels to show types of clouds, whether it is rainy or sunny, etc., can be bought, or a magnetic whiteboard with relevant images could be an acceptable alternative. Outdoor thermometers placed in different shaded areas around the grounds can provide useful data for some investigations.

The learning

One of the requirements of 'Seasonal Change' is to 'observe changes across the four seasons'. One such change could be the temperature. Using a large floor book, learners could record the temperature at particular times of the day throughout the year. Not only will this enable them to find relationships between temperature and the time of the

FIGURE 11.6
Home-made
weather
recording
device

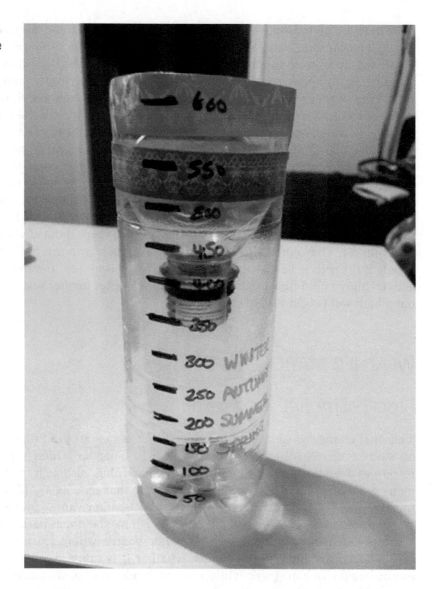

year, but it will provide a reason for using a simple measuring device. Another change that could be observed is what happens to the plants during the different seasons. Viewing points located at places around the outdoors area could be marked with signs. During each of the seasons learners can make observations from each of these viewpoints. Photos can also be taken and then used inside the classroom to show a time-line of events. In particular, learners can look out for: when plants are flowering, when there are leaves on the trees, and when there are fruits and seeds. In addition, learners could make a note of any rarer sightings, such as when spider webs were easy to see, when some ants were seen flying, when birds were seen making nests, when eggs were laid in a nest box and when frogs returned to the pond.

The second aspect of learning within 'Seasonal Change' requires learners to 'Observe and describe weather associated with the seasons and how day length varies'. Although a diary can be maintained in which learners help to record the weather on particular days, there also exist many opportunities to develop their observational skills further by studying several of the features of weather more closely. For instance, after looking at clouds and pictures of clouds (www.opalexplorenature.org/sites/default/files/7/file/Climate-survey-cloud-chart.pdf) learners could be challenged to draw their own cloud chart. Every day that there is some form of cloud they can record this on their charts. The amount and direction of wind is another feature of weather that might vary from season to season. Ideas as to how to construct an anemometer can be found on many websites including www.bbc.co.uk/learningzone/clips/measuring-wind-speed-using-an-anemometer/11172.html. Similarly with weather vanes: www.ciese.org/curriculum/weatherproj2/en/docs/windvane.shtml. Finally, learners could be required to construct and use their own rain gauges.

Learners could be provided with a two litre plastic bottle which has had the top third cut off and then reversed and inserted into the remaining part of the bottle (Figure 11.6). You may well need to part-bury these or place some heavy objects like bricks around them. A non-standard piece of measuring equipment could be created by placing a colour chart behind a small, narrow cylinder. Design the colour chart into sections vertically. When learners pour the water from their gauges into the cylinder they can see which colour the water is level with.

SUMMARY

This chapter has tried to show the reader that when planned well and supported with suitable resources, outdoor learning is the best way for learners to become familiar with and learn about the natural world. Through regularly visiting their learning zones and applying their skills and understanding of scientific processes, they will appreciate and become fascinated by flora, fauna and rocks. Whether they become naturalists, horticulturists, members of a nature organisation, or simply adults with an awareness of the living world around them, they should be able to look back fondly to the time spent exploring in their primary schools.

(Continued)

(Continued)

FURTHER READING

Knight, S. (2011) *Forest School for All*. London: Sage.
Ofsted (2008) *Learning Outside the Classroom: How Far Should You Go?* London: Ofsted.

Developing the outdoors for learning

Baines, C. (2000) *How to Make a Wildlife Garden*. London: Frances Lincoln.
Bardsley, L. (2007) *The Wildlife Pond Handbook*. London: New Holland Publishers.
Beddard, R. (2007) *The Garden Bird Year: A Seasonal Guide to Enjoying the Birds in Your Garden*. London: New Holland Publishers.
Lewis, P. (2003) *Making Wildflower Meadows*. London: Frances Lincoln.

Identification guides

Books

Olsen, L. (2001) *Small Freshwater Creatures*. Oxford: Oxford University Press.
Olsen, L. (2001) *Small Woodland Creatures*. Oxford: Oxford University Press.

Keys

Field Studies Council. www.field-studies-council.org/publications.aspx
Gatekeeper Guides. www.gatekeeperel.co.uk/guides.php
Woodland Trust. www.naturedetectives.org.uk

REFERENCES

Abrahams, I. and Millar, R. (2008) 'Does practical work really work? A study of the effectiveness of practical work as a teaching and learning method in school science', *International Journal of Science Education*, 30(14): 1945–69.

Adey, P. (2012) 'From fixed IQ to multiple intelligences', in P. Adey and J. Dillon (eds), *Bad Education: Debunking Myths in Education*. Maidenhead: McGraw Hill/Open University Press. pp. 199–214.

Adey, P. and Serret, N. (2010) 'Science teaching and cognitive acceleration', in Osborne, J. and Dillon, J. (2010) *Good Practice in Science Teaching: What Research Has to Say* (2nd edn). Maidenhead: Open University Press.

Aikenhead, G. (2001) 'Students' ease in crossing cultural borders into school science', *Science Education*, 85(2): 180–8.

Armstrong, H.E. (1903) *The Teaching of Scientific Method and Other Papers on Education*. New York: Macmillan and Company, Ltd.

Baines, E. (2012) 'Grouping children by ability', in P. Adey and J. Dillon (eds), *Bad Education: Debunking Myths in Education*. Maidenhead: McGraw Hill/Open University Press. pp. 37–56.

Barnes, J. (2011) *Cross-Curricular Learning 3–14* (2nd edn). London: Sage.

Barnes, J. (2015) *The Primary Curriculum: A Creative Approach* (2nd edn). London: Sage.

Beggs, J. and Murphy, C. (2005) *Primary Science in the UK: A Scoping Study*. Final Report to the Wellcome Trust, April.

Bell, B.F. (1981) 'When is an animal, not an animal?', *Journal of Biological Education*, 15: 213–18.

Bell, B. and Cowie, B. (2001) 'The characteristics of formative assessment in science education', *Science Education*, 85(5): 536–53.

Best, R.M., Dockrell, J.E. and Braisby, N. (2006) 'Lexical acquisition in elementary science classes', *Journal of Educational Psychology*, 98(4): 824–38.

Bingimlas, K.A. (2009) 'Barriers to the successful integration of ICT in teaching and learning environments: A review of literature', *Eurasia*

Journal of Mathematics, Science and Technology Education, 5(3): 235–45.

Black, P.J. and Harrison, C. (2004) *Science Inside the Black Box: Assessment for Learning in the Science Classroom*. London: GL Assessment.

Black, P. and Wiliam, D. (1998) *Inside the Black Box: Raising Standards through Classroom Assessment*. London: King's College School of Education

Black, P., McCormick, R., James, M. and Pedder, D. (2006) 'Learning how to learn and assessment for learning: A theoretical inquiry', *Research Papers in Education*, 21(2). (2006 Special Issue: Learning How to Learn, in Classrooms, Schools and Networks.)

Blatchford, P., Kutnick, P. and Baines, E. (1999) *The Nature and Use of Within-class Pupil Groupings in Primary Schools*. Final Report. London: Economic and Social Research Council.

Braisby, N.R., Dockrell, J.E. and Best, R.M. (1999) 'Children's acquisition of science terms: does fast mapping work?', in M. Almgren, A. Barrena, M.J. Ezeizabarrena, I. Idiazabal and B. MacWhinney (eds), *Research on Child Language Acquisition: Proceedings for the 8th Conference of the International Association for the Study of Child Language*. Somerville, MA: Cascadilla Press. pp. 1066–87.

Braund, M. (2015) 'Drama and learning science: An empty space?', *British Educational Research Journal*, 41(1): 102–21.

Broadfoot, P.M. (1996) *Education, Assessment and Society: A Sociological Analysis*. Buckingham: Open University Press.

Bruner, J.S. (1961) 'The act of discovery', *Harvard Educational Review*, 31: 21–32.

Cakici, Y. and Bayir, E. (2012) 'Developing children's views of the nature of science through role play', *International Journal of Science Education*, 34(7): 1075–91.

Camp, L. and Ross, T. (2008) *Why?* London: Andersen Press.

Campbell, D.T. (1974) 'Evolutionary epistemology', in P.A. Schlipp (ed.), *The Philosophy of Karl Popper*. LaSalle, IL: Open Court, pp. 413–63.

CBI (2015) *Tomorrow's World. Inspiring Primary Scientists*. http://news.cbi.org.uk/reports/tomorrows-world.

Chambers, D.W. (1983) 'Stereotypic images of the scientist: The draw-a-scientist test', *Science Education*, 67(2): 255–65.

Chow, A.F., Woodford, K.C. and Maes, J. (2011) 'Deal or no deal: Using games to improve student learning, retention and decision-making', *International Journal of Mathematical Education in Science and Technology*, 42(2): 259–64.

Coffield, F. (2005) 'Learning styles: Help or hindrance?', *NISN Research Matters*, 26(Autumn): 1–8.

Colburn, A. (2000) 'Constructivism: Science education's "grand unifying theory"', *The Clearing House*, 74(1): 9–12.

Core Education (2006) *The Quality Principles for Digital Learning Resource*. Available at www.core-ed.org.uk/activities/becta-2018inno-vative-approaches2019-quality-principle/becta-2018innovative-approaches2019-quality.

DfE (Department for Education) (2013a) *The National Curriculum in England: Key Stages 1 and 2 Framework Document*. London: HMSO.

DfE (Department for Education) (2013b) *Science Programmes of Study: Key Stages 1 and 2. National Curriculum in England*. September. London: DfE.

DfE (Department for Education) (2013c) *Science Programmes of Study: Key Stage 3. National Curriculum in England*. September. London: DfE.

DfE (Department for Education) (2014) *Statutory Framework for the Early Years Foundation Stage. Setting the Standards for Learning, Development and Care for Children from Birth to Five*. London: DfE.

DfEE (Department for Education and Employment) (1999) *The National Curriculum: Handbook for Primary Teachers in England*. www.nc.uk. net. Department for Education and Employment and Qualifications and Curriculum Authority. Norwich: HMSO.

Dorion, K.R. (2009) 'Science through drama: A multiple case exploration of the characteristics of drama activities used in secondary science lessons', *International Journal of Science Education*, 31(16): 2247–70.

Driver, R., Guesne, E. and Tiberghien, A. (eds) (1985) *Children's Ideas in Science*. Milton Keynes: Open University Press.

Duschl, R.A. (1990) *Restructuring Science Education: The Importance of Theories and Their Development*. New York: Teachers' College Press.

Dweck, C. (2008) *Mindset: The New Psychology of Success*. New York: Ballantine Books.

Elle, F. and Grudnoff, L. (2013) 'The politics of responsibility: Teacher education and "persistent underachievement" in New Zealand', *The Educational Forum*, 77(1): 73–86.

Evagorou, M. and Osborne, J. (2010) 'The role of language in learning and teaching science', in J. Osborne and J. Dillon (eds), *Good Practice in Science Teaching: What Research Has to Say* (2nd edn). Maidenhead: Open University Press. pp. 135–57.

Gagne, R.M. (1972) 'Domains of learning', *Interchange*, 3: 1–8.

Gibson, E.J. (1977) 'How perception really develops: A view from outside the network', in D. LaBerge and S. Jay Samuels (eds), *Basic Processes in Reading: Perception and Comprehension*. Hillsdale, NJ: Erlbaum. pp. 155–73.

Goldsworthy, A. and Feasey, R. (1997) *Making Sense of Primary Science Investigations* (Revised Edition, Revised by Stuart Ball). Hatfield: Association for Science Education.

Goldsworthy, A., Watson, R. and Wood-Robinson, V. (1998) 'Sometimes it's not fair!', *Primary Science Review*, Issue 53: 15–17.

Gott, R. and Duggan, S. (1995) *Investigative Work in the Science Curriculum*. Buckingham: Open University Press.

Gustafson, B., Shanahan, M. and Gentilini, S. (2010) 'Elementary children's shifting views of models and the nature of matter', *Canadian Journal of Science, Mathematics and Technology Education*, 10(2): 103–22.

Harlen, W. (2010) *The Big Ideas of Science*. Hatfield: Association for Science Education.

Harré, R. (1986) *The Physical Sciences since Antiquity*. London: Croom Helm.

Hart, S. (1998) 'A sorry tail: Ability, pedagogy and educational reform', *British Journal of Educational Studies*, 46(2): 153–68.

Hattie, J. (2009) *Visible Learning: A Synthesis of Over 800 Meta-analyses Relating to Achievement*. London and New York: Routledge.

HMI (2013) *Maintaining Curiosity: A Survey into Science Education in Schools*. London: HMSO. Doc. 130135.

Howe, C. and Tolmie, A. (2003) 'Group work in primary school science: Discussion, consensus and guidance from experts', *International Journal of Educational Research*, 39: 51–72.

Hume, A. and Coll, R. (2009) 'Authentic student inquiry: The mismatch between the intended curriculum and the student-experienced curriculum', *Research in Science & Technological Education*, 28(1): 43–62.

Huxley, T.H. (1905) *Hume*. New York: A.L. Fowle.

Johnson, C. (2011) 'The road to culturally relevant science: Exploring how teachers navigate change in pedagogy', *Journal of Research in Science Teaching*, 48(2): 170–98.

Johnson, J. (2005) *Early Explorations in Science* (2nd edn). Maidenhead: Open University Press.

Johnson, J. (2014) Chapter 1 'The development of emergent skills', in *Emergent Science: Teaching Science from Birth to 8*. Abingdon: Routledge.

Johnson, P. and Papageorgiou, G. (2010) 'Rethinking the introduction of particle theory: A substance-based framework', *Journal of Research in Science Teaching*, 47(2): 130–50.

Kambouri, M. and Michaelidas, A. (2015) 'Dramatic water: Using a drama-based approach to science in the early years', *Primary Science*, 136: 10–12.

Kirikkaya, E.B., Iseri, S. and Vurkaya, G. (2010) 'A board game about space and solar system for primary school students', *Turkish Online Journal of Educational Technology*, 9(2): 1–13.

Klahr, D. and Simon, H.A. (1999) 'Studies of scientific discovery: Complementary approaches and convergent findings', *Psychological Bulletin*, 125(5): 524.

Klappa, P. (2009) 'Promoting active learning through "pub quizzes" – A case study at the University of Kent', *Bioscience Education*, 14: DOI: 10.3108/beej.14.c2.

Kitcher, P. (1993) *The Advancement of Science*. Oxford: Oxford University Press.

Korzybski, A. (1931) The American Mathematical Society at the New Orleans, Louisiana, Meeting of the American Association for the Advancement of Science, December 28. Reprinted in *Science and Sanity* (1933): 747–61.

Latour, B. (1989) *Science in Action: How to Follow Scientists and Engineers through Society*. Cambridge, MA: Harvard University Press.

Latour, B. and Woolgar, S. (1979) *Laboratory Life: The Construction of Scientific Facts*. Beverly Hills, CA: Sage Publications.

Lawson, R.M. (2004) *Science in the Ancient World: An Encyclopedia*. Santa Barbara, CA: ABC-CLIO.

Lemke, J.L. (1990) *Talking Science: Language Learning and Values*. Westport, CT: Ablex Publishing.

Loxley, M. (2009) 'Evaluation of three primary teachers' approaches to teaching scientific concepts in persuasive ways', *International Journal of Science Education*, 31(12): 1607–29.

Ma, J. (2012) 'Exploring the complementary effect of post-structuralism on sociocultural theory of mind and activity', *Social Semiotics*, 23(3): 444–56.

Mant, J., Wilson, H. and Coates, D. (2007) 'The effect of increasing conceptual challenge in primary science lessons on pupils' achievement and engagement', *International Journal of Science Education*, 29(14): 1707–19.

Marshall, B. and Drummond, M.J. (2006) 'How teachers engage with assessment for learning: Lessons from the classroom', *Research Papers in Education*, 21(2): 133–49.

Matthews, M.R. (1989) *The Scientific Background to Modern Philosophy*. Indianapolis, IN: Hackett Publishing Company.

Matthews, M.R. (1994) *Science Teaching: The Role of History and Philosophy of Science*. New York: Routledge.

Medawar, Sir P.B. (1969) *Induction and Intuition in Scientific Thought*. London: Methuen.

Millar, R. (2004) 'The role of practical work in the teaching and learning of science', University of York. Available at: www7.nationalacademies.org/bose/Millar_draftpaper_Jun_04.pdf.

Millar, R. and Driver, R. (1987) 'Beyond processes', *Studies in Science Education*, 14: 33–62.

Muijs, D. and Reynolds, D. (2011) *Effective Teaching: Evidence and Practice* (3rd edn). London: Sage.

Naylor, R.H. (1974) 'Galileo's simple pendulum', *Physis*, 16: 23–46.

NCC (National Curriculum Council) (1993) *Teaching Science at Key Stages 1 and 2*. York: National Curriculum Council.

Newton, D.P. and Newton, L.D. (2009). 'Some student teachers' conceptions of creativity in school science', *Research in Science & Technological Education*, 27(1): 45–60.

Nussbaum, J. (1985) 'The Earth as a cosmic body', in R. Driver, E. Guesne and A. Tiberghien (eds), *Children's Ideas in Science*. Milton Keynes: Open University Press. Chapter 9.

Ødegaard, M. (2003) 'Dramatic science. A critical review of drama in science education', *Studies in Science Education*, 39: 75–101.

OECD (2012) www.oecd.org/pisa/keyfindings/pisa-2012-results.htm.

Ofsted (Office for Standards in Education) (2008a) *Successful Science*. London: Ofsted.

Ofsted (Office for Standards in Education) (2008b) *Learning Outside the Classroom: How Far Should You Go?* London: Ofsted.

Ofsted (Office for Standards in Education) (2011) *Success in Science*. London: Ofsted.

Ofsted (Office for Standards in Education) (2013) *Maintaining Curiosity: A Survey into Science Education in Schools*. London: Ofsted.

Ogborn, J. (1985) 'Understanding students' understandings: An example from dynamics', *European Journal of Science Education*, 7: 141–62.

Osborne, J.F. (1996) 'Beyond constructivism', *Science Education*, 80(1): 53–82.

Osborne, J. and Collins, S. (2000) *Pupils' and Parents' Views of the School Science Curriculum*. London: Kings College London/Wellcome Trust.

Osborne, J. and Hennessy, S. (2006) *Report 6: Literature Review in Science Education and Role of ICT: Promise, Problems and Future Directions*. Future Lab: http://archive.futurelab.org.uk/resources/documents/lit_reviews/Secondary_Science_Review.pdf (accessed 24 February 2015).

Osborne, J. and Simon, S. (1996) 'Primary science: Past and future directions', *Studies in Science Education*, 26: 99–147.

Osborne, J., Collins, S., Ratcliffe, M., Millar, R. and Duschl, R. (2003) 'What "ideas-about-science" should be taught in school science?', *Journal of Research in Science Teaching*, 40(7): 692–720.

Pan, W. and Tang, M. (2004) 'Examining the effectiveness of innovative instructional methods on reducing statistics anxiety for graduate students in the social sciences', *Journal of Instructional Psychology*, 31(2): 149–59.

Papert, S. (1998) 'Let's tie the digital knot', *Technos Quarterly*, 7(4).

Pollard, A., Broadfoot, P., Croll, P., Osborn, M. and Abbot, A. (1994) *Changing English Primary Schools? The Impact of the Education Reform Act at Key Stage One*. London: Cassell.

Pombo, L., Guerra, C., Moreira, A., Smith, M., Hoath, L. and Howard, D. (2011) 'Evaluation of the quality of science education programmes that use Web 2.0 tools – An Anglo-Portuguese Research Project', *Revista Educaco, Formacao and Tecnolgias*, April: 28–36.

Popper, K.R. (1965) *Conjectures and Refutations: The Growth of Scientific Knowledge*. New York: Harper Torchbooks.

Prain, V. and Waldrip, B. (2006) 'An exploratory study of teachers' and students' use of multi-modal representations of concepts in primary science', *International Journal of Science Education*, 28(15): 1843–66.

Roberts, R., Gott, R. and Glaesser, J. (2010) 'Students' approaches to open-ended science investigation: The importance of substantive and procedural understanding', *Research Papers in Education*, 25(4): 377–407.

Rorty, R. (1991) *Objectivity, Relativism, and Truth*. Cambridge and New York: Cambridge University Press.

Royal Society (2010) *Science and Mathematics Education, 5–14, A 'State of the Nation' Report*. London: The Royal Society.

Russell, T.L. (1981) 'What history of science, how much, and why?', *Science Education*, 65(1): 51–64.

Russell, T. L. (1988) *Science at Age 11: A Review of APU Survey Findings, 1980–84*. London: HMSO.

Sadler, D.R. (2007) 'Perils in the meticulous specification of goals and assessment criteria', *Assessment in Education: Principles, Policy & Practice*, 14(3): 387–92.

Scott, C. (2010) 'The enduring appeal of "learning styles"', *Australian Journal of Education*, 54(1): 5–17.

Sjøberg, S. and Schreiner, C. (2005) 'How do learners in different cultures relate to science and technology? Results and perspectives from the project ROSE (the Relevance of Science Education)', *Asia-Pacific Forum on Science Learning and Teaching*, 6(2): 1–17.

Skamp, K. (2004) *Teaching Science Constructively* (2nd edn). Melbourne: Nelson Australia Pty Ltd.

Smith, K., Loughran, J., Berry, A. and Dimitrakopoulos, C. (2012) 'Developing scientific literacy in a primary school', *International Journal of Science Education*, 34(1): 127–52.

Solomon, J. (2013) *Science of the People: Understanding and Using Science in Everyday Contexts*. Oxon: Routledge.

SPACE Research Reports (1990–1998) Scientific processes and concept exploration reports published by University of Liverpool. Available at www.nationalstemcentre.org.uk/elibrary/.../982/space-research-report

Stabler, M. (1988) 'The image of destination regions: Theoretical and empirical aspects', in B. Goodall and G. Ashworth (eds), *Marketing in the Tourism Industry*. London: Croom Helm. pp. 133–60.

Stephen, G.S. (2009) 'Scenario planning: A collage construction approach', *Foresight*, 11(2): 19–28.

Sulloway, F. (1985) 'Darwin's early intellectual development', in D. Kohn (ed.), *The Darwinian Heritage*. Princeton, NJ: Princeton University Press. pp. 121–54.

Tablets for Schools (2014) 'The use of tablets in UK Schools'. http://tabletsforschools.org.uk/new-research-launched-tablet-computers-in-69–of-uk-schools (accessed 10 February 2015).

TGAT (1988) *National Curriculum Task Group on Assessment and Testing*, Chaired by Professor Paul Black. London: Department of Education and Science.

Torrance, H. (2007) 'Assessment in post-secondary education and training: Editorial introduction', *Assessment in Education: Principles, Policy & Practice*, 14(3): 277–9.

Toulmin, S. (1953) *The Philosophy of Science: An Introduction*. London: The Hutchinson University Library.

Voogt, J. (2010) 'Teacher factors associated with innovative curriculum goals and pedagogical practices: Differences between extensive and non-extensive ICT-using science teachers', *Journal for Computer Assisted Learning*, 26: 453–64.

Vygotsky, L.S. (1978) *Mind in Society: The Development of Higher Psychological Processes*. Cambridge, MA: Harvard University Press.

Ward, H. (2007) *Using Their Brains in Science: Ideas for Children Aged 5 to 14*. London: Sage.

Warwick, P., Sparks Linfield, R. and Stephenson, P. (1999) 'A comparison of primary school pupils' ability to express procedural understanding in science through speech and writing', *International Journal of Science Education*, 21(8): 823–38.

Watson, J.R., Goldsworthy, A. and Wood-Robinson, V. (1998) *Interim Report to the QCA from the ASE/King's College Science Investigations in Schools (AKSIS) Project*. London: King's College.

Watson, J.R., Goldsworthy, A. and Wood-Robinson, V. (1999) *Second Interim Report to the QCA from the ASE/King's College Science Investigations in Schools (AKSIS) Project*. London: King's College.

Wellcome Trust (2008) *Perspectives on Education 1 (Primary Science)*. www.wellcome.ac.uk/perspectives.

Wellcome Trust (2010) *Attitudes of Children and Parents to Key Stage 2 Science Testing and Assessment: Final Report to the Wellcome Trust.* www.wellcome.ac.uk/stellent/groups/corporatesite/@msh_peda/ documents/web_document/wtx062721.pdf.

Wiliam, D. (2015) *Planning Assessment without Levels.* Teach Primary: www.teachprimary.com/learning_resources/view/planning-assessment-without-levels.

Ziman, J.M. (1976) *The Force of Knowledge: The Scientific Dimension of Society.* Cambridge: Cambridge University Press.

Ziman, J. (1978) *Reliable Knowledge: An Exploration of the Grounds for Belief in Science.* Cambridge: Cambridge University Press.

Ziman, J. (2000) *Real Science: What it is and what it Means.* Cambridge: Cambridge University Press.

INDEX

Bumblebee Conservation Trust 200, 203
bundles of three 168Fig, 169
Butterfly Conservation 196, 206
butterfly gardens 206

Cakici, Y. 140
carnivores, omnivores and herbivores 109,
    119–21, 120Fig
Carroll diagrams 75, 76Fig
cars down ramps 28
cave paintings 127
chain games 164Fig, 165
Chambers, D. W. 15
changes over time 8, 55, 74–5
    bean seeds 32–3, 79, 80Fig
    solutions 51–2, 51Fig
    see also seasonal change
charts 94–5, 94Fig
    progression 83, 86
child development 55
Chow, A. F. 164
Christ Church University Initial Teacher
    Education 18
Cinderella 89
circulatory system 109, 144–5
classification/classifying 22, 31, 46, 74, 75,
    76Figs, 91, 109, 171
    developing skills 41–2
    of living things 49–50, 62, 133
    matching objects and shadows 75, 76Tab
    using fiction 133
classification keys 50, 62, 109, 133, 171, 210
    role play 143
close-up photographs 44, 45Fig
cloze procedures 166
Coffield, F. 163
cognitive development 139
collaboration 140, 141, 164, 173
collage 15–19, 17Fig, 96
Collins, S. 138–9
communication 114, 138, 176
    developing skills 167, 177
    progression 83, 85
    of results 15, 87–8, 87Fig, 88Figs,
        95–6, 181
    see also recording strategies
comparative tests 31, 32–3, 56, 74, 79, 89
comparisons 41, 74, 130
    tree bark 118–19, 119Fig
compost zones 209–11
computer science 34
computers and Information
    Communications Technology (ICT) 36,
    174–92, 196
    background 175
    research evidence 175–6

computers and Information Communications
    Technology (ICT) cont.
    rules for using 176–9
    in science 181
conclusions/concluding 37–8, 79, 95–6
constructivist theory 99, 105, 140, 194
container zones 202–3
continuity 81
creativity 34, 49, 95–6, 138–9, 167
criterion-referenced assessment 99, 100,
    107, 114
critical observation 43
cross-curricular links 34, 38, 61, 77–8, 181
crosswords 166–7
Culturally Relevant Science Teaching 89–90
curiosity 4, 9, 138, 139, 194

Danny the Champion of the World (Dahl)
    125, 134
Darwin, Charles 7, 33, 125, 132, 133,
    198, 200
Darwin Walks ('thinking paths') 33, 198
data
    checking 33
    collection 28, 41, 43, 51, 56, 79, 87
    collection using data loggers
        184–6, 185Fig
    interpretation 22, 28, 36, 79
    recording 56, 79, 209
    recording apps 190
    tools for capture 181
    see also pattern-seeking; trend-seeking
data loggers 178, 181, 184–6, 205
data projectors 181–3
day and night role play 143
Deal or No Deal 164
Democritus 2
Department for Education 101
dependent variables 26, 27, 27Fig, 31, 79
detecting 75
diagnostic assessment 100
diagrams 34, 36, 74, 111
dialogue bubbles 87, 88Fig
diet and nutrition 130–1
differentiation 29, 45, 61
digestive system 131–2, 131Fig
digital cameras and films 44, 186–8, 196
digital literacy 175, 181
dinosaur footprints 77–8, 78Fig
discrepant events 116–18
dissolving 110
    'instant snow' 58
    vs. melting 57
    observing change over time 51–2,51Fig
    role play 143
diversity of learners 89–90
Dr Dog (Cole) 130–2

drama 131, 139–40 *see also* role play
drawings
    as assessment evidence 111, 112Fig
    as recording strategy 34, 88Fig
    of scientists 15, 16Fig, 18
    see also observational drawings
Driver, R. 23
Drummond, M. J. 102
Duggan, S. 23
Duschl, R. A. 7

Early Years/Foundation Stage (EYFS) 50, 64,
    183, 189
    classification keys 50
    Early Learning Goals 55
    equipment use 30
    exploration 41, 55–6, 82
    group work 91–2
    play and role play 140, 141, 142
    procedural understanding 81
    process skills 23
    question raising 55–6, 89
    sorting 46
earth and space
    apps 191
    big ideas 110
    changes over time 75
    deep questions 116
    games 162, 167
    questions from an alien 93
    role play 143–4
    simulations 183
    solar system 189
    talking tins display 189
    using fiction 128, 134, 135
Egg microscopes 183–4
Einstein, Albert 19
electricity and electric circuits 109, 110
    apps 191
    data logging 185–6, 185Fig
    deep questions 115
    learning intentions 195
    making things 75
    observation of light bulbs 42
    role play 142
    using fiction 129–30
energy sticks 185
English 34, 38, 77
    reading and writing prioritised 101
Enlightenment 2
Enormous Turnip, The 141–2
equipment
    Kim's Game with 167
    progression 83, 85
    selection and use 24, 30–1, 56, 79, 87
European Commission 175

evaluative questions 58
evaluation 36, 38, 79
evaporation role play 143, 152
evidence
    for assessment 34, 104, 111–14
    inductive vs. hypothetical approaches 9
    non-existent 4
    not fitting the theory 6
    and scientific ideas 11–15, 12Fig, 13Fig,
        14Fig
evidence-based approach 23
evolution 7, 74, 108, 110, 125, 194, 206
    using fiction 132, 133

fair tests 56, 79, 89, 127–8, 129
    bouncing balls 87–9
    dominance in primary science 8, 31–2,
        73–4
    planning 90–1
Feasey, R. 90
feely bags 45
filtering role play 143
Finding Nemo 121
fish, observational drawings 47, 48Fig
five-minute science 170–1
Flamsteed, John 4
Flat Stanley (Brown) 134
fleece 35Fig
Fleming, Alexander 9
floating and sinking (water
    resistance) 109
    discrepant events 116–17, 116Fig
    soft drinks cans 14–15
    using fiction 134
floor books 91, 189, 189Fig, 211
Flotsam (Wiesner) 132
focused observation 43
food chains/webs 110, 190, 208
    apps 189
    role play 143
    using fiction 132, 133
footprints and tracks 12–14, 12Fig, 13Fig,
    14Fig
    dinosaur 77–8, 78Fig
forces and motion 165, 167
    apps 191
    balancing cola can 117–18 117Fig
    role play 141–2
    using fiction 125, 127–8, 134
    see also Newton meters
formative (covert) assessment/assessment
    for learning (ASL) 60, 101–2
    recording system 121
fossils 110, 127, 133
frames ('peepholes') 42
friction 109, 127–8

Second Word War 175
secondary sources 14, 25, 31, 63, 74, 75, 79, 89, 211
Secret Garden, The (Hodgson Burnett) 132
seeds
  collecting 206–7
  deep questions 116
  observing change over time 32–3, 79, 80Fig
  tree fruits and seed dispersal 204Tab, 205
senses 43, 45, 50–1, 55, 61, 104, 203
'senses survey' 51
separating mixtures 52
sequence drawings 34
shadows 75, 110, 128
  matching pictures and 75, 76Fig
  role play 143
shells 46
  in the fields 7–8, 8–9
shoes 142
similarities and differences 23, 42, 46, 55, 62
Simon, H. A. 23
simulations 183
small animals *see* invertebrates; mini-beasts
Smart Slides 182
Smith, K. 139
smoking 130, 164, 168
solids
  'I can think of three' 166
  role play 146–7
solids, liquids and gases 109, 169
  role play 146–54, 147Fig, 152Fig
solutions *see* dissolving
sorting 46, 49, 75, 91, 114, 118–19, 171
sound/s 55, 109
  recordings 184
  role play 143
space *see* earth and space
special educational needs 144, 179
specific learning needs 182
Statutory Framework for the Early Years Foundation Stage 140
Stig of the Dump (King) 126–8
Stonehenge 128
stories and fiction 123–36
  developing science from 125–6
  selecting 126–35, 132–5Tabs
  why use fiction? 124–5
story boards 96
summative (overt) assessment 101, 114
surveys/ surveying 8, 32, 73, 77–9, 91
  best cup of tea 74
  and fair tests 32, 89
  invertebrates 210–11
  and letter writing 96
  nature 196

surveys/ surveying *cont.*
  outdoor sites 195
  school dinners 130
  'senses' 51
  woodlice habitats 28–9
sustainability 195
synthesis questions 58
systematic observation 43

tables 34, 87, 87Fig, 94–5, 94Fig
  progression 83, 86
tablets (iPads) 44, 179–80, 182, 183
  apps 189, 190–1Tab
  everyday use 180
  picture collages 180Fig
Tadpole's Promise, The (Willis and Ross) 124, 132
'talk about' games 168–9
talking partners (pairs) 105, 115
  and 'thoughtful fours' 58–9
Talking Science (Lemke) 163
talking tins 189
target setting 114–15
Task Group on Assessment and Testing (TGAT) 99, 100
tea and tea bags
  blackcurrant investigation 74, 187–8, 188Fig
  identifying variables 90–1, 90Fig
  types of investigation 74
'teacher in role' 141
teachers
  attitude to questions 25, 56–7
  controlling learning 80
  deficit model 19
  fixed vs. growth mindset 114
  lack of confidence with tablets 179
  questions about bubbles 65Tab
  reducing support over time 26, 82
  as role models 55–6, 57
  roles 22, 43, 52, 56, 58, 61, 70, 82, 142, 207
  sharing of assessment practice 113–14
  see also modelling; scaffolding
teaching approaches 138–41
teaching to the test 101, 102, 103
'twenty questions' 171
theory development 6–9
thermal insulation role play 143
time-lapse photography 183
Tomorrow's World (CBI report) 25, 103, 104
topic work 61, 132
torches investigation 91
Torrance, H. 102
transects 133
tree and hedgerow zones 202Fig, 203–5